THE GOLDEN WING
A SOCIOLOGICAL STUDY OF CHINESE FAMILISM

by

LIN YUEH-HWA, Ph.D.
PROFESSOR OF SOCIAL ANTHROPOLOGY,
YENCHING UNIVERSITY

NEW YORK
OXFORD UNIVERSITY PRESS
1947

First published 1947

THIS BOOK IS PRODUCED IN COMPLETE
CONFORMITY WITH THE AUTHORIZED
ECONOMY STANDARDS

Printed in Great Britain by Butler & Tanner Ltd., Frome and London

THE GOLDEN WING

INTERNATIONAL LIBRARY OF SOCIOLOGY AND SOCIAL RECONSTRUCTION

Editor : Dr. Karl Mannheim

Advisory Board: HAROLD BUTLER, C.B., Minister in Charge of British Information Service at H.M. Embassy, Washington, D.C.; SIR ALEXANDER CARR-SAUNDERS, Director of the London School of Economics; SIR FRED CLARKE, Chairman Central Advisory Council or Education; LORD LINDSAY OF BIRKER, C.B.E., Master of Balliol College, Oxford.

Owing to production delays this book was not published until 1948

TO

MY FATHER

ON HIS SEVENTY-FIFTH BIRTHDAY

IS THIS BOOK

DEDICATED

CONTENTS

CHAP.		PAGE
	Foreword	ix
	Introduction, by Professor Raymond Firth	xi
	A Genealogical Table of the Hwang and the Chang Families	xvi
I.	Dunglin's Early Life	1
II.	Emerging from Poverty	13
III.	The Lawsuit	25
IV.	The House of Chang	36
V.	Primary Education	49
VI.	Village Festivities	60
VII.	The Agricultural System	71
VIII.	The Rice Trade	82
IX.	The Store Business	93
X.	Fenchow's Fate	103
XI.	Educational Ambition	113
XII.	A Split	122
XIII.	Division in the Store	133
XIV.	The Bandits	142
XV.	The Fraternal Conflict	153
XVI.	The Expansion of the Store	165
XVII.	The Chang versus the Hwang	175
XVIII.	Local Politics	187
XIX.	River Transport	200
XX.	The Deadlock	210
XXI.	Putting Seeds into Earth	223
	Index	230

FOREWORD

In the winter of 1934, I returned to the province of Fukien in South China. I was extremely surprised, in my native village, by the difference in the development of two households with which I had been closely associated since my childhood. The heads of these two households, Hwang Dunglin and Chang Fenchow, were brothers-in-law. Twenty-five years ago they were business partners and equally prosperous. Their newly-built houses, standing within earshot of each other, had long been the subject of chattering praises by the travellers who passed along the trading road that ran between the two big residences. Now their situation was totally different. Dunglin was enjoying the peak of his prosperity. He had many lineal and collateral descendants; he had acquired a certain amount of fortune and fame. Fenchow was dead. In his house there remained only his daughter-in-law, a widow and her adopted son. When I went back again for a second time, in 1937, I found the house of Chang deserted and the widow lost in loneliness and poverty. She and her son had even been compelled to return to their ancestral place far off among distant kinsfolk.

How could two households, which were once of equal standing, have been so transformed by two entirely different fates within only a little more than a score of years? How could it be? I have been told by many persons that the rise and fall of a family is determined by the good and evil of " wind and water ". Human will is nothing against the force of fate and fortune. Must I believe this? Certainly not, for I am an educated man, who must take his truth from life and not from fairy-tales. Then what is the truth?

In telling of the fate of empires, or families, or individuals, we deal with human relations. Can we ever understand these? Can we follow carefully year by year and day by day the changes that take place in men and women when they adjust themselves to one another? Can we ever learn the ways of fate otherwise? Take the smallest child : from the moment of his birth, he responds to his parents, his nurse, and his relatives. At the same time they respond to him, little as he is. During all the time of his growth, this child acts with others and the character of this interaction provides the force that moulds him. Think what a continual process of adjustment and conditioning this must be! Scientists say now that human existence is thus a continual process of learning to respond to stimulation. Man's behaviour, like that of all animals, is under the spell of these processes that science has at last begun to describe. Here now are the fates of these two related families, the Chang and the Hwang. What is their story, in the light of truth and circumstance, and the events to which they had to adjust themselves, in order to learn and to survive?

The nature of this study as stated involves the growth of a viewpoint incorporated from many scholars and individuals with whom I have made close contacts, both in China and abroad. Mention can be made of only a few who have contributed, in one way or other, to the progress of the work.

I owe, first of all, my initial training in sociology to Professor Wu Wen-tsao of Yenching University at Peiping, whose instructtion has constantly been my inspiration for researches in science.

My acknowledgment should be made to the grant of a fellowship, 1937-40, by the Trustees of the Harvard-Yenching Institute, without which my advanced studies at Harvard University would not have been possible. To Professors E. A. Hooton, A. M. Tozzer, C. S. Coon and Clyde Kluckhohn, I owe my general training in ethnology and social anthropology.

In the preparation of this book, I am deeply indebted to Drs. Eliot D. Chapple and Conrad M. Arensberg, who have given invaluable advice and criticism. My friend Gabriel Lasker has shown his utmost interest in its development. Special thanks should also be made to Messrs. Bruno Lasker and William L. Holland of the Institute of Pacific Relations, who have read the manuscript and rendered assistance to bring it to publication.

I wish to acknowledge my gratitude to Professor Raymond Firth of London University, who writes an Introduction to the book. My friend, Mrs. Douglas N. Sargent, has helped to polish the English during the revision of the manuscript in Chengtu. Much credit should go to my wife, Jao Yusu, who, in years abroad as well as at home, has most helpfully criticized my work.

DEPARTMENT OF SOCIOLOGY,
YENCHING UNIVERSITY, CHENGTU.

INTRODUCTION
By
Professor Raymond Firth

The Golden Wing is a sociological study written in the form of a novel. Its theme is refreshingly simple in conception—but like the painting of a bamboo leaf, its austere form conceals a high degree of art. The story sets out to examine why, of two families living side by side in a Fukien village, and related by kinship and business interests, one should continue to prosper through adversity and the other should first flourish and then decline. Its central character is the head of the first family, Hwang Dunglin. No hero, he is nevertheless emblematic of the industry, thrift, business acumen and toughness of the best type of Chinese peasant. "The Golden Wing", the house that he built, was so named because the side of a nearby mountain that resembled a pheasant stretched round like a wing towards the new dwelling. In terms of "wind and water"—a traditional part of the Chinese geomancer's art—this might well have made the family prosper. But to the sociologist the influences are of another kind. Chance in the form of accident—a sudden death; a meeting with an old school friend; the happy discovery of a document which wins a lawsuit—plays some part. But the real destiny is that which every man carries within his own bosom—that with which all great dramatists and novelists, as a Euripedes or a Dostoievsky, have presented us. A man's choice of good or evil, wisdom or foolishness, really depends not on the whim or chance of the moment, but on all those previous inclinations and habits of himself and others which so weigh down the scale that in reality the issue has been chosen long before. As Professor Lin puts it in other terms : " For the ' Heavenly Gods ' we can nowadays read human beings themselves and for ' Fate ' human society."

The author is faced by the problem inherent in all serious literature, of rendering the general through analysis of the particular. He has deliberately set himself the task of examining and illustrating a social process by recounting a chain of events in the lives of small groups of individuals. Only occasionally, therefore, is he at liberty to couch what he has to say in abstract terms. But he has most successfully avoided the obvious danger

—of making his narrative no more than a pedestrian chronicle of some obscure Chinese villagers. On the contrary, he has managed with skill to lift the story on to the plane of true sociological interest, and to make almost every event the epitome of some process in Oriental rural society. The method Professor Lin has chosen, moreover, does not merely attract the interest of the reader. It also has the advantage of freeing him from some of the ordinary rules of scientific procedure, not least from the obligations of documentation which normally weigh upon the sociologist or historian. The author can tell us what every character did or said—whether in the medicine store, the inner chamber, or the bandit's stronghold—with as much assurance as if he had been by their side. He can even pry into the recesses of their minds and explain their present motives and their past feelings. How true is all this? we must ask. I fancy Professor Lin would not shirk this question, but would point out, as he has hinted in his Foreword, that he is writing of his own village, of people he knew in boyhood and in later life; that if he was not always by their side, at least he had often been in similar situations. For example, one may perhaps be allowed to think that the author himself has passed through some of the experiences he describes—those of a scholar leaving his native land, studying abroad, and then returning with enhanced reputation to take up positions of responsibility. However, no matter what may be the combination of faithful observation with imaginative reconstruction, the skill is such that the events of the story bear the stamp of authenticity.

But I have not been asked to write this preface in order to vouch for the correctness of the author's material and the adequacy of his generalizations. For this, his early association with Professor Wu Wen-tsao and his own reputation are sufficient evidence. My rôle is only to give a few words of appreciation as a colleague who has not yet had the opportunity of working in China, but who has long been interested in studies of Chinese culture, and has shared the general admiration of the democratic world for the struggle of the Chinese people, including the academic groups, against the invader.

I have found the narrative and accompanying analysis absorbing. One is accustomed in the conversation of one's Chinese colleagues and friends in this country to delight in their polite but pithy observations on English social life, and in the novel angle from which they view our admittedly at times somewhat eccentric behaviour. One senses also a certain dispassionateness and objectivity in their judgement of affairs in general—even when those affairs may be events in their own war-torn country. Western readers already have some acquaintance with fictional or real Chinese family biography, mirroring also the changes that have taken place in China as a whole. Translations such as the *Red Chamber Dream*, original tales such as *The Good Earth* and its successors, or the still more charming *House of Exile*, have given us vivid portrayals of various aspects of Chinese social life. But one has long wished that to these could be added the work of Chinese scholars, familiar from childhood as participants in the scenes they describe as well as versed in the disciplines of modern social science. Here we have one such story.

For all its natural style the tale has been carefully rounded out, one suspects, by systematic study and orderly presentation of the different facets of the community life. This material is extremely rich, since the author has taken the occasion to develop the analysis of a full set of institutional relationships around events —even quite small ones—in the lives of his characters. The provision of timber for Hwang Dunglin's new house involves him in a dispute which becomes a peg on which to hang an exemplification of the local system of law and justice ; dissension between two brothers provides the basis for an analysis of the processes of " division of family " which breaks up a corporate household and lineage into smaller autonomous groups. One by one other important aspects of the social life appear in the same apparently artless way—the agricultural cycle ; a wedding ; a funeral ; the workings of the steamboat company, or even, unhappily, those of a system of banditry.

Throughout all this analysis one becomes more and more conscious how unreal is the conventional view of Chinese family and other institutional life as a placid affair, rigidly restrained from personal exuberance by rules of politeness, filial obedience, respect for old age, and other social and ritual conventions. These rules do operate, but side by side with them expression of individual personality takes a very definite and sometimes even violent form. Of the many features illustrating this, one may be cited. As against the common view of the Chinese woman as a suppressed being, subordinate to her menfolk and her mother-in-law in ways which render her almost a chattel, we are given here examples of a woman with money of her own, investing it in business ; of sisters-in-law fighting beyond the control of their husbands' uncle ; of a man being nagged by his own wife for defending his daughter-in-law ; of a daughter-in-law committing such outrageous acts as chasing her husband round the room with a knife and slashing the wrist of an aged relative who interferes. That such breaches of filial regard are not to be taken as unique is shown by the emergence of similar themes in the relations between younger and elder brothers and nephews and uncles, while passing reference is also made to a breach of clan exogamy rule and to a threatened breach of a rule of generation endogamy. It is true that the total picture of Chinese society so presented is one where every effort is made to heal a breach of rules or social relations, and where the mechanisms of healing are themselves elaborate, well known and almost codified. The effect of this to a Western reader is of a very tortuous social process, but as every anthropologist knows, this is an impression which tends to disappear as one becomes used to the procedure. All this may be no novelty to one who knows China, nor to the social anthropologist, to whom the discrepancy between theory and practice, between rule and its observance, is almost a standard hypothesis. But it does provide one set of data which will help to destroy any remaining legend of Chinese impassivity and inscrutability in social affairs.

An interesting question for the social scientist is raised by the integrative concepts with the aid of which Professor Lin binds together the varied materials of his story. The concept which he favours most and which he elaborates in theoretical form in his final chapter, is that a system of human relations is in a constant state of balance, or equilibrium. This equilibrium is disturbed from time to time by external forces and a new equilibrium is later set up. " Human life swings between balance and disturbance, between equilibrium and disequilibrium." Such an integrative concept is, of course, but one of a number of possible ways of attempting to comprehend and represent a complex reality, and it is still a subject of discussion by social scientists. Some may ask, for instance, whether such a view of states of equilibrium, derived by analogy from the physical sciences, is not an over-simplification—whether such states are in fact ever attained. It may be argued that social activity is characterized by antagonism of forces working simultaneously for and against a balance, which is never reached. Again, using the concept, could one not distinguish between the attainment and preservation of personal or psychological equilibrium and that of group or social equilibrium? The former may be maintained when the latter is destroyed, as in the moving last scene of the novel, when the old man preserves his calm and his sense of the real issues of life amid the roar of a Japanese 'plane. But that sociologists may wish to enter into such arguments is itself a tribute to the stimulus of the book.

Above all, Professor Lin has admirably shown that the changes which take place in the two families he has chosen for analysis are not haphazard, but are illustrations of general principles which are of importance for an understanding of social processes. And even to the reader who is interested more in the story than in the underlying sociology, *The Golden Wing* will appeal as a dramatic novel of rich experience, giving a calm, dispassionate analysis of moral issues, yet infused with a broad sympathy.

A Genealogical Table of the Hwang and the Chang Families

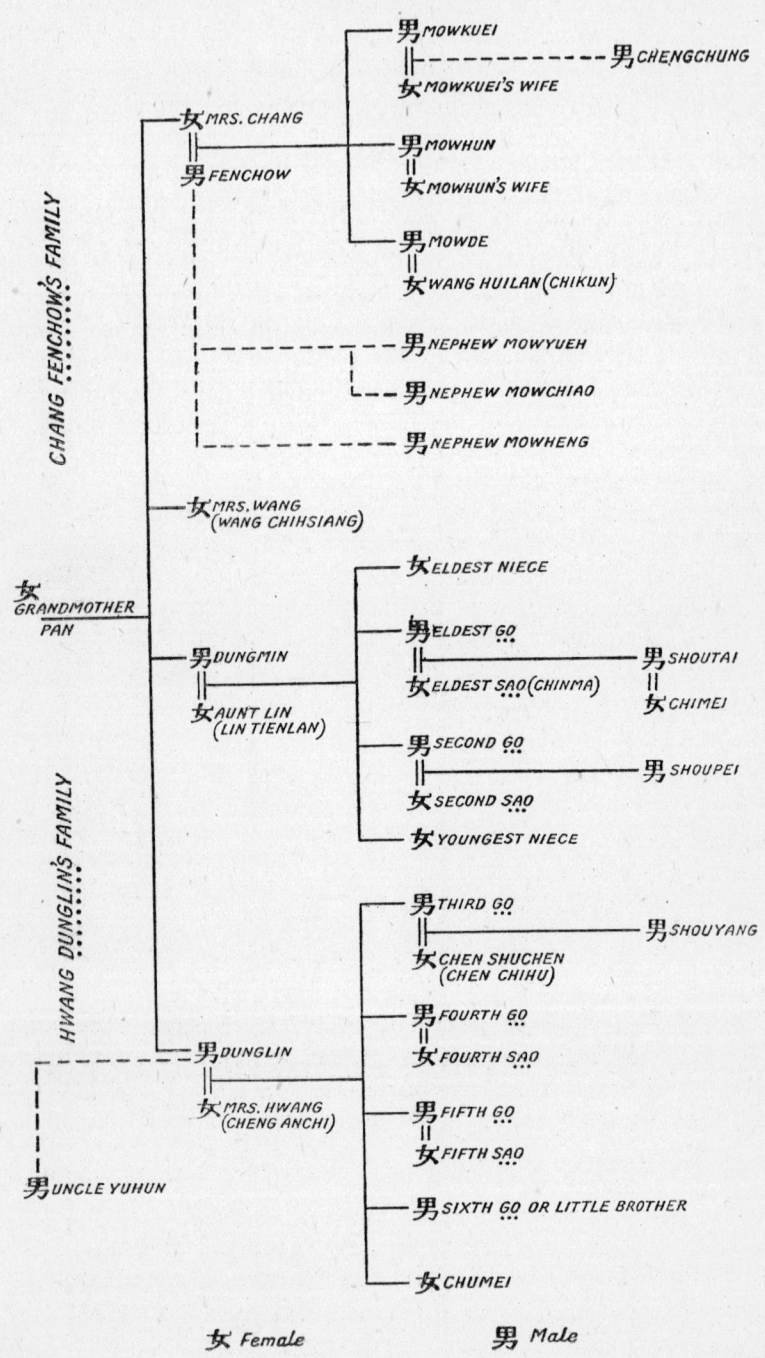

THE GOLDEN WING

CHAPTER I

DUNGLIN'S EARLY LIFE

Once when Hwang Dunglin's grandfather was still alive, a tax collector came to the village of Hwang and did some injustice to a family there. Dunglin's grandfather was a forthright man. He beat upon a gong to call up the men of the clan in order to resist the tax collector and his men. If apologies had not been made right then, there would certainly have been a bloody battle. Since then the Hwang village has had a title. It is called "the barbaric village".

The barbaric village lies on the lower slopes of the lofty green mass of Pheasant Mountain. Below the village there is a valley cradled by precipitous mountains. Several hundred inhabitants, whose main occupation is to cultivate the rich soil on the gentle slopes and level surfaces, dwell in the valley. The black forest stretches up the steep hillsides above them. Whenever the skies are cloudless and clear, if one looks sharply amid the verdant splendour on the lower half of Pheasant Mountain, one can detect roof-tops covered with grey tiles that overlap one another like the scales of a fish.

A great trading road, which passes just below the village, leads westward only two miles to the river port of Hookow, where boats sail downstream to the coastal city of Foochow. Eastward this same trading road leads from the village to the district city, Kutien, a distance of twenty-five miles. The road is called the Western Road because it leads off to the west from this district city. Transport between Hookow and Kutien, before the road was widened into a public highway for buses, was very difficult. People used to carry their goods along the road in bags and baskets suspended on shoulder-poles. Many of these people, trading and carrying their goods, used to stop for a rest in the teashop of the Hwang village, sitting there for a good while each trip, and gossiping of the happenings of the district.

Hwang Dunglin's grandfather, the stubborn man who routed the tax collector, was a farmer who acquired a certain reputation by his hard work and an accumulation of wealth. He had three sons, of whom Dunglin's own father was the eldest. When the young Dunglin was four years old, his father, the eldest son, died suddenly at the age of twenty-eight. The little boy's mother never remarried. She took care of her four children, two sons and two daughters, and lived on with their grandfather. The old man was especially fond of Dunglin, who was his youngest grandchild. He often said the boy had the kind of face that destined prosperity for him in later life. The boy's face was square with wide, bright eyes and long, thick ears. In later life it was the face of a merchant—quick, shrewd, and a little hard.

When Dunglin was fourteen, the old man died. It was the first time the boy had experienced grief. He was very much shaken by his grandfather's death. When alive, the old man used to take him to visit friends and relatives, to walk with him across the fields, and to tell him legends and folk stories. The ties between these two were very close. The boy learned a great deal of life and of old tales from the old man, and the old man leaned on him as a constant companion, young as he was.

There is no reason then to be surprised that Dunglin was so upset. The pattern of his life was rudely dislocated. Our lives, after all, can be coldly charted out. The circle of our daily associations is like a delicately-poised network of bamboo sticks tautly connected by elastic rubber bands. Pull one band too hard, to the snapping point, and the whole network tumbles into ruin. Each tautly connected stick is one of the human beings to whom our life has tied us. Pull one of them completely away, and we tumble, too, in pain, to ruin, and all the ties go temporarily slack.

Thus it was with young Dunglin. For more than a year he mourned his grandfather. But gradually his life with his mother and his elder brother pulled him back to normal again.

His elder brother was Hwang Dungmin, now the head of the family, the eldest male. Dungmin was a hard, earnest, and able young man. He threw all his energies into working the meagre land inherited from his ancestors. All day long he worked very hard in the fields, even though his brother Dunglin was too lazy to work with him.

With the deaths of father and grandfather, the family declined. The farms the grandfather had acquired had been divided into three sections, Dunglin's two uncles, his father's brothers, taking their shares. Even though all who remained worked as hard as they could, the produce from the meagre land could hardly support a family that still numbered seven people. For there were still the two brothers, their mother, and though the two girls had married and gone off, Dungmin now had a wife of his own and three small children.

As the family's means dwindled, they postponed the expensive ceremony of burying their grandparents, and left their remains in their coffins in a cabin on the farm. Likewise, they were forced to postpone Dunglin's marrying, for though he was now at the marrying age, he could not take a wife in the face of the family poverty.

Under the pressure of such a fate, the Hwang family was either doomed to further decline until it reached its ultimate ruin, or a new horizon had to open up. Let us see the new adjustment that took place. Its agent was Hwang Dunglin.

Dunglin was restive now under the urgings of his mother and his brother Dungmin. They kept plaguing him to work but paid no attention to his needs. Dungmin openly declared his brother was a laggard and dullard and would never get a wife. Under this goading he began to hang about with the people who ran the teashop on the trading road and with the travellers who rested there.

In the teashop on the trading road, Dunglin noticed that the passers-by needed some sort of refreshment when they took their rest. He suggested to the shopkeeper that he sell them peanuts. But he got no support, and the selling of peanuts did not materialize until one day Dunglin won several dollars at gambling with the local village toughs. With this money he bought raw peanuts from a farmer of the neighbourhood. For two or three years thereafter he carried on his peanut selling. He often slept in the shop instead of going home. He made friends with the shopkeeper, the traders, and the village toughs.

This shifting of his life from family to teashop broadened Dunglin's contact with the world. It gave him a little release from too close surveillance at home and found him a new place among the teashop people.

One day, when he was sitting beside his peanut stall, he noticed a man approaching. It was his brother-in-law, Chang Fenchow, his eldest sister's husband. Chang was an old-fashioned Chinese doctor who often practised in the villages. His native village was Chenyang, up on the mountain beside the Western Road, midway between the district city of Kutien and the town of Hookow.

As Chang Fenchow came near, Dunglin stood up and they greeted each other. After a brief interchange of conversation about business, Dunglin invited his brother-in-law to his house, where they spent a day and a night, talking about setting up a store in order to make some money. Fenchow told him how promising enterprises were springing up in the town of Hookow where the population was increasing and the people gathering to exchange their goods. On hearing the news, Dunglin was only too glad to ask his brother-in-law to draw up a definite plan for the store. He offered all the capital he had gained from the selling of peanuts. Chang Fenchow was really interested only in setting up a medicine shop, in which he could practise healing and sell medicines. But Hwang Dunglin insisted he add some other lines such as wine and peanuts. In the end the point was agreed upon.

The project planned by the brothers-in-law was not realized, however, until half a year later. During all this time Dunglin and Fenchow went to call on each other very often, for they not only planned the use of their capital but they also threshed out the details for managing the store.

They visited Hookow. The town, as we have said, is a river port, but situated in a valley pocket so that it cannot be seen from the river. The stream, which flows parallel to the Western Road from the district city, joins the river at the left foot of Hookow Mountain where the slopes are steep. The port thus finds its wharf at the right foot of the same mountain. From the wharf the stone steps lead upward to the mountain gorge where the main street begins. This street descends gradually by stone steps for some distance, extends into the heart of the town and ends at a triangular piece of ground before the town temple. Eastward from the temple the Western Road goes off, and south-eastward across a bridge over the stream a road runs downward along the far bank of the Min River, the river along which the history of the province, its trade and commerce and its life blood flow.

After looking around the town, Dunglin and Fenchow rented a place midway along the main street. It cost them fifty dollars a year. It consisted of a main hall with an earthen floor, a counter with a platform, a small room at the back of the counter, an earthen stairway leading to an upper room used for storage, and a kitchen at the rear. In the main hall they placed the medicine cases and boxes on the left and the big wine bottles, peanut bags, and other utensils on the right.

When the store opened there were four persons working in it. Although these four observed no strict division of labour, yet they did have somewhat different tasks. Fenchow, the senior partner, was naturally the general manager. At the same time he did most of the work dispensing medicine. He also went out often to practise his healing. Dunglin, though a partner of Fenchow, acted more like an employee. He was strong and healthy and thus willing to do all the hard labour in the store. Chang Mowkwei, the eldest son of Fenchow, though a boy of only twelve years old, acted as accountant and did other chores. A man named Yao Yunseng was cook and apprentice.

The store soon began to work smoothly and systematically. The four persons fell into an easy co-ordination. Usually a customer would come into the shop and ask the price of wine. When Dunglin gave him his answer he would buy or go away. But very often he would want to see the head man, Chang Fenchow, in order to get him to reduce the price. After a long argument back and forth, when they arrived at an agreement, Fenchow would turn to Dunglin and ask him to pour out as much wine as the customer wanted. While Dunglin was measuring the amount on the scale, he would call it out in a loud voice. The accountant, Mowkwei, would write it down. Then the customer would go up to the counter and ask the accountant how much he was to pay. While the customer was paying his money, Dunglin would pour the wine into the customer's pot or bottle. Then the customer would come over again to Dunglin, who handed him his bottle. They would say good-bye, and the customer go out.

This was the normal way the store worked, but it was not the only way. Sometimes Fenchow might be absent, and Dunglin was then the final determiner of the price. Sometimes Dunglin might be engaged in other business, and then Fenchow or Mowkwei would become the measurer of the wine. Even the apprentice could measure the wine, if he were asked. But usually he did only the cooking, carrying water, washing, sweeping the floor, and running errands.

The new wineshop took Dunglin from the Hwang village to the town of Hookow. It cut him off from the people of the teashop and separated him almost completely from his family.

Occasionally his brother Dungmin came to town to see him and to buy things for their mother and the family. But Dunglin himself seldom went home at all. For the time being the shop, not the family, became the centre of his life. The wine and goods for sale, and the dealing with customers, gave occasion for a bustle and an activity that filled his days. For the first time since his grandfather's death Dunglin's hours were fully occupied.

But while Dunglin was busy in the store, he could not help but notice the rapid growth of the life of the town outside the door. The people were flocking into Hookow from all directions, from places both inside and outside the district boundaries. Many new stores were going up. Junks were sailing more often on the Min River between the town of Hookow and the city of Foochow. At this period the Western Road became more convenient for trade and commerce than the once prosperous Southern Road that connected the river port of Shuikow with the district city of Kutien, because the Southern Road was mountainous and had become the haunt of bandits who plundered the passers-by.

With business increasing and the town growing prosperous, Fenchow and Dunglin began to grow interested in expanding their store. In those days the most important commodities transported from the coastal city of Foochow to the inland towns were salt and salt fish. Salt was a government monopoly, but the merchants of the town could buy the salt fish in the Foochow city markets and bring them in for sale to the townspeople and the villagers. In turn the villages and towns supplied Foochow with rice, the most important staple food of South China. The peasants from the villages along the Western Road used to transport their rice to Hookow, where they sold it to the rice stores, from which the merchants shipped it in quantity on to Foochow.

Many stores in Hookow dealt in both salt fish and rice, buying the rice in from the peasants and selling them salt fish in return. Consequently, the partners decided to expand their shop by adding these lines. By this step, their store carried more business, but to make it possible, they had to arrange connections in Foochow.

Dunglin was twenty-two years of age, a tall and handsome young man, when he first went to the city of Foochow. He went on board a junk with two of his friends, Cheng Lugo and

Wang Yiyang. Yiyang had been a pedlar of ducks along the Western Road and Dunglin knew him from his peanut-selling days at the teashop in the Hwang village. But before Dunglin had ever set up his shop in Hookow, Wang Yiyang had grown from a pedlar to a merchant of salt fish and rice, in a store set up by himself and his brothers. He had already gone to Foochow several times, and so knew many people there. The other companion, Cheng Lugo, was a native of the city and had a shop in Hookow selling seafood, cloth, candles and other things. His shop was right across the street from Dunglin and Fenchow's store.

After three days of sailing, they arrived at Foochow, eighty miles from the town of Hookow. The city is situated at the centre of a plain or basin, in area about three hundred square miles, walled by high, steep mountains. The Min River, flowing from west to east, cuts across this basin, dividing at Nantai Island which breaks the river into two branches. The northern branch runs through the Hungsan Bridge and the Long Life Bridge and meets the southern branch again at the point of Lo Star Pagoda. The Long Life Bridge, fourteen hundred feet in length, is famous. It was first built of stones in the eleventh century and rebuilt of cement in 1931. It connects the main part of the city with Nantai Island, where stand many foreign shops and banks, missionary schools, and consulates, also the main post office and custom house.

In Foochow, Yiyang and Lugo introduced Dunglin to some fish-shop owners in Pavilion Street, whose southern end runs into the Long Life Bridge leading to Nantai Island. The street was given over to shops specializing in salt fish, for it was near the wharf from which the fish could be shipped in from the coast upstream past Lo Star Pagoda. From the shops of Pavilion Street, Dunglin bought various kinds of fish, which he stored temporarily in a warehouse, waiting for boats to take them up to Hookow. He lived at the warehouse and went out through the city every day to look over the business of the city, following the changing prices of fish, and visiting friends and business acquaintances. Each night he wrote his partner Fenchow a report of the state of the market and gave him the fish prices. In turn Fenchow wrote to him telling him what fish were in demand at Hookow and what prices they would get.

After a stay of nearly a year or so in Foochow, Dunglin became accustomed to the business life there and knew better the mechanics of commerce. As he often experienced difficulty in getting money from his store in Hookow, he talked one day with Yiyang about making connections with the native banks. Wang was already associated with two or three of these banks. He went therefore with Dunglin to one of them known as the Tienchi Bank. On meeting the owner, Wang introduced Dunglin and suggested opening an account for the Hookow store Dunglin represented. On looking at young Dunglin, who seemed a man of enterprising spirit, the bank owner was willing to do so. Furthermore, Wang had been associated with him for many years and they had a great deal of confidence in one another. This first connection with a city bank was to mean a great deal in the future development of the store.

A little explanation may be needed about the native banks. These banks did not necessarily have much capital. There were many of them before the establishment of a modern banking system. They issued their own banknotes, in denominations of one dollar, two dollars, five dollars, and sometimes of ten. On the face of notes the name of the issuing bank was printed. But the statement of the amount of the note was left blank, to be filled in by an officer of the issuing bank, in order to avoid forgeries. The banks also carried accounts with different merchants and traders, with the understanding that these clients could overdraw up to the amount of their deposits. This loan, or debit, was to be repaid within a certain time, usually not later than a fortnight.

With his connection with the Tienchi Bank, Hwang Dunglin found business much easier. From then on he no longer had to have cash on hand when he ordered fish from the shops in Pavilion Street. He would buy on short-term credit and tell the labourers to carry his fish to the warehouse without further ado. The shops settled their accounts twice a month.

All this time Dunglin had also to arrange the transport of the fish from the warehouse to Hookow. There were about twenty junks that plied back and forth between the town and Foochow city. Each junk was owned by a family who carried on the job generation by generation. These junks carried the rice down the Min River.

The junk men and the shopkeepers of Hookow were business associates, depending upon each other to carry on trade. On each trip on the river the junks carried goods for the stores they were connected with following arrangements made between the junk owner and the representatives of the inland stores in Foochow.

Another class of people with whom Hwang came into contact, and whom he came to know, were the transport coolies. There were thousands of them, waiting on the wharves or walking the streets in Foochow, looking for casual jobs. It was these coolies, wearing bamboo hats and clothed in rags, who carried salt fish from Pavilion Street to the warehouse. It was they who carried it again from the warehouse to the junks scheduled to sail up-river to Hookow. Yet these two groups of coolies, those who did the one job, and those who did the other, never competed or interfered with each other. Each group had its own monopoly. A coolie who carried fish from fish shop to warehouse could not carry it from the warehouse to the junks. Any intrusion of a member of one group on the territory of the other always led to fighting. But the relations between these coolies and the dealers such as Hwang Dunglin, ending impersonally each day when the coolies were paid off, were limited to their work. So Dunglin never came to know these men except as labourers.

The varied life of the city spelled further change in Dunglin's life. He was cut off almost entirely from his family and his village. Though he was still the business partner and agent of Chang Fenchow, his brother-in-law in the store at home in Hookow, yet he became more and more absorbed in his life as a fish dealer in Foochow. His new life took him increasingly into the stores on Pavilion Street, into the banks like the Tienchi, among the associates of Wang Yiyang, among the owners and captains of the junks, and the noisy transport coolies. Occasionally nostalgia turned his thoughts homeward for a moment, to the life of the farm and the village under green Pheasant Mountain, and the paths he had walked in his boyhood at his grandfather's side. But most of the time his days were filled with business and with city life. The buying and selling, the coming and going, the bargaining and conferring about trade in fish became a balanced, even life for him in which he found himself active and content. On that day twice a month when all the shops settled their accounts, Dunglin would walk into the Tienchi Bank and draw out his money. He would go down to the warehouse and there pay off the clerks sent by all the fish shops to settle his accounts. He could sit there in the satisfaction of having met his debts and having acquitted himself well and strongly in the struggle to keep the business going day after day and fortnight after fortnight. He could feel that in the endless stream of fish and rice going up and down the river, and in the endless effort he must make to meet his debts, arrange for new credits, and make the profit on his buying and selling that would help keep the stream of commerce flowing, he had achieved that satisfaction that comes to a man adjusted to the world he must inhabit.

In his leisure time Dunglin often went out with Cheng Lugo, who was very much at home in the city. Once they went to one of the near-by warm springs to bathe. Beside a group of volcanic springs bathing houses had been built. These houses acted as a sort of club, an important social institution in fact, as all sorts of people went there to take baths and talk business. On this visit, while Dunglin and Lugo lay resting on their long chairs after a bath, they began to talk lazily. Lugo took the opportunity to tell Dunglin he should get married.

"You are just the right age," he said. "There is a family of my own name living in the village of Chaotien. This Cheng family has two young daughters about twenty years old who are expected to marry soon."

Dunglin replied, "I have heard of them, but I should have to know more about the real situation of that family before I could take your suggestion seriously."

Knowing thus that Dunglin was interested in the Cheng family, Lugo came again several days later with the information.

"The father of the Cheng girls is a peasant, but he has a smattering of education in the classics. He has three sons besides the two daughters. It is a 'clear and white' family, neither rich nor poor. The first daughter is the best, for she is clever, diligent, filial, honest and capable."

Hwang said, "That is the very kind of wife I would like."

When Dunglin returned to Hookow, he made further inquiry about the Cheng family. As soon as the discussion began to take shape, Dunglin went home to ask the advice of his family. He laid the matter before his uncle Hwang Yuhun, now the only surviving male member of the elder generation of his lineage, and also before his mother and brother. They made no objection, and a betrothal was effected between the two families.

During these years, Dunglin travelled often between Hookow and Foochow. Once when he was on a boat crossing the river, his boat arrived outside Chaotien village, which is situated on the bank of the Min River, ten miles downstream from Hookow.

He happened to be talking with another passenger, an old man, who sat beside him. As the boat drew in, he learned that the old man was his future father-in-law. But he dared not introduce himself. During their conversation the old man asked Dunglin what his native place was. On learning that, he asked about Hwang Dunglin. Dunglin was in a quandary. Tradition discouraged all contact between a young man and his fiancée's family before the marriage took place. So he found himself forced to say that the Hwang the old man asked about was his brother. On hearing this the old man immediately invited him to his house. But Dunglin, now in a deeper quandary still, was forced to refuse. Had he told his real identity, he could not have refused the invitation without great discourtesy. But if he accepted, even under false colours, he would be impolitely intruding in the house where his future wife dwelt !

Dunglin was twenty-four when he married. Yet he had proved himself a mature man. The fact that he chose his wife himself and conducted the arrangement through a friend of his own age and generation made his marriage very exceptional in the village. Ordinarily, a proposal of marriage began only on the initiative of a family head, and the betrothal and wedding were both arranged by older people. But since his brother Dungmin, the formal head of his own family, had long ago publicly despaired of his getting a wife, and had washed his hands of his responsibility, Dunglin had decided to make his own arrangements. Public opinion in the village offered no objection. His success in the business world made the elders look upon him as a man with a future.

Dunglin after his marriage went back to work in the original store at home in Hookow, and his position as fish dealer and representative in the city fell to Chang Fenchow's eldest son, Mowkwei. At home Dunglin took ever more responsibility in fish-selling and rice-buying, while Fenchow devoted most of his time to the sale of medicines and healing. They dropped their original business of selling wine and peanuts and concentrated on the three lines of fish, rice and medicine. Of course, more men were employed in the store : an accountant, and some clerks and apprentices.

At home again in the store, Dunglin often wrote to Mowkwei about what he had learned of the mechanics of commerce during his years of experience in Foochow. He liked to drop in across the street to Lugo's shop in order to enjoy a cup of tea there.

When the annual festivals came, with all the village world renewing its ties of home and family, Dunglin had merely to walk out of the store, carrying two bags of gifts for the occasion, and go home. Once more he could take his meals with his family, with his mother, his brother, his sister-in-law, his wife and his nephews and nieces. He was home again from the outer world, a man of substance among his own kind.

CHAPTER II

EMERGING FROM POVERTY

Accustomed as Hwang Dunglin was to the life of the store in the town, he was nevertheless not totally indifferent to the agricultural life of his people and the work of his brother Dungmin at home in the village. Round the table at family gatherings, at the festival seasons or on special occasions, the Hwang brothers discussed both business and farming. They talked about the seasonal rains and water for irrigation; they planned ploughing and hoeing the fields, sowing and harvesting the crops and paying the taxes and rents. As the family had not been officially divided, the capital and money income of the store, as well as the family lands and their produce, were still common property, belonging to both the brothers. Thus the two young men took an interest in each other's work and planned together for the good of the whole family.

Occasionally Dunglin took up a hoe and walked around the fields in order to help his brother look for water, as all the farmers must do in the irrigation seasons. After several years of having been away from farming he came now to look upon the green fields with much affection. Strolling along the footpaths between the fields, in the quiet and peaceful atmosphere where the singing birds in the woods and the murmuring waters in the ravines made a natural music, he felt very much released in heart after the strident, bustling life of the town.

The Hwang brothers were tenants, though they had a certain kind of ownership of their land. Under the local laws of land tenure, the ownership of land assumes different forms. The landlord owns the " bottom " or subsoil of the land and has a right to collect the ground rents. He is legally holder of title to the land and his name is registered with the government, to whom he pays the taxes on the land. But the man in possession of the land itself, the " root-holder " as he is called by the villagers, has the right of permanent occupation. The word " root " obviously signifies that part of the land, the soil, where the roots of crops grow. These leaseholders or " root-holders " usually farm for themselves, in which case they are called " self-tenant " farmers. Yet sometimes a " root-holder " may lease his permanent tenancy to another farmer, giving to him a temporary right of cultivation. The sub-tenant farmer would then have to pay rent to the leaseholder.

This system is called locally the "bottom-root-tenant" system of land tenure. The landlord, who owns the "bottom", usually gets one-half of the produce as his ground-rent, while the "root-holder" gets a quarter for his interest, and the tenant, the actual working farmer, gets another quarter. The distribution is, however, not absolute, and much variation can be found. Theoretically only the landlords pay the taxes, but sometimes the leaseholders are forced to pay also. The leaseholders' taxes are called the "small taxes", to distinguish them from the "large taxes" paid by the landlords.

The Hwang brothers, then, were "self-tenant" farmers, that is, leaseholders working their land themselves, like most of the people in the village, and their landlords dwelt in the city of Kutien and the town of Hookow. At harvest-time, the landlords sent their agents to the village to collect rents in kind. During the years after his return home, Dunglin would hasten back from his store when the landlords' stewards came and entertain them in an urbane and careful manner. His city training had made a difference in his manners. As the stewards grew more and more impressed by the conversation and the manner of Dunglin, they came to behave somewhat more restrainedly, and after a time they were no longer so harsh as they had been previously.

So fate worked out a nicely balanced programme for Dunglin during the early years after his marriage. He went to and fro between his shop and home. The expanding store stimulated him and took up most of his time in business. Yet the pull of a growing family and an active home life often drew him out of the noisy, hurried shop where he gave so many hours to bargaining, calculating, giving orders, and much talk. A birth, a ceremonial, a religious service, a harvest, a festival, each was an excuse to walk homeward to his native village. This relaxation with his clan renewed his energy for a new trial in his business transactions. The changes between home and store, between village and town, between farm life and business, in short, between peace and struggle, gave Dunglin the most balanced existence that he had ever enjoyed.

Yet this balance of life did not last long. The Hwang brothers soon divided up their family property. They set up two separate hearths with only their mother as a connecting link between the two households. The new arrangement meant a new burden upon each family. Mrs. Hwang, Dunglin's wife, found herself toiling early and late to keep the new smaller household going and to take care by herself of a small daughter and a baby son.

Hardly a year after this division of the family, Dungmin suddenly got very ill. His brother Dunglin had to leave his business and come home. The old doctor, Chang Fenchow, their brother-in-law, was immediately called in. Several medicines had been tried, but with no effect. Yet one day after he had lain ill for a considerable time, Dungmin suddenly vomited all the medicines that he had had, and announced he felt quite well again. He got up and recited to the people around him a vision he had just had.

"I left the house and walked to the underworld," he said. "Hardly had I arrived at the gate of the city of Kutien, when I met my grandfather, walking with a bamboo stick. As soon as I got near him, he raised his stick to punish me, and ordered me to come back at once. That is why I am still here now. I shall not die."

But Dungmin's vision was borne out in reality for only three days more. On the fourth day he lay down again and quietly passed away. He left his wife, Aunt Lin, and four children, two sons and two daughters. His eldest son was then only eleven years old.

Dungmin's funeral was held immediately, and he was buried beside his deceased father. Yet mourning for the dead was not ended with the burial. Aunt Lin, who now had become a widow in the prime of life, wept day and night, complaining bitterly of her bad luck. Her children followed her about, crying and wailing, though the youngest two did not even understand why she cried. Dunglin's mother wept also, her face bathed in tears. Yet she was a practical woman. Her first words to Dunglin, after the death of his brother, were to demand that he reunite in one household the recently divided family. Dunglin well understood there was no other way out. It was not merely a duty. Pity demanded it, too. How could he bear to see his nephews and nieces, the direct descendants of his own father, left to starvation!

Dunglin himself was of course shaken by the death of his brother. Once more the pattern of his life was rudely dislocated. Yet this time the dislocation was greater even than the one which had overtaken him on the death of his grandfather. The reunited family was bigger now and Dunglin took up more responsibility than ever before. He was the only adult man to whom a family of three women and six children could look for support.

As soon as he got home after the burial, he had to rent out his family land to sub-tenants, since he could not work the whole farm himself. He arranged matters with both the tenant farmers and the landlords. Remember a "root-holder", as Dunglin now was, gets only a quarter of the produce of the lands! How little, then, he received from the rents of his family lands! He looked about him at the crowd of children around the table, asking for food. How could he support such a family? Dunglin sighed deeply. He said, "I have only two hands. What more can I do?"

But the question did not long seek an answer. The whole family turned to meet the crisis. As Dunglin was occupied mostly with the store in town, his mother, Grandmother Pan of the family, became matriarch of the household. Although grey hair covered her head and furrows lined her face, she had kept, because of her very experience of hardship, a very industrious spirit. She was an orderly woman who managed her household affairs clearly and in orderly fashion. In company with her two daughters-in-law, Aunt Lin and Mrs. Hwang, she took up spinning and weaving, besides carrying on the household work. The three women made cloth from a hemp that was cultivated on the poorer lands. The cloth was sold at the market and added somewhat to the family income.

To help cut the family expenses, Aunt Lin availed herself of an old local custom and gave her youngest child to another family, as a betrothed daughter to be adopted into the other family's household. A betrothed daughter is a young girl, not yet at a marriageable age, but sent away to live with the family of the boy to whom she is betrothed. The practice is very common among villagers of the poorer classes.

The women of the family took every means they could to save money. They went often to the mountain at the back of the village to cut wood and collect dry leaves and branches for fuel. They gathered pig-dung for fertilizer for the fields. Nothing was wasted.

One day when Grandmother Pan was collecting pig-dung, Dunglin's seven-year-old daughter, a pretty, active, cheerful little thing, came running to her. The little girl took a piece of white candy out of her pocket. It was the first time in her life she had been given any such candy and she kept it to play with rather than to eat. But when Grandmother Pan saw the candy, she grew very angry. She stalked home and snatched up a bamboo whip. She demanded angrily the story of the candy. Mrs. Hwang knew nothing about it. But Aunt Lin came out to confess. She had found some cash in an old dressing-case and had bought just that one small piece of candy for the little girl from a pedlar who came by chance to the house. How could Grandmother Pan believe it? She knew very well there was no money in the house. All the money there was, was invested in the store. She was convinced her daughters-in-law were buying sweets with the household rice money. Furious, she flogged both young women and the little girl. As she did so, she muttered she had been a widow for more than twenty years and never once had had a bit of candy. The young women had no further explanation to give and took their whipping calmly.

But the little girl could not bear the pain of punishment and broke out into loud crying. An hour or two afterwards she got badly chilled, and fell ill. Three days later, before any of the women noticed how serious her illness was, the charming little girl was dead. Mrs. Hwang, clasping the cold little dead body, wept for a whole day and a whole night. The little girl was her first-born daughter, so sweet and lovely, never to be forgotten. Mrs. Hwang always kept the memory of this little figure and her pain and hurt. She told her future children time and again about her first-born girl, and the little girl became a legend of the time of hardship for the family.

Yet there were other losses still to come. Some time later Mrs. Hwang gave birth to another girl who was immediately given out as a betrothed daughter. By giving away her child, the young mother could save her energy for household work. Local custom provided this means of easing the load of family cares, but it was not a happy way. One must bear in mind that only girls were given out. All boys were taken care of by their own parents, no matter how poor the family might be.

About the same time Dunglin got unhappy news about his youngest niece, another girl the family had had to give out as a betrothed daughter. Her future husband, a boy of a Hsu family in the neighbourhood, was working as an apprentice in

B

the town. But her parents-in-law, the boy's father and mother, died in quick succession so that she, who was only six years old, was left to live alone. Dunglin could do nothing except to send a man to bring her back home again. When she arrived, the little girl described herself and the situation she had been left in, in broken words. Of herself she said she was " a handful of rice in a kettle of water . . . the kettle above the burning stove ". She spoke so plaintively, in so peculiar a brogue, the dialect of the Hsu clan, that the members of the house of Hwang laughed heartily, and welcomed her back again.

All this time Dunglin carried on his store business as usual. He and Fenchow rented a neighbouring shop, a building of two stories separated from their store only by a thick wall. By excavating a doorway through the wall, the new building was incorporated with the store. They moved all the medicines to the new building, where Fenchow now took up his main activities. He began to teach Yao Yunseng his medicinal knowledge.

At home Dunglin also made some new arrangements. His two nephews were growing into their teens and were ready to follow their uncle who was head of the family. The elder nephew was the more alert. He used to tell his uncle in his sweet little voice, " When I grow up, I shall earn money to help you, Uncle, to repay you for having brought us up and done so much for us." But the future gave him the lie, as we shall see, and the boy turned out to be a bitter enemy of his Uncle Dunglin.

But since his nephews were still too young to do all the farm work, Dunglin employed a farm labourer, a man by the name of Nanmin. He engaged Nanmin to manage the family lands, which he now took back from the sub-tenants. Usually villagers help each other in farm work. A day's labour is paid back by a day's labour, on a basis of reciprocal co-operation. Very few of them have hired hands. Nanmin was, however, a long-term employee, who was paid in actual money, a wage of forty to fifty dollars per year. He received food and shelter from his master, who also supplied him with farming implements. Nanmin was a man of more than forty years of age ; a distant relative of the Hwang family by marriage. The tenuous relationship was enough, however, to make Dunglin call him " uncle ", and he was well treated and honoured on that account.

It took almost ten years after the death of his brother for Dunglin to bring his life back again to a proper readjustment. They say it is a man's " wind and water ", the power of chance beyond his control, that builds a man's life up or tears it down. Perhaps so. But we must reckon with the man himself and with the system of life's ties that binds him to his fellows and pulls him this way and that. A family is a system of such ties, a strong web of bonds woven around a man, who is held delicately poised in habit, duty, emotion, and desire. Tear away a member of the family, snap off the powerful bonds that bind him to the others, and them to him, and the family faces a crisis. So it was with Dunglin and his family. Blow upon blow fell upon them and shook the web of their lives almost to the point of destruction. The hunger of the children, the necessity of renting out the family lands, the enforced giving away of the little girls, the hard, unwonted discipline of rigid household economy, the death of the little daughter, these were all further crises rudely shaking the pattern of their lives.

"Wind and water" control those things, perhaps. But there is a resiliency in human life which they do not yet control. There are other ties in the web of life that come into their full influence, when those torn by a crisis lie limp and ineffectual. So it was here. Not all the strands of Dunglin's life were involved in these crises, and the ties which were not involved gradually came to pull him back upon his feet and set a new pattern for his family's existence.

Ever since Dunglin and Fenchow had expanded their business by adding lines of rice and salt fish, the store had become more and more prosperous. It acted as an exchange market between the rice moving downstream and salt fish moving upstream. This was a busy, never-ending commerce by which local commodities flowed from village to town and from town to city, and the urban commodities flowed back. From this commerce, in which they came to be very skilled, the brothers-in-law Dunglin and Fenchow began to accumulate more and more money.

So the Hwang family passed once again into industrious and peaceful days. It was about the time of the birth of Dunglin's fourth son. As this son was the youngest of all his brothers, he was called Little Brother. The name became his given name. Family tradition had it that all the males of the same generation should be called by number in the order of their birth. Little Brother, the youngest male of his generation, was called Sixth *Go*, since " Go " was the word for both brother and cousin by which all the males of a single generation were designated. His two eldest cousins, the sons of Dungmin, were, therefore, Eldest or First *Go*, and Second *Go*. Third, Fourth, and Fifth *Go*, thus, were his elder brothers.

When Little Brother was about to be born, his old grandmother sent Nanmin to Hookow. Dunglin, instead of returning home himself, sent back his eldest son, Third *Go*, who was studying in a private school in town. Third *Go* was to officiate in his father's stead in the ceremonies of birth.

Third *Go* went first to the town temple. There he worshipped the mother goddess, taking out one of her incense burners on which incense sticks were kept burning continually. On the way home, Third *Go* opened an umbrella to cover the incense burner, for in it the spirit of the mother goddess was supposed to dwell. When he arrived home, he took the incense burner into his mother's bedroom. The midwife was already there, helping his mother through the delivery. As soon as the incense burner of the mother goddess came into the room, the new babe came into the world and began to cry.

When Little Brother came into the world, a tiny new member of the Hwang family, Aunt Lin at once set about preparing eggs and noodles in the kitchen so that every person in the house should have a bowl of noodles and an egg to celebrate the occasion. All the neighbours and relatives who came to hear the glad news were offered eggs and noodles. The noodles signified long life and the eggs, peace. The eggs were dyed in red, for that is the colour that represents happiness.

On the third morning after his birth, the new babe was given his first bath. That, too, was a ceremonial occasion. Grandmother Pan carried out the principal rites, assisted by other women. Sitting beside the bathing vessel, she took up an egg dyed in red and encircled the little fellow's head with it three times. As she did it, she sang a folk-song, praying that the little head would become as round as the egg. When Little Brother was a month old, attaining " Fullness of the Month " as the occasion is called, once more noodles and eggs were prepared for entertainment.

On this occasion Dunglin's second daughter, who had been given out immediately after her birth and was now in her teens, came back home. She was short, homely and timid; her timidity the result of living as a maid in the family of her betrothed. Fourth and Fifth *Go*, her younger brothers, used to tease her, but she would just warn them if they kept it up they could not expect to be properly treated as brothers, when they should come to her house. This time they teased her once again, and she turned and spoke to the new baby, embracing it, " Sweet Little Brother, you are the only one who will be welcome at my house. I'll always have a big bowl of noodles and two round eggs ready for you."

Unfortunately her prophecy was not fulfilled, for the news came a year later that she had died, from an unknown cause, in the house of her betrothed's family. Such was the end of Dunglin's second daughter. Her fate was no better than that of the first one, but she, too, was remembered.

On his first birthday, " The Rounding of the Year ", Little Brother was dressed up beautifully and brought up to the main hall of the house. While his mother, Mrs. Hwang, hugged him to her breast, his old grandmother offered him a lacquer tray on which many small objects were spread at random. There were a seal, an arrow, a bow, a brush pen, an inkstand, a bit of paper, a silver dollar, a balance, some peanuts, a pair of chopsticks, a red egg, some rice stalks and several miniature replicas of real things. Little Brother stretched out his small hands and clasped a brush pen in his right hand and a bit of paper in his left. All the spectators in the hall shouted from happiness. They knew the baby would become a great and learned scholar and would pass the literary examinations his present choice forecast. They recalled once again how his father Dunglin had taken up the balance and the silver dollar at his Rounding of the Year long before. The symbols he had taken up had indeed forecast the future ; for Dunglin had grown up to be a merchant.

On such occasions as the Fullness of the Month and the Rounding of the Year, a baby's mother's family should play an important rôle. But Little Brother was very unfortunate in his maternal family. Not only were his maternal grandparents no longer alive, but a sudden fire had destroyed their dwelling-houses, and taken away his three maternal uncles. One member of the family alone remained, a betrothed daughter of that family who would have become the wife of the uncle second in age in his generation, who had barely escaped the fire. Now, with all her fiancé's family dead, she would have been sold by her kinsmen if Dunglin had not been alert enough to adopt a husband for her. He thus assured a continuance of the line of the Cheng, their family name.

This was just the time of the Chinese Revolution, the year

1911, when the Manchu government was overthrown. The disturbances which arose in the cities soon spread to the towns and villages. One day about this time a village elder suddenly gave warning of the coming of a band of the " Long Hair Bandits ". They were coming towards the Hwang village, so that all the people had to flee the village to the deep mountains. Carrying Little Brother on her back and clasping Fourth and Fifth *Go* by the hand, Mrs. Hwang ran out, as fast as her bound feet would let her, through a back door of the house. But it turned out the revolutionists were not bandits and did not plunder. The so-called Long Hair Bandits, as the villagers still recalled, were the insurgents of the " Taiping Rebellion " of 1850–64.

Third *Go*, Dunglin's eldest son, was not at home at the time of the revolutionary incident. After his two years' schooling in town, he went to live with his aunt, Dunglin's second sister, who had married into a family named Wang. The Wang family had a cousin, Wang Chihsiang, who was the master of the primary school in which Third *Go* enrolled as a student. Chihsiang had passed a provincial examination and had obtained the degree of *Chujen*. Later, as we shall see, he played an important rôle in politics. Two years later, Third *Go* was called back home and Dunglin asked him to join Chang Mowde, Fenchow's third son, who was studying in a missionary school, Yinghwa College, situated on Nantai Island in the city of Foochow. Third *Go* stayed there for the next six years.

Shortly after this, Dunglin arranged the marriage of his nephew, Eldest *Go*. Early on the morning after his wedding, the nephew rushed into his uncle's bedroom and demanded that he send the bride back. Eldest *Go* said he had made a test and the bride was not a virgin. He said his brother-in-law, the husband of his elder sister who had come to celebrate the wedding, had told him how to make the test. Dunglin was very angry with both young men, Eldest *Go* and his brother-in-law, and berated them for their stupidity about such a test. While Eldest *Go* was trying to justify himself with further argument, a terrible shout came from the bride's room. Aunt Lin discovered the bride trying to commit suicide. She had swallowed poison. All the women rushed in and set about making her vomit. Soon the bride recovered consciousness, and broke into bitter cries at her disgrace.

The bride was tall and pretty. Being a clever woman she behaved tactfully in the household. Later on, Eldest *Go* became very much attached to her, and they both hated their mischievous brother-in-law from that day on.

About this time Dunglin took advantage of the New Year vacation, and went to call on his uncle Yuhun to discuss the burial of his grandparents. Their remains had been left in their coffins in a cabin on the farm awaiting final burial. The two men set out next day with a geomancer to look for a suitable place. A lucky site was found. The geomancer set his compass on a spot at the head of a hill from which there was a view of broad farm land below. He explained the hill looked like a mouse with its head extending into the farm land where crops were growing. The site was accordingly called A-Mouse-Facing-A-Barn. A man's descendants should be very rich and prosperous with such a lucky site chosen.

The choice of a burial site based on divination and geographical configuration was a necessary step in any burial, for the belief in " wind and water " was deeply rooted in the hearts of the villagers. Therefore, as soon as Dunglin had bought the lucky site, he built a tomb on it, all of bricks, fifty feet in length and thirty feet wide. The funeral ceremonies were carried out there and the remains of his grandparents were finally buried in the brick chamber of the tomb. He often took pride later in having chosen such a fine burial-site for the grandfather whom he had so much respected.

The final disposal of the remains of his grandparents had been troubling Dunglin's mind for the past twenty years. It was not merely a filial duty. We remember how much Dunglin in his youth had been bound to his grandfather ! To-day he could see that the old man lay at peace resting in the lucky site. What a great joy it was to him, the living, too. He too felt released and at peace.

Nevertheless time brings changes continually. The more one keeps old memories, the more one collects new ones. Dunglin's duties towards the older generation were only one part of life. The older he grew himself, the greater became his responsibilities to those of the younger generation. Human life goes in cycles. Occasions like birth, education, marriage and death, as we have briefly noticed in the Hwang family, are the stages that ever tend to throw out of gear the normal way of life. Each stage begins with a crisis. Each crisis stirs up change and is accompanied by the ritual which pulls life back from its deviation to a normal course.

Meanwhile store business took Dunglin to Foochow, where once again he met his old friend Cheng Lugo. Lying on long chairs placed side by side, the two friends reclined in the bathing-house where they had formerly visited. Once while they were talking lazily, a fortune-teller, dragging a long blue gown and beating a horn instrument, came up to them. Lugo signalled the fortune-teller, who stopped beating the horn. As the man in the long blue gown moved a chair near them, Lugo turned to Dunglin and asked him to name his " eight characters ", that is, the year, month, date, and the hour of his birth, in order to have a basis for calculating his fortune.

Having taken this record of Dunglin's birth, the fortune-teller opened his secret book and meditated for some minutes. Then he wrote a few phrases on a piece of red paper. Turning to his customers, he said, " If you don't mind, sirs, I will explain very frankly what I have written."

" We don't mind at all. Please go on with your explanation."

" To begin from the beginning," the fortune-teller said, " the person whose fortune I am telling must have gone through many troubles during his life. He could not have seen the face of his father except in babyhood. Yet his mother lived a long life. In his teens he must have suffered loneliness, conflict, insecurity, poverty and much else. When he was just on the right track a great misfortune must have befallen him. That probably was the death of an important member of his family, from which point he began to bear further burdens.

" At the present stage of his life, he must be enjoying a state of progressive prosperity. He must now be a merchant dealing with trade balances and credits all day long. While he is managing his business in the outside world, his wife, faithful and devoted, helps him manage the household affairs, so that peace rules in his family. He has or will have at least four sons who will help glorify this family in the future.

" His family and business have been prosperous so far, yet there will be a very dangerous time within the next five years. This danger will probably take his life. If not that, he then will be involved in some great trouble, in which much of his property will be destroyed. If he can pass this dangerous period, his future life will be as smooth as the surface of the sea."

After he had left them, the friends Lugo and Dunglin laughed at what the fortune-teller had prophesied. Would fate really carry Dunglin into a period of danger ?

CHAPTER III

THE LAWSUIT

As time went on, Fenchow and Dunglin, the brothers-in-law and partners of the Hookow store, accumulated a considerable amount of money and they decided to make good use of it. They were thinking of building houses for themselves. They both went with a geomancer to look around the village of Hwang for suitable building sites. Starting from the village, which is situated on the lower half of Pheasant Mountain facing south, they worked to the west towards Dragon Mountain, which protects the valley like a western wall. The stream and the Western Road both pass below the Hwang village and run parallel from east to west for a time, but they begin to separate once more at the foot of Dragon Mountain. The Western Road passes over the top of the mountain, leading directly westward, but the stream flows south-westward and turns round below the peak of the same mountain. When the expeditionary group came to the mountain peak they saw the slopes fall away abruptly below them and noticed a piece of farm land occupying a considerable space between the foot of the mountain and the turning point of the stream. The geomancer set his compass and took his bearings. Suddenly he screamed with joy. He had found a very beautiful site. He named it " A-Dragon-Vomiting-Pearls ", the mountain of course representing the dragon, the field and its crops the pearls, and the stream the saliva.

Fascinated by this lucky site, Fenchow at once called the labourers from his village of Chenyang and ordered them to build a house on the land right before the dragon mouth, but without the knowledge of Dunglin. When Dunglin came to the spot, he saw at once that the plans left no room for erecting another house, and he was very much disappointed. He was far from satisfied with this arrangement of his brother-in-law Fenchow, but as a junior he dared not complain.

So, very unwillingly, Dunglin looked again for another site on which to build his house. Finally he found a suitable spot to the right of the other Hwang houses and standing aloof from the village. From this spot, looking south-westward, the house-site Fenchow had taken could clearly be seen.

Dunglin hired labourers to erect his house and employed his

kinsmen as helpers. For the building material he needed timber. It was on account of the timber that Dunglin became involved in trouble once again. It is true, the seed of the trouble had been sown in the middle part of the previous century in his grandfather's time, but the harvest came to Dunglin.

Dunglin's present house was of respectable dimensions, that is to say, it was one big enough to accommodate fifty persons. It had been built by his grandfather. Yet at the time the grandfather had completed the house he had had only his wife and a daughter. So, to fill the newly-built house, he had invited his two elder brothers and their families to live with him. The three brothers had always been friendly; they co-operated in farm work and in the management of the household. But the arrangement nevertheless gave rise to the future trouble that was to beset Dunglin two generations later.

These three brothers were also on good terms with an uncle, their mother's brother, who was a headman among the clan Ou. This man came very often to the big house as a visitor. The clan of Ou were a prosperous group who lived in the village of Ou, ten miles along the trading road—the Western Road. Their houses were to the east, just across a wooden bridge, known as the Flower Bridge, which crosses the stream that flows to Hookow and joins the Min River there. The Flower Bridge is a toll-gate on the trading road. All the people living to the west of this bridge make up about twenty villages, including the town of Hookow itself, and they form a natural cultural group. They refer to themselves as the People Below Flower Bridge in contrast to the People Above Flower Bridge, those of the villages upstream. But the people of both sides have always been closely related through marriage.

Dunglin's grandfather's mother belonged to this clan of Ou. Her brother, as we have said, was a village headman. But he was fond of his Hwang nephews, and one day he told the three of them to plant trees on the mountain—in his own clan lands, right beside the Flower Bridge. This was, of course, a beautiful gesture on the part of the uncle, but he never dreamt that this bit of timber land would be a source of conflict between the two clans in the future.

For by now the trees on this timber land had grown up, and Dunglin wished to use them as building materials for his new house. With permission from Yumen and Dungchien, the two elders of the line descended from the two brothers of Dunglin's grandfather, he planned to go ahead and fell these trees. He asked Dungfei, a cousin once removed, to head the labourers doing the job.

But when Dungfei led his group of labourers to the mountain beside the Flower Bridge and began to cut the trees, a band of men from the clan of Ou suddenly appeared claiming the right to possession of the trees. They prevented Dungfei from proceeding with his work.

On hearing of the incident Dunglin sent more men to the mountain. But the other faction also increased its numbers and again interfered. Epithets and curses flew back and forth and the two parties soon began to resort to force. There was a clash and some men were wounded.

Immediately after the bloody clash, Ou Asui, then the headman of the clan Ou, rallied a band of his kinsmen, all armed with big knives on long shafts, and led them in a sudden rush to Dunglin's house. They caught him, but instead of doing him harm contented themselves with warning him, backing their warning of course with a display of arms. He must not ever again send his men to the timber land which they claimed was the property of the clan Ou. Dunglin argued his case singlehanded against the lot of them with his usual eloquence and courage, though all the other males of his household had hidden themselves away. But Ou Asui paid no heed to his defence and simply threatened him with danger to his life and property if he were to persist in going further.

At the time of this conflict over the timber land, the clan of Ou was wealthy, prosperous and prolific. There were altogether four lines descended from Dunglin's grandfather's maternal uncle, the very man who had originally allowed his three nephews to plant the trees on his land. Asui, the headman of the four lines, was a man of wealth and reputation. His position as headman, his wealth and a new house he had just recently completed all swelled his own self-pride and the pride of his family in him. When Asui heard that Dunglin also was building a new house, he took offence at Dunglin's rise in the world. The building of a house of respectable dimensions is considered a great mark of eminence and success in the village world. Ou Asui saw a little peanut-seller, whom he had always despised, come to position and honour comparable to his own. His pique soon turned to wrath.

Asui thought he could count upon the fact that Dunglin was inferior to him in all qualities—wealth, fame, experience, age, and the manpower of his following in family and clan. He thought Dunglin would simply yield to his threats and that soon he would have the trees cut for his own use without further ado. That is the usual way that a wealthy man becomes still more wealthy.

But Ou Asui miscalculated. Dunglin neither yielded nor showed the slightest weakness. Threatened and offended, he grew angry and excited. He swore such a thing would never happen under the blue sky. He swore everybody knew that the trees on the timber land belonged to the clan of Hwang and that Asui's claim was simply unjust and dishonest. In order to seize the advantage by striking the first blow, he resolved to take the matter to court. So Dunglin petitioned his case at the district yamen in Kutien. By this action, a long and important litigation began and a new turn of events opened up.

The case disputing the timber land, which Dunglin had presented rather impetuously to the government, was a very important turning-point in Dunglin's life. Fate brought Dunglin to meet his opponent Asui directly. The older man was proud and sour, but very experienced, while the younger was industrious, energetic but imprudent. Both were obstinate personalities, a pair of well-trained players ready for a giant game of chess.

This was the greatest crisis that Dunglin had met in his life. As soon as the district prefect had issued summonses for the first trial, both parties of the clan Ou and of the clan Hwang sent representatives to his yamen. The pleaders were Yumen, Dungchien, Yuhun and Dunglin himself. The result of the trial came speedily enough : Asui and his three men were immediately clapped into prison. As a matter of fact, the prefect had no right to hold them till after final decision. But in practice arbitrary injustice was the rule in this corner of the world where the people, mainly villagers and farmers, were ignorant of the law. The corrupt prefect only wished to threaten any litigants who were among the common people, clapping them into prison in order to extort more bribes.

A great fear came over the clan of Ou when they learned that their headmen were imprisoned. All the Ou kinsmen gathered together and swore they would stand together to the last on behalf of their leaders. They collected money from all the four lines of which Asui was headman and returned to carry on the suit.

Meanwhile a new prefect took the place of the one who had been in favour of Dunglin. The people of the clan Ou were soon able to approach the new man with a petition for a second hearing. Again the result came as speedily as before. But this time Asui and his men were set free, and Dunglin and his Uncle Yuhun were taken off to prison.

Dunglin entered prison with a heavy heart. He was kept isolated from friends and home until the second trial should be held. While the kinsmen of the clan Ou stood together behind their headman, a cleavage grew up among the Hwang families. Yumen and Dungchien, the elders of the other two branches of the clan, fearing they would be involved in further complications, withdrew from the lawsuit and relinquished their property rights to the trees. These two were related to the clan of Ou because one of Dungchien's daughters had married a grandnephew of Asui, and Asui had a son-in-law who was in turn a nephew of Yumen. The nephew, more attached to his wife's family than to his own, kept them informed of every detail of the secret plans of the clan of Hwang. Dunglin thus found himself deserted and betrayed. There was left to him only his Uncle Yuhun. But Yuhun, though poor and aged, would fight for ever for his nephew, Dunglin. And so he went with him into gaol.

The news of Dunglin's imprisonment struck the family at home like a thunderbolt. The helpless women, Grandmother Pan, Aunt Lin and Mrs. Hwang, wept and wailed. They could depend on no one except Dunglin, their only grown man and the sole support of the family, yet he was now in gaol. Gaol, in the minds of the villagers, was a sort of half-way step to the netherworld; the next door beyond gaol was hell itself.

Eldest *Go*, Dunglin's nephew, then a young and inexperienced man, immediately went to see Lei Wuyun, one of the most powerful men of the district. As an adviser of a district prefect, Wuyun was said to be very influential in politics. Earnestly begging Wuyun to use his influence to release Dunglin, Eldest *Go* offered him some money, which he accepted. Wuyun promised he would do his best. But no one knows whether he did ever try to do anything or not. It is certain that when Eldest *Go* went to visit Wuyun a second time, he talked as encouragingly as before. Dunglin, however, stayed on in gaol.

Still another old uncle of Dunglin's, his mother's brother, made the journey afoot, in spite of his age, to see Dunglin in his prison. This old man, unlike the others, was faithful and made the trip three times, a fact which heartened Dunglin. It was he who kept Dunglin informed and who carried Dunglin's messages home.

He calmed the agonized feelings of the women, especially those of his sister, Grandmother Pan. An old and experienced farmer, this kind uncle did all that he could.

We must not forget Fenchow, Dunglin's brother-in-law and business partner. The old saying is a true one : " Happiness does not come twice but misfortunes never come singly." The store did not escape while Dunglin was in gaol. In the middle of one night a group of bandits broke in and stole all the money in the till. They carried off Yao Yunseng, then the accountant of the store, who slept behind the counter. Thus Fenchow found his hands full : he had to build up the store business after the theft and he had to make plans for ransoming his accountant.

Yunseng's wife, upon hearing that her husband had been kidnapped from the store, moved into the house of Dunglin. Kneeling before Grandmother Pan, the matron of the Hwang family, Yunseng's wife laid her head upon the breast of the old woman and wailed. The old grandmother, already deeply concerned about her son in gaol, thus had to bear the additional burden of the young woman's constant crying for her kidnapped husband. She felt as if she stood on the brink of an abyss.

After a time Fenchow received a letter from the bandits. They called themselves " The Black Money Association ". Yunseng must be ransomed, otherwise he would be shot. Fenchow then sent a middleman to the camp of the bandits to negotiate the ransom and release. The bandits demanded a large sum. Most of the spare capital of the store had already been used up by the building of the new houses, the expenses in the lawsuit and the theft by the bandits. Fenchow had nowhere to turn to get more money. He stood between the devil and the deep sea.

In all this desperate situation was there really no way out ? If there was none, then Dunglin, his family, and his store were doomed to ultimate and not too distant ruin. Only a new turn of fate could bring a new day, and let them make a new adjustment. Some new compensatory force must be set in motion to save the precarious balance of their lives.

The new force was not long in getting under way. Third *Go* was enrolled as a student in Yinghwa College in Foochow. When news of the misfortunes that had befallen his family reached him, he could not help but hurry back to his native place to visit his father and grand-uncle in their prison and to discuss ways of submitting the case to a higher court. This time they decided they would take it up to the provincial court at Foochow, the capital of the province of Fukien.

Once the case was in the hands of the provincial court, a transfer of documents from the district of Kutien to the capital city was effected. In due course Dunglin and Yuhun were sent for trial to Foochow. The defendants, Ou Asui and his men, were summoned there as well. The court called for the testimony of the two previous trials and sat in judgment upon the conflict between the clan of Ou and the clan of Hwang.

At the final trial both plaintiffs and defendants claimed the right of possession of the trees growing on the mountain land beside the Flower Bridge. Dunglin presented the documents he had to support his claim. His chief exhibit was the document showing a contract written by his grandfather's mother's brother, then the headman of the clan Ou, leasing the mountain to his three nephews, Dunglin's grandfather and two grand-uncles. The document was signed in 1849 and had been sealed by both parties.

The defence, represented by Ou Asui, argued that Dunglin's document was a false one. They asserted that on the date designated in the alleged contract, the ancestor allegedly contracting was in fact already dead. In support of his assertion, Asui presented in evidence the record of his clan book, in which the death of the ancestor in question was entered for the year 1846. If his evidence were good, then the contractor would in fact have died three years before his alleged contract was made.

In the trial, therefore, the decision hinged upon establishing the date of the death of the common ancestor. Once the true date was proved, the validity of the contracts could be determined. Fortunately for his case, Dunglin was able to get hold of a supplementary bit of evidence which threw much light on the question. This was a document embodying a contract of land conveyance made by the same contractor, the headman of the clan Ou, to a cousin of Dunglin's grandfather. The date of the contract was 1851, two years after the first lease. It proved that the contractor was not dead in the year 1849, the time at which he wrote the contract with his three nephews.

Now the question was whether the lease itself was forged or not. There was no doubt that the land conveyance was genuine. Finally, under careful examination, the seals, the signature, the style of writing as well as the quality of the paper showed that both contracts were genuine and could not have been forged.

Thus all the evidence was in favour of Dunglin. At long last, he won his case. Asui was fined, and having lost his case, he was in much disgrace among the villagers.

Gold is purer after passing through an intense heat; jade is more precious after a careful polishing. In the same way a man is stronger after surmounting a crisis. Thus it was with Dunglin. In his dull gaol life he had often dreamt that he had been killed and his soul taken to the netherworld. The destruction of his store and the ruin of his family filled his mind. He passed the days in pain and sorrow.

Free once again, Dunglin did not regret what had happened. He recalled the prophecy of the fortune-teller on the day when he was with Lugo in the bathing house. He told his friends and fellow-villagers that his imprisonment and the waste of money over the lawsuit had all been destined by fate. These things were prearranged by the heavenly gods. For the " heavenly gods " we nowadays can read human beings themselves and for " fate " human society. But however they might attribute them to destiny or the work of the gods, Dunglin and his villagers knew by trial and error how to manage their own lives.

Free now from prison and the threat of the lawsuit, Dunglin immediately took up his business again. As a first step he borrowed some money from the Tienchi Bank, with which he had been originally associated. He used it first to help Fenchow ransom Yunseng, the store accountant, from the bandit camp. The shop had come to the edge of bankruptcy, but Dunglin's victory won over his former creditors and customers, and brought him new associates.

Dunglin's popularity grew more and more as the villagers, travellers, and passers-by gossiped in the teashop of the Hwang village about the building of his new house and about his victory in the lawsuit. Yuhun, Dunglin's old uncle and companion in gaol, was a marvellous reciter of the story of the litigation. A well-educated farmer, he could sit in the teashop hour after hour describing, in detail, how he and Dunglin had argued before the prefects and had defeated their opponents. He repeated it again and again, but his audience always listened wide-eyed.

Thus Dunglin finally got the timber he had sought, and his new house was completed. It was by far the largest house in the village. But before he could move into the new house, he had to set a lucky date for carrying out the task.

Finally on the day chosen, in the morning when the sun had

just come up, each member of Dunglin's family was ready and neatly dressed. They fell into a straight line, as in a parade, and marched one by one out of the main gate of the old house originally built by Dunglin's grandfather. But instead of going directly to the new house, they made a wide détour by way of the big Western Road, the main road below and through the village of Hwang. The procession was not only a show for the villagers. The main road was considered most proper for such happy, prosperous occasions of ceremony and grandeur.

The parade proceeded slowly and solemnly. Dunglin, the head of the family, led the group. He carried in his hands a steelyard with a large beam and heavy weights. It was a symbol that he could weigh rice and collect rents. Grandmother Pan followed closely behind her son. She carried an incense burner, symbol of the continuance of the family line. Eldest and Second *Go*, the two nephews, came next, carrying upon their shoulders a plough and a hoe, the most important tools and symbols of farming. Next came Third *Go*, with his classical books, Fourth *Go* with his case of legal documents, and Fifth *Go* with a box of four literary treasures, namely, a brush, some ink, some paper, and an inkstone. Sixth *Go*, the Little Brother, now six years of age, came next, carrying a pair of small red lanterns suspended at both ends of a small shoulder-pole. Mrs. Hwang, in her turn, carried upon her back her little daughter, Chumei by name, and in her hand, a silver wine-pot and the cups used for festive occasions. She was followed by her sister-in-law, Aunt Lin, who carried a big pan, the symbol of food. Eldest *Sao* came next. Eldest *Sao* was the wife of Eldest *Go*. The word " Sao " was used to designate *Go*'s wife. She had her little son Shoutai on her back, and also carried a dressing-case, the container of a woman's most precious things. Nanmin, the long-term labourer of the family, took up the rear. He carried on his shoulder an old-fashioned gun as if he were protecting the whole group on the march.

The spectators of the parade were mostly the Hwang villagers, all related to Dunglin. They all greeted him, some with shouts of joy. As soon as the parade arrived at the new house standing with its gate wide open, there broke out a crackling of fire-crackers as a sign of welcome. Thus did the group enter their new residence in great excitement and followed by a crowd of the village lads.

The house of Dunglin was built upon a gently sloping hillside which had been levelled into three successive terraces. These terraces were encircled in a square by high walls of stamped earth, painted white on the outer surface. The house differed from the other Hwang houses in one important respect : it had two fortified towers, one in the left corner of the front wall and the other in the right corner of the back wall. These towers made it possible to watch for bandits and to defend the house in case of attack ; for the walls of the tower were pierced at intervals with rows of small gun clefts.

If one wished to enter into the interior of the house, one first passed over the threshold of the main entrance to the front terrace, where a large open court occupied the middle of the enclosure and rooms lined both sides. These were studies and guest-rooms where guests might stay overnight. There was a path built of flagstones laid evenly across the open court. The path ended with ten stone steps leading upward to the main hall of the second terrace above.

Here was the main and the most important part of the house. At each side of the main hall, there were two series of apartments built of wood. In theory the house was supposed to be divided between Dunglin and his dead brother Dungmin. According to custom rule, the elder brother should take the left half and the younger the right half. Consequently, when the Hwang family moved into the new house, Eldest *Go*, being the eldest son of Dungmin, took up the first apartments at the left and lived there with his wife and their son. The second suite of apartments, the future property of Second *Go*, were occupied by him and his mother, Aunt Lin. Dunglin, his wife and children lived in two suites of apartments at the right of the main hall. Grandmother Pan took up a rear chamber and shared it with Mrs. Hwang, her favourite daughter-in-law.

On the central terrace, there were side doors where wooden staircases led upward to a second story taken up by storage rooms. This second story was on a level with the third or rear terrace on which the kitchens and dining-rooms were built. There were also side doors to the third terrace. From them, a steep staircase of more than twenty steps, all of stone, led down from the rear terrace to the back hall of the second terrace of the house.

Since the earliest days when the Hwang ancestors had settled in the village, there had never been a house so large and so magnificent as Dunglin's new residence. He had surpassed his ancestors, even his beloved grandfather, in this, his creation. Remembering the hardships of his youth, the struggle of his rise in business, and the disaster of the lawsuit, Dunglin could look long at this new house and smile a smile of triumph.

CHAPTER IV

THE HOUSE OF CHANG

Some time before Dunglin moved into his new mansion Chang Fenchow, his brother-in-law, had completed his house at the site A-Dragon-Vomiting-Pearls. The Chang house was very like Dunglin's except that the former, having been erected on level ground, did not have three successive terraces. It did contain, nevertheless, three parts : the front patio, the main dwelling-house, and the kitchens. In the rear there was a garden bounded on two sides by high walls with the back open. The arrangement followed the advice of the geomancer, and the natural wall of the steep mountain slope lay open to receive pearls from the dragon's mouth above.

Fenchow was now a man of fifty. He was slender, bony, and square of face. His eyes, sunken and dark, looked very sombre and fearful. As a doctor he wore a long bluish-white gown and walked along gently but upright. He always wore on his head a " bowl cap ", with a red button on top, and carried with him a two-foot pipe with a mouthpiece of false jade.

When about twenty Fenchow had already begun to practise, among the people both below and above Flower Bridge, the healing he had learned from his father. Once long ago when Dunglin's grandfather met Fenchow for the first time, the old man had been so taken by the little gentleman who was so serious in his attitudes and so devoted to his profession, that a marriage between him and the old man's granddaughter, Dunglin's eldest sister, had been arranged.

Though Fenchow had always been a successful doctor, he could never rely upon his profession for the support of his family. A shrewd and far-sighted man, he always seemed to foresee developments before others did. It was he who noticed the coming business development of the town of Hookow and suggested to Dunglin that they open a store there. The store had been very successful under joint management. Fenchow was always thoughtful and looked into the future. It was he who figured out the fluctuating trends of business while Dunglin, the more energetic and the stronger of the partners, carried their plans into effect. The brothers-in-law had learned to work perfectly in harmony, and they made plans, carried on business, accumulated money, bought their farms and built their houses in an amicable and profitable co-operation.

In all the twenty years Fenchow and Dunglin had been carrying on the business of the store in such perfect agreement and such close friendship, the moment of the house building, when Fenchow intended to monopolize a lucky site for his own house instead of sharing it with Dunglin, was the first time in which Fenchow had shown himself mean and a little selfish.

Now Fenchow lived in his new house. One day when he was alone in his study in the front patio, a man came in and greeted him. It was Chang Mowheng, Fenchow's nephew once removed. Mowheng was an educated man who had studied for years in the elementary school in the Wang village under Wang Chihsiang and had known the brothers Wang Yiyang and Wang Liyang. The village of the Wang clan, along the Western Road, seven miles from the district city of Kutien, is large. It contains a population of several thousand and divides them, according to location, into the Upper Wang and the Lower Wang. Wang Chihsiang, the master of the primary school, belonged to the former. He was, as we remember, the teacher of Third *Go*. The Wang brothers, Yiyang and Liyang, on the other hand, belonged to the Lower Wang. Yiyang was Dunglin's old friend who had introduced him to the business stores and the Tienchi Bank in Foochow. The Wang brothers had two big houses placed side by side. Liyang's house stood on the right and Yiyang's on the left. They had made their money from their store in Hookow and had become the richest family in the village.

Mowheng was returning from a visit to the Wang brothers, and he presented his Uncle Fenchow with a red envelope containing a card with characters written on it. The characters were the names of Liyang himself, of his father and of his grandfather, and the name of his daughter, Huilan—the last supplemented by her "eight characters", that is, the year, month, date and hour of her birth. Such a card was the first step in the arranging of a marriage. Mowheng was acting as a go-between, as a man associated with both the family of the boy and that of the girl.

Taking the red card, Fenchow placed it under the incense burner standing before his ancestral shrine on the big table of the main hall. By this act he sought the advice of his own ancestors on the matter of this marriage between the girl proposed and his own third son, Mowde, now a student of Yinghwa

College in Foochow. Fortunately, a full three days passed without any unlucky omens. There had been no breaking of bowls and plates in the home, no cawing of crows over the house outside, no disputes and quarrels among the kinsfolk. All the signs led Fenchow to think his ancestors would consent to the arrangement of this marriage.

As a further step Fenchow took the girl Huilan's date of birth and that of his son Mowde to an astrologer, to determine once again the fitness of the young couple. Although Mowde was born in a Pig-year and Huilan in a Tiger-year, yet a pig and a tiger never quarrel. Such an augury was considered good. All this done, Fenchow then sent off a similar envelope containing a similar card on which the name and birth date of Mowde and the names of his three most immediate forebears were written. At the house of Wang, Liyang similarly examined the credentials of the prospective groom.

This marriage was an important occasion for the two families. The examination of omens was only one consideration. There was the equality of the status of two families to be considered. Fenchow and Liyang were both merchants and the standings of their families were roughly equivalent. Through Mowheng's position as an associate of both families, the betrothal could easily be arranged.

Before the betrothal ever took place, however, Mowheng, as go-between, had to make many trips between the families. The size of the dowry and the kinds of marriage gifts had to be arranged most carefully. Fenchow first drafted a list on a sheet of red paper, which was presented by Mowheng to Liyang, who then revised it, adding some items and deleting some others. It was then returned and a final agreement was arrived at.

This done, they selected a date for the engagement. It was not until this date came that Mowde was notified and called back home from his school.

On the day of the betrothal, the house of Chang was thoroughly cleaned and beautifully decorated. Red lanterns were hung up, new couplets of appropriate poetry were posted up and red tablecloths set out, covering the feasting tables half-way to the ground. For the feast was to gather in all the kinsmen and friends of the family. They all raised their wine cups and toasted their hosts and each other.

The local name for the betrothal was " exchanging the big cards ", because the " male card " of the groom's family was exchanged with the " female card " of the bride's family. Both cards were red and written in a ceremonial style, wishing good luck upon the betrothal and saluting each of the family heads. Mowheng as go-between was the carrier of these cards.

Mowheng also carried to the bride's house half of the dowry, a sum agreed upon between the two families beforehand. He went there with four labourers, each carrying gifts to the bride's family.

As soon as Mowheng and his four labourers appeared in front of Liyang's house, fire-crackers went off in a loud and noisy welcome. The feasting and the celebration had begun. Noodles, fruit, cakes and eight-cornered dumplings specially made for the occasion were spread before the family.

This celebration over, the groom's family and the bride's family were considered bound by the ties of a betrothal, but they still avoided communicating and meeting one another. Neither the family heads nor the future husband and wife could yet come face-to-face.

A year was to pass, however, before Fenchow again sent Mowheng, this time to request a date for the wedding and to present the bride's family once again with gifts and dowry. This new portion was known as the second dowry payment in contrast to the first dowry payment made at the time of betrothal. The gifts this time consisted mostly of silks and other cloth to be used by the bride for her dresses.

As soon as the wedding date was fixed, bridal cakes were presented to the bride's family. The weight of the bridal cakes was carefully measured to an amount which had been agreed upon before the betrothal. Bridal cakes, indeed, were so indispensable that wealthy families used to insist upon a large number of cakes rather than additional dowry payment. Such cakes were made of rice dough mixed with sugar and bits of pork. The cakes were three inches square, and half an inch thick. The house of Wang distributed all these bridal cakes to its friends, relatives and neighbours. They in turn gave Huilan, the bride, such gifts as earrings, bracelets, dresses, shoes, hairpins and clasps, dress cases and other ornaments to complete her trousseau. For the first time she could do her hair up in a roll instead of plaiting it, for now she could safely count herself a bride.

As the wedding drew near, the work of preparation in the villages became enormous. Relatives came from all sides to stay in the house of Chang for the week before the wedding. They divided among themselves the work of sending wedding cards and receiving and recording wedding-presents, engaging musicians and the bridal sedan chair and decorating the house.

Twenty labourers were sent by Fenchow to the house of Wang in order to bring back the trousseau of the bride. For the trousseau consisted now of four huge, high cases of clothing, four leather chests, two bamboo caskets, two wooden boxes, two sets of tables and chairs, a basin stand, a clothing stand, and four dressing-cases, two big and two small. In these cases, boxes and caskets there were many things: needles, pins, cords, threads, ribbons, palm fibre, bracelets, pendants, necklaces, earrings, finger rings, hairpins, brooches, curtain hooks, lacquer trays, lacquer vases, clocks, mirrors, bronze mirrors, candlesticks, yarn, sheer gauge material, silk, wool, blue cloth, tassels, shoes, and many kinds of garments. And lastly the dowry money which the groom's family had paid was wrapped in red paper and put in one of the dressing-cases.

Just before the trousseau was carried out of the house of Wang clan, a lighted brazier was set on the floor of the main hall. The family gathered to carry out the ceremony called "sifting the evil eyes". Each item of the trousseau was passed over the fire, piece by piece. Two specially-hired bridal maids, professional performers on this occasion, carried the rite out. As the things passed over the fire, they chanted: "Let millions and millions of eyes be sifted out; let gold, silver and treasures be sifted in."

In the house of Chang in the village of the groom a bridal room was prepared for the trousseau that was to be carried into it. Everything was new and clean. There was a big wooden bed with a frame lacquered on three sides with legendary pictures on it in different colours. Old Grandmother Pan, who was considered a lucky person because of the many descendants she had, was invited to conduct the ceremonial setting-up of the bridal bed. She came into the bridal room and hung a red curtain over the bed. She put a cluster of taro, with a mother-taro at the centre and the cluster of young taros adhering to it, under the bed. This was a symbol of fertility, for taro is one of the important foods in this corner of the world. Then she put several rice stalks and five copper coins on the bed, symbols of productivity and wealth. She directed that a pair of lanterns, bearing the characters for "hundreds of sons" and " thousands of grandsons " be hung from the curtain hooks. And lastly she ordered several male babies to be brought in to sleep on the new bed in order to complete the magic of fertility.

On the eve of the wedding day the Chang family sent a group of men to parade the bridal sedan-chair over to the village of Wang, to fetch home the bride. The chair itself was carried by four bearers and escorted by a theatrical troupe playing pipes and drums. Men of the household carried brilliant reddish flags and vari-coloured lanterns with long handles, and bore baskets of foods to be eaten at the feast to take place at the bride's house. A cock and a hen were carried in one of the baskets, for it was the ritual that the bride's family should accept only the cock and send back the hen, as a token of their future hopes. In the rear of the procession, ten men carried burning torches in case darkness should descend before the parade reached its destination. Whenever the procession came to a village, fire-crackers exploded in three prolonged bursts, followed by a final burst of music to attract the attention of all spectators. Mowheng, the go-between, led the procession, wearing a long blue gown, black jacket, and a " bowl cap " on his head. Only late at night did the procession reach the house of Wang, where the guests were entertained and where they passed the night.

The following morning, the day of the wedding, Huilan got up early and took a ritual bath. Into her bath tub three things were put : some early rice stalks, some barley and some garlic. The rice stalks symbolized bearing many sons early ; the barley, changing a bride's bad temper ; and the garlic future prosperity and good luck. After her bath the bridal maids helped the bride into her wedding-dress. Once again each garment and ornament had to pass over the ceremonial fire as all the trousseau had. The hired bridal attendants fixed Huilan's hair roll and put her new red shoes on her tightly bound feet.

Huilan was a charming and beautiful girl of nineteen. She was precocious and bold, and as the only daughter of the family she was rather spoiled by her parents' indulgence. At times she had a bad temper and broke things wilfully. Different from other girls, who wept many tears during the days before their wedding, she took the occasion rather lightly. When her mother advised her to change her temper in her new surroundings,

Huilan curtly replied there was no need for her to worry about that.

As soon as Huilan was fully dressed in all her finery, her father Liyang came to carry her from her room to the main hall, now crowded by the relatives who were going to escort the bride to her new home. The father asked his daughter to step into a bamboo sieve which was placed on the floor. He must literally carry her on his back to the meeting-place of her kindred. The symbolism of the ceremony had it that she must not stand directly on the floor lest the " wind and water " of her home be carried by her into the husband's family into which she was going. Then Huilan knelt down to thank her parents and to weep at her departure. Her father placed a bridal crown on her head and her mother put a pretty artificial flower into her hair. Huilan turned to the ancestral shrine and kowtowed before her ancestors.

A noisy crowd filled the main hall of the Wang house. Huilan, the central figure in the ceremony, walked from one bamboo sieve to another without setting her feet to the ground. She turned to each of her relatives and neighbours, one by one. To each of them she made an obeisance. Huilan was not a typical old-fashioned village girl who usually composed folk ballads expressing her love and hatred towards each of her relatives at this moment. But Huilan did her duty creditably.

Just before Huilan went out at last to take her seat in the bridal sedan-chair, several additional rites were carried out. First, one of the bridal maids burnt a piece of hempen cloth, a magical precaution against death, as hempen cloth is used in mourning. Next a boy baby was put in the chair for a little while as a hope that the bride might give birth to sons. And lastly, torches were lighted and carried round the chair to drive away every kind of evil spirit.

The theatrical troupe started its playing of music as soon as father Liyang had put his daughter Huilan into the bridal sedan-chair. The chair is an enclosed box with only a single door on one side. When the door is closed, the bride simply sits in darkness. But the outside of the chair is very beautifully decorated with vari-coloured curtains, cloth flowers, tassels, and embroidered pictures, all topped with a flowery pyramid. As soon as one of the bridal maids had closed the single door, Huilan's mother threw grains of early rice and barley over the roof of the chair. Then the bearers lifted it up and carried it away, and a chopstick was thrown after it to act as an arrow to ward off evil.

Thus the bridal sedan-chair was carried out of the house. The young men of the household took up torches burning in the bright sunlight, and accompanied the procession which the day before had come into the village. The procession consisted of the people previously sent from the house of Chang in addition to the bride, and her two bridal maids who walked beside the chair.

It was about dusk when the bridal procession arrived at the house of Chang. Mowyueh and Mowchiao, nephews of Fenchow, each carried a big red lantern on a long handle and received them at the half-way point. Amid the continual explosion of fire-crackers and the accompaniment of music, the home-coming procession, the crowd that followed it, and the bridal sedan-chair made their slow way into the main hall of the bridegroom's house.

Now the most solemn ceremonies of the wedding began. The bride was the centre of attention. All the people crowded round the bridal chair. The maids struggled with difficulty to break a way for Mrs. Hwang, Dunglin's wife, up to it. She had the honour of opening the door, and she brought her little son, Sixth *Go*, to bow before the bride and proffer her a mirror. The bride had a " bag of five happinesses " to reward Sixth *Go*, who officially invited her to come out of the chair. In the bag, there were five kinds of fruit : peanuts, red dates, hazelnuts, watermelon seeds and dried longans. The five fruits were called " the five sons "—symbols of marital happiness. In the vernacular they had special names : the peanuts were called " Bearing-Sons ", the red dates " Early-Sons ", the hazelnuts " Increasing-Sons ", the watermelon seeds " Many-Sons ", and the longans " Dragon-Sons ".

The bridal maids helped Huilan to step out of the chair. She was crowned and veiled down to her shoulders so that she could not see at all. They led her over a red carpet spread on the ground, chanting a rhythmic couplet as they walked :

> As soon as the bride stands in the middle of the hall,
> There is luck, long life, wealth and happiness for all.

Mrs. Hwang, as matron of honour, led the bride over to a pair of dragon-and-phœnix candles which she lighted. They proceeded then to the bridal room. Mowde the groom, dressed in a blue gown and a black jacket, was already there sitting on the left side of the bed. He was a handsome young man with a round face and a dark complexion. Whenever he smiled, he showed off a gold tooth gleaming like an electric-light bulb. Although he had been educated in the city and had learned many new ways, he did not object to his father's arranging his marriage. He rather felt like an adventurer and was burning with eagerness to look at his bride to see whether she was beautiful or ugly. The bride was brought to sit on the right side of the bed. She was still veiled and her head and face could not be seen. Here now was his life companion who sat beside him still unknown to him. It is said that if during this rite of sitting together, which lasts about fifteen minutes, the bride sits on the border of the groom's gown, he will become a henpecked husband. Sometimes a daring groom slips the hem of the bride's garment under the hem of his own, expecting thus to be dominant over her. But Mowde certainly did not believe this nonsense. He just sat there, meditating.

The crowd waited outside in the main hall to see the most solemn part of the wedding ceremony carried out. Next, the matron of honour led the bridal couple out of the bridal room. They were made to stand behind an offering table facing outward, the groom on the left and the bride on the right. Yao Yunseng, acting as master of ceremonies, came out and spoke a single word to them. "Kneel," he said. The groom and bride followed his order and went down upon their knees. "Kowtow," he said. They touched their foreheads to the ground three times. "Stand up." They got up. They paid obeisance to Heaven and to Earth. Turning inward, the bride and groom performed the same obeisance to the ancestral shrine of the house. After that they bowed to each other face-to-face. All during the performance the bride was helped by the maids and occasionally bursts of applause broke out among the spectators. The music of the threatrical troupe, the songs of the bridal maids, the loud directions of the master of ceremonies and the cheering and applause of the crowd all helped to make a joyful din.

Finally the bride and groom retired to the bridal room. The maids closed the door and shut out the noise of the company. Here now came the private ceremony to which the couple had secretly looked forward with such curiosity. As soon as the bride was asked to kneel down, Mowde came over to lift her veil. His heart beat heavily as his trembling hands lifted off the veil.

But the first glance assured him of his bride's charms. Huilan in her bridal finery was as beautiful as the full moon. Mowde was very lucky. He quite forgot what to do next until the maids reminded him he must lift the bridal crown from the bride's head. As he performed the rite the maids continually repeated rhythmic couplets :

> When the bridal crown is lifted up
> Then the family's luck will fill the cup ;
> When the crown is raised above her head
> Let the groom buy land, and barn and shed ;
> When the crown is set upon a tray
> Jewels rich will all be theirs one day.

Mowde heard nothing the maids were telling him. His whole attention was fixed on this bride whose beauty he beheld and whose fragrance he smelled. His happiness was beyond words.

Next the maids took Huilan behind a screen and helped her take off the ceremonial garments and put on a fashionable flower-printed robe. The groom stood waiting before a small red table on which ten dishes of dainties, a pot of wine, two wine cups and two bowls of rice were arranged in a traditional fashion. A ceremony of eating and drinking together had next to be carried out by the bride and the groom. Mowde and Huilan sat down face to face at the table. One maid poured wine out into the cups which were tied together by a red ribbon. Another maid took up a second cup and gave Mowde the first half to drink and Huilan the second half. Still another cup was handed first to the bride and then to the groom. In this way Mowde and Huilan exchanged wine six times.

Huilan kept her eyes cast down all the while and tried hard to avoid smiling. But in the midst of exchanging the wedding cups, she seized a chance to look at her groom out of the corner of her eye. " Oh, he is handsome ! " she thought. She felt very happy and smiled a little. It was the beginning of mutual understanding between the husband and wife.

Next there was a brief kitchen rite to be carried out. The couple offered obeisance to the kitchen god. For the kitchen would be an important place for the bride, who shortly would have to cook for the whole family into which she was marrying.

During all these rites guests were gathering in ever-greater numbers. The men were entertained in the study and the rooms off the front patio and in the main hall, while the women were brought back to the back hall and inner chambers. Fenchow and Mrs. Chang, the parents of the groom, were very busy receiving all the guests, each of whom extended his congratulations to the parents rather than to the groom himself.

The main hall was so arranged that the groom and bride could come out to make their obeisance to all the older relatives of the family before the assembled company. In front of a big table on which the ancestral shrine was placed two big armchairs covered with red blankets were set side by side. Deep-red carpets were spread on the ground. The groom stood on the left and the bride on the right, both facing inward towards the armchairs. As they took up their positions there was a surge among the crowd as everyone tried to get a look at the bride who appeared now for the first time without her crown and veil. Report of her charms and beauty spread from the front line of spectators back to the outer circles so that an audible hum of admiring comment sprang up.

Soon Chang Fenchow and Mrs. Chang, father and mother of the groom, came out, in full ceremonial dress. They sat down in the two armchairs, Fenchow on the left, facing his son, and Mrs. Chang on the right, facing the bride. Both groom and bride made obeisance to the older couple. The groom's parents sat there motionless, smiling and feeling very proud. After three genuflexions and nine kowtows had been finished, the parents got up from the armchairs and withdrew, leaving behind them a gift, wrapped in red paper, for the young couple. The next persons to be honoured were Mowkwei and his wife. The third in turn were Mowhun and his wife. Mowkwei and Mowhun were the two elder brothers of Mowde, the groom. When all the members of the Chang clan had been honoured, elder relatives outside of the clan but connected with the Chang family were also honoured one by one. The ceremony took a very long time, extending until midnight.

After this the wedding dinner was served. There were four tables in the main hall, six tables in the open yard, and five tables for the women guests in the back hall. Midway through the dinner, after three courses had been eaten, there was a burst of fire-crackers. It was a signal for the groom to kneel down in the middle of the main hall and kowtow to all the guests, thus thanking them for taking part. All during the meal the bridal couple went about from table to table to drink the health of their guests.

Most of the guests dispersed after dinner, but a few young men rushed to the bridal room in order to " tease the bride " as the custom went, their object being to make the bride laugh by all sorts of jokes, and to submit the bride and groom to all kinds of merry embarrassment. At long last they left, but not till the bride had bribed them with the gift of some of her handkerchiefs.

At last the bride and groom could be alone in their room, happy and tired. When Mowde asked his bride, " How do you feel ? " Huilan was too shy to answer and hid her face in the curtains. The bridal maids came in for the last time, their faces wreathed in smiles. They brought the groom the " good luck cloth ", a piece of square and reddish silk to be displayed on the morrow as the traditional test of virginity, and demanded their tips. Only then were the young pair left to each other.

Next day there were further ceremonies. Wang Chihkun, Huilan's younger brother, arrived at the house of Chang. He brought with him two ordinary sedan-chairs and invited his sister and her newly-wedded husband to go back with him to the house of Wang. There were further ceremonies performed in the presence of the bride's family. The new son-in-law was received ceremonially by Liyang, who offered him three times a brew of special tea and a puff of special tobacco.

Mowde and Huilan made their obeisances to the ancestors of the bride's family. They again went through the ceremony of kneeling and kowtowing to clan members and relatives, this time those of the house of Wang. All the gifts they received this day became their private property because for the first time now they were deemed capable of owning private possessions, where before their marriage all their goods and money had belonged to their parents. Their wedding was thus an important day in which trousseau, furniture and money were laid down as a foundation for a family of their own.

In the days that followed, Mowde and Huilan enjoyed many celebrations and many parties in the house of Wang and passed the most delightful time that they had ever known. Being a handsome, well-mannered, pleasant, well-educated young man, Mowde brought joy to his parents-in-law. Later on the newly-wedded couple went back to live in the house of Chang. Fenchow asked Mowde to stay at home to help manage family affairs instead of returning to school, and Mowde accepted gladly.

The marriage of Mowde was over and the life in the house of

Chang could return to normal. Mowkwei went once again to Foochow as the fish dealer for the firm. Fenchow came and went between the Hookow store and his new house. The family lands were cultivated now by Mowhun, Fenchow's second son, and their hired labourer, Peimin.

Here now was another link in the circle of associations which Fenchow had built up gradually during his life, by his medical practice, by his partnership in opening up the store with Dunglin, by his business connections, by his building of the house, and last but not least, by his alliance with the house of Wang through his son's marriage. Two circles of associations, that of Fenchow and that of Dunglin, were now equally extensive and equally robust and prosperous and honoured in the villages, and both were closely interrelated. But were they going to differ as they grew apart, and finally to meet different ends?

CHAPTER V
PRIMARY EDUCATION

One day while Dunglin was sitting at the counter an old gentleman entered the gate. Dunglin recognized the old man walking with the help of a stick. He was Wu Sungnan, an influential man of the town. Dunglin stood up to greet him and politely offered him a chair.

"Uncle Wu, what wind sends you here to-day?" asked Dunglin as he went to get a water-pipe for the old man.

"I have been wanting for a long time to come and congratulate you, Brother Dunglin," answered Sungnan. "You are certainly the foremost man in town now."

"Oh! no, I am not good enough for that! You flatter me too much, Uncle."

With this complimentary overture Sungnan and Dunglin both sat down to discuss the business of the selling and buying that had been carried on in the store. As they sat there Fenchow happened to come over from the medicine department. Seeing Sungnan, he immediately brought him a cup of tea as a mark of courtesy. Sungnan expressed to both partners his admiration at the success of the store and the completion of their new house. He expressed to Fenchow in particular his regret at not having been able to attend Mowde's wedding. He had heard, he said, that it had been a great and splendid occasion.

In the course of further talk Sungnan told the partners that he had hired a teacher and was organizing a primary school to which he hoped they would send their children. Dunglin had long felt the importance of modern education for his children, especially after the litigation, and gladly agreed to co-operate. Without losing a moment Dunglin looked over to his cousin Dungheng, Yuhun's eldest son, who was standing at the other side of the counter and sent him off to carry the message back to their home village that Sixth *Go* should come to town to attend school.

As soon as Sungnan had left the store, Fenchow said privately to Dunglin: "It seems very curious to me that a man like Sungnan should become an important man in the town. Do you remember how sudden his rise was and how many rumours it stirred up? He was originally only the owner of a bakery.

Someone told me a certain cousin of his was a chief of one of the Black Money Associations and used to cache his money in Sungnan's bakery. Then this cousin came to live with him after he retired from his life of robbery. They say Sungnan murdered his cousin and got hold of all the money that the bandit had stolen. That is, they say, how he got rich."

Dunglin answered: "I have heard that, but I never knew how much truth there was in it."

"Anyhow," Fenchow continued, "Sungnan built a new house after that and took a wife and a concubine. They say the house was haunted by the ghost of his cousin. Then he met a Western missionary who drove the ghost away for him and whose preaching of the Gospel converted him to Christianity. He offered his house to be used as a church in which services were to be held every seventh day and school on the other six days. Now the Chinese preacher and the school-teacher both live with him."

Dunglin said: "If that's the case, his school is a missionary school." He continued after a pause, "That is all right. I got a letter from Third *Go* recently, which says that he has been baptized. At any rate, that's the way to get to associate with the influential foreigners and church-people."

At this point an apprentice lad from the medicine department came to call Fenchow away, so that the talk between the two brothers-in-law came to an end. But a decision had been reached.

The following day Dunglin's second son, Fourth *Go*, took Sixth *Go*, the Little Brother, to town to see their father. Dunglin did not take his young son to school himself. He asked Yao Kaituan, a newly appointed accountant, to do it for him. Kaituan took Little Brother by the hand and walked with him up to the main gate of Sungnan's house. No sooner had they stepped into the house than they saw that both the right and left patios were crowded with children, each sitting beside a desk. The school-teacher was a middle-aged man dressed in a long gown. He welcomed Kaituan by putting his hands together and bowing his head. Kaituan performed the same courtesy in return. Then he asked Little Brother to kneel before the teacher as all students do when they first meet their teacher. In the meantime, Fourth *Go* had brought a desk for Little Brother from the store, and the teacher ordered it to be put in the second row in the right-hand patio.

Sixth *Go*, the little boy who had officiated at Mowde's wedding by carrying out the rite of inviting the bride out of her sedan-chair, was now eight years old. He was a weak, pale child, and as he had been brought up in small home-village, he was very shy and afraid of strangers. As soon as he had sat down at his own desk he began to regret his having come to school. He did not want his elder brother Fourth *Go* to leave him. When the elder brother left through the school-house door, the little one's eyes filled with tears. He felt so lonely among strangers, like a young goat lost in the wilderness. The preacher's son who sat in the first row looked back at the country child and ridiculed him. " Look at the miller pressing out the oil," he said, referring to Sixth *Go*'s tears. Little Brother could endure it no longer. He ran out of the school-house after his brother and demanded to be taken back with him.

Dunglin, however, was a stern and severe father. All his sons looked upon him as the tyrant of the family and tried to keep as far as possible away from him. But they always obeyed his orders like imperial edicts. Pale little Sixth *Go* of all the brothers feared him most and did not feel any affection for him. It did not help, then, that his father mercilessly told Fourth *Go* to return home to the village as soon as the two of them appeared back at the shop, and ordered Little Brother to go back to school alone. The second day of school life for Little Brother in fact was more frightful than the first, when the teacher began to examine him in his lessons.

So the third day after breakfast Little Brother lied to his father when he promised he would go straight to school and instead simply turned off in a homeward direction. After a little while he saw Dungheng in the main street of Hookow and watched him closely, intending to follow him to the village. As soon as Dungheng left the town, Little Brother followed him at some distance behind, and thus they both walked towards the village of Hwang. When Dungheng finally discovered him, it was too late to stop him because they had already arrived at the edge of the village.

When Little Brother thus made his sudden appearance before his mother, Mrs. Hwang, she welcomed him warmly because she had missed him so very much. He clung to her, crying and swearing that he would never go to school again. He would gladly feed water-buffaloes his whole life long if only he might stay and live with her. Mrs. Hwang was a tender and warm-hearted woman. She took him up into her arms and soothed him. She began to tell him a story that she well knew would please him. Gradually the fears of his school life were pushed out of his little mind and his heart was full of happiness. Mother and son chatted and laughed together and all seemed well again.

But happiness reigned only till word came that Dunglin, too, was coming back to the village. They were greatly startled at the news of his coming back. Little Brother felt the threat of punishment hanging over him. His cheeks burned and his heart beat painfully in his breast. As swiftly as he could he left his mother's side and fled through the back door of the kitchen, intending to run deep into the forest on the mountain behind the house. But Mrs. Hwang followed him out and pleaded with him to return. Little Brother was thus led back to be the victim of his tyrant father.

In the heat of his anger Dunglin broke a bamboo stick beating his son for disobeying. The little boy was ordered to leave for school without a moment's delay. Sixth *Go* cried for help. Mrs. Hwang, who usually obeyed her husband, to-day remonstrated with him for the sake of her little son. "It was not Little Brother's fault," she said, "I asked him to come back."

Dunglin turned upon his wife and shouted, "Shame on you! Don't you understand that I am sending your son to school for his own good? I am not putting him in prison!"

Mrs. Hwang fell silent and dared not try any further to stop the father's beating of his son. But Grandmother Pan and Aunt Lin came running out together and they tried to stop Dunglin. But no sooner did they get near him than he picked up the crying boy and carried him out of he house. The women called after Dunglin to come back and take lunch at home, but he refused. The boy cried louder and louder as his father carried him upon his shoulder, walking away to the Western Road.

The three women, Grandmother Pan, Aunt Lin and Mrs. Hwang, came out of the house and stood outside at the main gate watching father and son. Not far from the house Dunglin put Little Brother down again upon the ground. But the boy refused to walk and lay down in the road. Snatching up a stick, Dunglin beat his son once more, but this time with heavier blows, so that his victim screamed out at the top of his voice. The three women, in spite of their bound feet, ran along quickly to them. But to their disappointment, the father picked up the boy once more and carried him farther away as soon as they got near.

At sunset Fourth *Go* came home from his work on the farm and learned how Little Brother had run away from school and how he had been punished and carried away. Mrs. Hwang urged Fourth *Go* to go to see Little Brother. She knew he was good to the boy, who had been his bedmate since the birth of their youngest sister Chumei. So the two brothers, Fourth *Go* and Sixth *Go*, met in the store, and the little one showed his swollen hands and feet, hurt in the punishment that he had got. The elder brother soothed him and advised him to be a good boy from then on.

Yet when Fourth *Go* was about to leave the store, Little Brother, who dared not run away again, clung to him and would not let him leave. The two brothers had always been very fond of each other. But Dunglin came out and snatched the little boy away from Fourth *Go* and carried him into the back room. Hearing the crying of the little voice from the bedroom, Fourth *Go* left the store with a heavy heart. He broke into tears when, arriving home again, he was asked by his mother about his little brother.

It may seem strange that Dunglin was so stern about putting his little son into school. Having himself experienced many difficulties and handicaps, Dunglin realized how essential it was that the boy be educated in order to make his way in life. His hopes of moulding his little son were certainly to prove effective for Little Brother, who as we shall see later became a highly educated man. If Dunglin had allowed his son to follow his own wishes, Little Brother might for ever have remained a mere buffalo boy. With the bitter lesson of the litigation in his mind, Dunglin could insist that his plans be carried out. With the best interests of his son and his family at heart, Dunglin enforced his personal authority, and made the boy conform to his new environment.

Indeed a few days later Little Brother began to take an interest in his school life. The first boy to whom he spoke was Wei Chenchin. Chenchin was older but not so bright as he. Soon they became friends and also occasionally enemies. In the arithmetic class Little Brother always showed his quickness by solving the problems long before the others, so that his schoolmates all came to him for the answers. He was also quick to learn in his other courses—history, geography, penmanship and composition. The preacher's son, who had despised him at first as a country child, soon became friendly with him.

The school was planned by missionaries and preachers. Under the school organizer, Sungnan, and the teacher, a modern curriculum had been adopted. But the old traditions which still existed in the family and village schools were more or less maintained. Once when Chenchin was about to recite an essay, he turned his back on the teacher as an old-fashioned student would. He stopped half-way through his recitation, for he had not memorized the other half. Little Brother, who sat beside him, tried to help him by whispering to him. Unfortunately the teacher heard him. The teacher at once took a white chalk and marked two circles on the ground. Chenchin and Little Brother had each to stand in one of them for some hours as punishment. The punishment was a modification of " kneeling incense " before the shrine of Confucius. Confucius was no more ; for in the missionary schools the Church prohibited the worship of other gods than Jesus Christ. But the punishment remained, though in a modified form. A student who had had to do " kneeling incense " in former days had knelt down before the shrine and held an incense stick in both hands. Not until the incense stick had burnt completely away was he allowed to stand up.

Little Brother often won rewards for his diligence in study. If the teacher drew with his red brush pen a mark in the shape of an egg on the palm of Sixth *Go*'s hand, this indicated he should be rewarded with an egg. The boy would then show the " egg " or his palm either to his Uncle Fenchow or to the accountant Kaituan. One of them would certainly buy an egg for him that very evening. Little Brother never showed his eggs to his father ; he was afraid of him. But Dunglin grew more fond of his son Sixth *Go* as the boy made progress in his school studies, especially as he never failed to get his name listed first among all his schoolmates in the final examinations.

Besides studying well, Little Brother became active in outside activities. There was an athletics class at school. Each student had a wooden gun modelled after a real gun. The teacher, acting as commander, called out orders to the students, marching and stopping them as in an army. He taught them to sing war songs. Then in the evening after school the students themselves practised what they had learned in the athletics class. In addition, they copied details of organization from a troop of soldiers stationed in the town of Hookow. They kept a book recording the office of each person of their group. During one period Chenchin tried to compete with Little Brother for the commandership. The students proposed to vote by secret ballot. Two candidates, Little Brother and Chenchin, had their names written on a piece of paper. Those who favoured Little Brother wrote their names under his. When the ballots were opened, no names were found under that of Chenchin, and he was thus defeated. Chenchin, however, tried to make up by studying diligently, in order to win back his place with his fellow-students. But this proved in vain, for he never won favour even for studying hard.

One evening Little Brother, as commander of the group, ordered his army to march into the store belonging to his father Dunglin and his Uncle Fenchow. Every one at the store was greatly surprised, and people came from the neighbouring stores to look at the " army ". Surrounded by the spectators, Little Brother called out his orders and the troop practised the exercises which they had learned at school. In addition, they went through the new drill they had copied from the real army squadron, who drilled in the village every morning. The performance of the students brought up a roar of laughter from the crowd. Dunglin, sitting at the counter, looked at his little son's army with great pleasure, and at last felt proud of him.

There was a girl named Chang Yuehying in the school, sitting in the row behind Little Brother. She was the eldest daughter of Mowheng, the go-between of Mowde's marriage. Mowheng was the owner of a grocery store in the town of Hookow. His business had been so prosperous that he had moved his family from the village of Chenyang to live in the back room off the store. As an educated and " modern " man, Mowheng sent his daughter to the primary school to study among the boys. Yuehying was a very well-behaved little girl and never mixed much with the boys. She had a face as round as the full moon, clear bright eyes and crescent eyebrows. A very beautiful dimple appeared on her left cheek whenever she smiled. Yuehying and Little Brother were very friendly, not only because of their family relationship, but also because they were both interested in their lessons.

Once Yuehying went to wash her hands in the washroom at the side of the school-house, and Chenchin, the boy who was a rival of Little Brother's, came after her and tried to embrace her.

She grew very angry, but because of her timidity only told the story privately to Little Brother. He immediately reported it to the teacher. The teacher got very much excited, because that kind of action was most vulgar and one of which an educated child should never be guilty. He seized a bamboo stick and beat Chenchin on the head with it. He was so furious that he used the bamboo stick, which was ordinarily used only to beat a student's palms, to strike the lad's head.

When in the store Little Brother did not spend much time in his studies but asked people to tell him stories or amused himself making water-mills, bird-cages and grass baskets. One day he even stole a box from the medicine department to make one of his inventions, and as a result he was again severely punished by his father. This time he thought the punishment was unfair. For he had just begun not to fear his father so much as before, because now Dunglin was beginning to indulge him somewhat over his school successes. After this new punishment Little Brother cried the whole afternoon. As he was crying, Mowheng, who liked him very much and who by chance happened to pass the place, came in to soothe him, but even he could not stop the boy's crying. Mowheng left in disgust. He told the store people that he had spent two hours with him and had still been unable to stop the stubborn boy from weeping. His fondness for the boy lessened. Later, as a result, when Third *Go* asked Mowheng to betroth his daughter Yuehying to Little Brother, Mowheng flatly refused him.

Meanwhile Little Brother grew accustomed to a life divided between the store and the school. For the time being he forgot his life in the village. Gradually his father, instead of his mother, became his constant associate. His father grew more and more attached to his little son. In the end not only the relationship between the father and son changed considerably, but others too began to note the change and to come to regard the boy in a new light.

Little Brother, however, did not completely lose all association with his family and village. At the Dragon Boat Festival, Dunglin sent his little son back home. Little Brother was extremely glad to see his mother and elder brothers and to enjoy family life again. When he reached the house, he saw new couplets posted on the sides of the gate. On the lintels of the gate there hung branches of calamus with their sword-shaped leaves to ward off evil influences. He entered the house amid the clamouring of the children, his sister Chumei and little nephew Shoutai, who crowded round him asking for cakes.

Mrs. Hwang, Aunt Lin and Eldest *Sao* sat in the hall in the third terrace, preparing three- and four-cornered dumplings. The dumplings were made from glutinous rice and mixed with meat, fruit and beans. Bamboo leaves were used to rap the dumplings together, which were tied with grass strings to form bundles. The bundles of dumplings were boiled, and then hung from the ceiling, whence they would be taken down from time to time to be eaten as delicacies.

When Sixth *Go* came in, he showed his mother a dozen handkerchiefs and a paper fan on which several lines had been written. The paper fan had been given to Sixth *Go* by his school-teacher. It was the tradition that at the Dragon Boat Festival a feast was held to which the students invited their teacher. Afterwards the teacher distributed gifts of fans and handkerchiefs to the students. Fifth *Go*, who had gradually become a leader of the village youngsters, wanted the fan in order to show it to his companions, but Little Brother would not give it to him. In the tussle Fifth *Go* snatched the fan and tore it to pieces. Sixth *Go* cried in dismay. Fourth *Go*, on good terms with Little Brother, came to the rescue and grabbed Fifth *Go* and the two brothers fought. Although Fourth *Go* was two years older than Fifth *Go*, he was small for his age, so that their strength was almost equal. Mrs. Hwang, their mother, tried to separate them, but she could not stop them from wrestling. From that day on the two brothers fell out and fought each other.

To appease her children Mrs. Hwang took out some embroidered incense-bags and distributed them as festival gifts. The bags were all very small, embroidered in the shapes of birds, tigers, wolves, fish, drums or fans. Each bag was filled with fragrant incense powder and carefully sewed together. Each was tied with a ribbon so that it could be hung around the neck.

The family celebration was held at noon on the fifth day of the fifth moon, the proper day for the festival. Although Dunglin and Third *Go* did not come home for the occasion, the other members enjoyed the feast much as usual. They drank realgar wine, which was made by putting realgar powder into ordinary wine. They used the realgar mixed with water to smear the foreheads of the children, Sixth *Go*, Chumei and Shoutai, in traditional fashion. Fourth *Go* even made a realgar powder cylinder which was lighted up and whose fumes it was said would ward off poisonous influences. After it had burned out, he took the smoky cylinder and wrote a few words with it on the walls for good luck. There is nothing like realgar powder to ward off calamities such as plagues or other diseases, poisonous snakes and insects.

In the afternoon Fourth *Go* and Little Brother went to the town of Hookow. There on the Min River Dragon Boat racing was carried on for several days. The story has it that the Dragon Boats commemorate a loyal minister and poet of Ancient China who was drowned. Four-cornered dumplings were thrown into the water to feed the spirit of the faithful man. Racing was very popular at this time in the region around Foochow.

Soon after the festival the summer vacation began. Third *Go* came back from Foochow and brought with him Chen Shankai, his classmate and a sworn brother. Shankai was a man about twenty, of great stature, square-faced and broad-shouldered, stout and energetic. He liked to talk, tell stories and make jokes. The members of the Hwang family all soon liked and respected him.

Once that summer, strolling along with Third *Go* and his three younger brothers up the hill behind the house, Shankai looked up at the mountain ridge and exclaimed, " Here is ' wind and water ', brothers ! The mountain which looks like a pheasant, from which fact it gets its name, has its head and face on the other side, but it twists one of its golden wings toward your house. That must be the reason why your family is prosperous. Let me call your house ' The Golden Wing '." Third *Go* and his brothers were delighted by this suggestion. They repeated what he had said to the members of the Hwang family, who took it with great seriousness because Shankai was a well-educated man. They thought his words carried more weight than those of a common village geomancer. The phrase spread from the family to the villagers and from the villagers to the townspeople, so that in the end the house of Dunglin became known as the House of the Golden Wing.

Vacation life is always very pleasant for students. That of the Hwang brothers was more so because of the company of their sworn brother Shankai. They often went out under the moonlight to steal peaches and grapefruit from the neighbouring villages. Coming to the bank of the stream, they would sit down on the grass to talk and consume their spoil. They spent their daytime hours swimming, climbing the hills, and collecting wild fruit, or paying visits round about. Sometimes they went to see Mowde and to have lunch with him in the house called A-Dragon-Vomiting-Pearls. After stealing sweet potatoes from mountain terraces, they would hold their picnics merrily high up on the peaks. In the village world, the stealing of fruit and potatoes was so frequent and so accepted that no one regarded it a crime.

Time when it is pleasant flies like an arrow. So Shankai and the Hwang brothers thought at the end of the vacation when once again the students had to leave for their schools. Everyone was saddened at their going. Shankai had been treated like an adopted son. He made the round with Third *Go* when he went to pay his respects to each of the family. Grandmother Pan took out two boiled eggs and some horse-beans and gave them as her parting gifts to him, because she loved him as a grandson. When he went to say good-bye to Dunglin in the town, Dunglin insisted again and again that he must come back again later. Thus began the relationship between Shankai and the family, started in such an ordinary way, but to become immensely important in the future life of the family, as we shall see.

CHAPTER VI

VILLAGE FESTIVITIES

Shortly after the departure of Shankai and Third *Go*, the season of tomb sacrifices arrived, an occasion to be participated in by all the families of the Hwang village. The first sacrifice —to the first ancestor—always took place on the first day of the eighth moon. Their first ancestor, in the case of the Hwang, was the great-great-great-grandfather of Dunglin's own grandfather, the man who had migrated out of South Fukien up along the Min River and had settled down so long ago in this little village of the Hwang. It was his misfortune that at the time of his arrival, all the land surrounding the village was already occupied by earlier settlers. Yet, by dint of hard labour, he had gained a foothold in the village. He certainly could never have imagined that several centuries later ninety-nine per cent. of the population would belong to the clan of Hwang, and only one house, the village inn, be left to be run by others. To-day the Hwang villagers, all of the same descent, are closely bound together in so fierce an allegiance to each other against outsiders that their settlement is named " the barbaric village ". Moreover, the clan still retains a special brogue of the dialect of South Fukien which the neighbouring villages do not understand. When the Hwang villagers do try to communicate with outsiders, they must use the dialect of the whole district, the Kutien dialect, named after the chief city of this part of the province. To this very day the first ancestor's descendants, in their hearts as well as in their language, are truly a clan.

The rites of tomb sacrifice have been developed through tradition. The first ancestor is said to be the nominal owner of a piece of land, usually called the ancestral plot, and cultivated in rotation by the different families among the different lineages of the clan. Each year, whichever family is temporarily the tenant in charge of the ancestral land gets the right to the produce of the plot. But it also has the duty of making sacrifices and preparing a feast for the whole clan for that particular year. The ancestral plot is of course never permitted to be sold, and the whole clan has a collective responsibility towards it.

The tomb of the first Hwang ancestor is situated on a mountain-top half-way between the clan village and the town of Hookow. On the day of sacrifice Fifth *Go* and Little Brother, the family representatives chosen to do so, went up early to the tomb to preserve for their family the better seats for the noon feast. Though they arrived at the tomb by mid-morning, there were already many village children there. The surface of the tomb had been cleared, weeds uprooted and earth cleared away. Seats were placed on the left and right wings of the tomb yard. About twelve seats formed a circle around a depressed space, round but level, which was to serve as a table.

Having arrived a little too late at the tomb, Fifth *Go* and Little Brother had to look carefully here and there for a suitable place to set their own family's table. A place shadowed by the tall trees that grew about the tomb was pleasant. The experiences of each year had taught the village boys where to look for the more desirable places.

While Little Brother carried on the search for a suitable place, Fifth *Go* fell to quarrelling with a village boy of about his own age. Fifth *Go* wanted to occupy a space which the village boy claimed was his. The boy had laid his belongings on the space as a token of his occupation, but Fifth *Go* argued that he himself had put down green branches on the seats, an act traditionally recognized as the sign of first occupation. In the heat of their argument the village boy and Fifth *Go* began to wrestle. Little Brother, the potential enemy of Fifth *Go* at home, now became his sole ally. He flew to help Fifth *Go* by throwing away the possessions of the village boy and by using a stick to beat the boy's feet. Attacked by the two brothers, the boy felt himself defeated and retreated. He could have beaten Little Brother up if he had wished, but he would not do so because Little Brother was too young to be his match.

By and by more village people assembled and soon some thirty casks and as many baskets of food appeared, brought up to the tomb by the family conducting the sacrifice. Among the crowd of people who climbed the mountain to the tomb were many members of the House of the Golden Wing. Little Brother called out to Chumei, who rode upon the shoulders of Fourth *Go*, and to Shoutai, who was carried on the back of his father, Eldest *Go*. The two children answered the call of Little Brother and came over to where he stood at the top of the tomb entrance waiting for them.

Dunglin and his clerk Dungtzu, the brother of Dungfei, came up to the tomb from the direction of the town. The children rushed down to receive them and led them to join the space reserved for their family. Dunglin was certainly conspicuous among his fellow-villagers, standing out like a crane among a flock of barnyard fowl. He was heavy and strong. His countenance was bright, and his carefully trained moustache made him look impressive. He was simply clothed in a suit consisting of a short upper garment and broad trousers, all made of lustrous black silk. In this he was more elegantly dressed than the other men, who mostly wore hempen clothing produced by the village women. But Dunglin's superiority was not simply to be judged from his outward appearance. His choice of words, his quick speech and command of argument, his nimbleness of thought, his great experience in the outside world as well as his tact in dealing with people of all kinds, all gave him authority and leadership. As perhaps the most successful and able man of the village since the days of the first ancestor, Dunglin was on this occasion greeted respectfully on every hand.

After a while fire-crackers were exploded and echoed across the mountain. The village children shouted to each other and raced about. Their elders greeted each other, smiling and laughing together. Every face seemed full of delight and happiness. Suddenly a leader beat upon a big gong, a sign to summon all the descendants to pay their obeisances to the ancestor and ancestress who lay in the tomb before them. The silent mountain-top now suddenly became at this moment a great stage, on which was to be enacted a solemn play accompanied by solemn music.

On the ground before the tomb the village people, old and young, knelt down and kowtowed thrice. As the space was too small for all the people to perform the ceremony at the same moment, they came and went like water flowing in a stream. Late-comers quickly took up the places left vacant by the earlier celebrants. On a great stone table before the inscribed tablet of the tomb, delicacies were spread, wine cups filled up with wine, candles and incense sticks lit and finally paper money and paper ingots set together to make a bonfire.

After the obeisances the family conducting the sacrifice began to distribute the food to the different dining places and the people took their seats to begin their picnic. Whenever the village elders raised their wine cups to toast one another, they added words to their toasts celebrating the merits of their forefathers. All the males of the clan, from those first able to walk to those of old age, participated in this sacrificial feast. There were no women, though a few girls under the age of ten had straggled along and were also present. This was one of the greatest gatherings the clan of Hwang had ever known.

The tomb sacrifice of the clan of Hwang lasted for about ten days. Each day the people swept only one tomb, and each day they progressed from the tomb of more remote ancestors to those of the more recent ones. Like the branches of a tree, different lineages of a clan deviate from a single ancestral trunk. So in respect to the more recent ancestors the different lineages separated to sacrifice at their proper tombs. Dunglin's family certainly did not forget the tomb of Dunglin's grandfather, the site of which was A-Mouse-Facing-A-Barn. When Dunglin and his Uncle Yuhun took the younger members to sweep the tomb of the lucky site, they carried along the sacrificial delicacies. Yuhun knelt down before the tomb and read aloud a prayer composed by himself. He was a literary man who had formerly been a teacher in the village school. Dunglin, who did not read or study much, cared little about the composition of a prayer. He climbed up to the top of the tomb to get the view and was satisfied to see once more the spread of rich crops in the lands right below before his eyes. The party had only some cakes and sweetmeats at the tomb. The real feast was held at home where all the men and women, old and young, of this lineage could take part.

The season of tomb sacrifices was a great occasion for all the villagers. They took this occasion to enjoy a rest after their summer of hard work on the farms and before taking up the final harvest of the year. Like other villagers Dunglin never failed to be present at tomb sacrifices. He considered attending an act of filial piety. Likewise, he knew that the reunion of the clan, in which all their personal ties were renewed, was one of the great integrating forces of the village. He had respect for the life of his people.

This cheerful season having passed, life soon returned again to normal. In the House of the Golden Wing the men worked on the farm each day and the women managed the household. Whenever minor festivals came, celebrations were always carried on within the household itself.

In the case of the Winter Festival, for example—the day of winter solstice—every family of the clan of Hwang performed its own little ceremony. On the eve of that festival Dunglin and Little Brother came back to join the family in an assembly in the kitchen at which all the members were required to be present. All of them took part in making round rice dumplings, a special food for the festival.

When Mrs. Hwang took out a basket of rice dough ground from glutinous rice, she mixed the dough with water and kneaded it to form a big mass. She then divided the big mass into smaller blobs and let each person have one of them. The members of the House of the Golden Wing crowded into the small kitchen, some sitting on benches, some standing, and some leaning against the walls. Merrily they broke their blobs of dough into little pieces and rolled each piece in their palms to form a round dumpling. The saying is that a family will have complete happiness if the dumplings are rolled into perfect spheres. Little Brother, feeling naughty, kneaded his blob of dough into various figures of dogs and cats, balance weights, and mortars and pestles. When all the family had finished the work of rolling the dough, they put all the dumplings into a large open-mouthed basket. Everybody took his turn at holding the rim of the basket and shaking it as a token of the transmission of happiness from one generation to the next.

At dawn on the festival day Eldest *Sao* boiled the round dumplings and added black sugar to them. The family first offered the food to their ancestors and to the kitchen god before they themselves ate it. They hung two of the round dumplings up over every entrance of the house and every door into every room. The practice was said to be connected with a legend about filial piety. Once upon a time a man was lost on a wild mountain and had to live among the animals. He met a she-ape and occupied the same shelter with her. Some time later the ape gave birth to a son and the man took the son back to his home with him. When the son grew up, he became a high official. He wanted his mother, the ape, to come to live with him. He gathered his kinsmen together and led them to the mountain, and there he had them hang every tree with the round dumplings, all the way back to the door of his house where he hung still more of them. The mother ape, old and hungry, followed the trail of dumplings from the forest to the house, where her son came out to meet her and welcomed her to live with him. In memory of this filial son, the custom of hanging dumplings is kept to this day.

The New Year season was really the greatest festivity in the village world. The festive round of activities began with a ceremony in the kitchen, where articles of food for the festival had been prepared several days ahead of time. The members of the House of the Golden Wing once again assembled to do honour to the kitchen god. They offered ten cups of tea, ten kinds of cakes, and ten dishes of delicacies, as well as ten cups of wine. They spread some yellow beans on the roof of the kitchen, in order to provide feed for the horse of the kitchen god. At this time a new god succeeds the old one, who rides off on a horse over the roof up to the heavens. The offering has the purpose of bribing the parting god not to report ill of the house to the gods in heaven, so that they will not be angry and will refrain from sending calamities to visit the family down below.

Little Brother, who had a winter vacation, was the first one of the family to arrive home from the outside world. Once at home he was surprised to see how everything had been cleaned up. New couplets, written by his grand-uncle Yuhun on red paper, were posted at each side of the doors, on the posts in the main hall and on the walls of the ancestral shrine.

Two days later, Dunglin and Third *Go* arrived home together. Mrs. Hwang and Grandmother Pan were greatly pleased. Third *Go* had brought some special cakes from Foochow, which were distributed to all the members of the family. Dunglin gave some money to each child under sixteen, their " growing-up money ".

The real ceremony began in the House of the Golden Wing on New Year's Eve. At sunset, before dinner, the main hall was decorated with red curtains and red lanterns. Before the ancestral shrine, which was placed on a table in the middle of the hall against the centre wall, delicious dishes were set out as offerings and red candles lighted. Dunglin asked Third *Go* to offer the incense sticks and to bow at the ancestral shrine. On hearing the order, Third *Go*, who had become a Christian and sworn never again to worship ancestors, cast a glance toward his brother Fourth *Go*. Fourth *Go* understood his silent message at once and went to perform the offering of incense. As soon as Fourth *Go* inserted the incense sticks into the incense burner, Dunglin was satisfied that his order had been carried out, and he did not inquire which of his sons had done it.

It was at this moment that Eldest *Go* placed a flat-bottomed cauldron on the floor of the main hall. In the cauldron he arranged a pagoda of wood splinters. A fire was set at the bottom of the pagoda and some salt was sprinkled upon it so that a crackling noise came from the fire. This is called " burning the fire-crackers ". The custom is said to have originated at the end of the Ming dynasty, in the seventeenth century, when the coast of Fukien was ravaged by the Dwarf Pirates. The pirates were savages, murdering, burning, and plundering the possessions of the people, capturing and raping their women. Soon these pirates occupied the land. Each conquered household on the coast was ordered to support one of the pirates. Then the people decided in secret to kill all the pirates in a single massacre on New Year's Eve, and the burning of a bonfire was set as the signal for the massacre. The plan was carried out successfully, and all the pirates were killed off. The people still keep the custom of " burning the fire-crackers " in memory of the glorious event.

At the House of the Golden Wing the wood burning was carried out in the cauldron in the main hall. The children of the family, headed by Little Brother, put on their paper masks and danced around the fire, singing folk-songs. They were warned not to pull off their masks until the last wood splinters had been burned up, lest illness, especially smallpox, get them. The family members, male and female, old and young, all assembled, looking on and making merry around the sacred fire. Laughter and jollity welled up from among them and a warm, happy feeling reigned in the house. The ceremony came to an end when Dunglin, the family head, took three pieces of the charcoal from the burned-out fire and carried them to the fireplace in the kitchen.

After that, the delicacies set before the ancestral shrine were removed to the kitchen to be cooked. The whole family assembled to enjoy for their dinner the same dishes that they had offered, a while before, to their ancestors. After the feast they made several offerings to various gods of wind, of rain, of heaven and earth. All this was done in the main hall.

Under the bright light of the lanterns and candles the Hwang household, from the old grandmother to the little children, stayed up as late as possible, in order to keep vigil. They talked of pleasant things and behaved as properly as possible, to be sure of entering the New Year in the proper spirit. The children were specially warned not to use dirty language and unlucky words. If they did, the grown-ups wiped their mouths out with toilet paper, to rid them of whatever ill omens they had uttered.

Just before midnight a table was set up for the offering of the " New Year Rice ". The things set out on the table consisted of a box of rice, a pair of porcelain vases with flowers, candles on the candle stands, an incense burner, and wine pots and wine cups. The table was placed in the centre of the main hall. Of all these things the box of rice was the most important. The box was specially made for the purpose. It was round, fifteen inches high, and lacquered in gold and red. Steamed rice filled half the box. On top of the rice a big tangerine was placed in the centre and " the five sons " were spread about on all sides. Around the inner sides of the box, ten pairs of lacquered chopsticks were stuck into the rice. Also planted in the rice were two juniper branches. Coloured flowers, paper money and paper ingots, flowery tassels, a miniature almanac and other lucky things hung in profusion from the branches.

When everything was properly arranged, Dunglin, as family head, took up a wine pot and poured out wine into the cups three times. Fifth *Go* set off the fire-crackers and Fourth *Go* set fire to some paper money. The family members began one by one to kowtow from behind the table toward the open court. Only Third *Go* did not perform any rite, on account of his new religion, though Little Brother made his obeisances to the familial and heavenly gods as usual, despite the fact that he, too, had been baptized.

At dawn on New Year's Day, Nanmin, the hired man of the House of the Golden Wing, fired a gun off three times. Everybody was awakened by the gun-shots, and they all said " Happy New Year " to each other. The children were dressed in new and beautiful clothes and started their New Year celebration with full pockets of peanuts and horse beans.

After breakfast a group of villagers rushed into the house and demanded a look at the bride of the family. Second *Sao*, the wife of Second *Go*, had married into the family just a little more than a month before and was still considered a bride. It was the tradition of the village that any bride of the year should welcome visitors on New Year's Day. Consequently, Second *Sao* was beautifully dressed for the occasion, and she came out into the main hall carrying a lacquered tray. On the tray there were cups of tea, " the five sons ", horse beans and candies. As she offered the tray to the visitors, she was so shy she dared not look up, but the visitors each politely took something off the tray and gave her their thanks. Some of them praised her strong and tall figure, her beautiful dress and her charming manner.

In the afternoon of New Year's Day, Dunglin begged Grandmother Pan to dress herself up in special finery, to receive honour from her descendants, because she had now arrived at seventy years of age. The Chinese always count one's age from the New Year rather than on one's actual birthday. Grandmother Pan put on a fine, sweeping, embroidered gown covering her to her ankles, and took her seat in a broad armchair covered with a red spread and placed in the centre of the main hall. Before her another red spread was placed on the floor. Aunt Lin knelt down first on the spread and kowtowed thrice before her mother-in-law. Dunglin and other family members made their obeisance to Grandmother Pan one by one in the order of their generation and age. The last one of all to perform the ceremony was little Shoutai, the son of Eldest *Go*, the first member of the fourth generation of descent from the old grandmother.

Meanwhile several visitors had knocked at the gate, which had been closed to ensure privacy at the ceremony. These visitors were Mrs. Chang, Grandmother Pan's eldest daughter, her husband Fenchow and their sons Mowhun and Mowde. They arrived at an auspicious time and took their turns in paying respect and making obeisance to Grandmother Pan, who received them gladly and smilingly. They were cheerfully entertained afterwards with fruit, peanuts, sweetmeats, wine and tea.

One can imagine how happy Dunglin was to see his old mother, who had been a widow through more than forty hard and troublesome years, now sit proudly there in the main hall with her face so full of contentment. The sun, streaming into the main hall, gave clear and vivid colour to the red spreads, the flowery embroidered dresses, the new couplets and the other decorations of bright new paper. The eyes of every person in the house sparkled with delight. Happiness reigned in the house. There was no business to-day, no school, no farming, no routine household work. This was the perfect day of enjoyment, rest, talk, and relaxation, all in a flood of warm sentiment. Thus Dunglin passed the happiest time since his childhood.

The New Year period was indeed a gay and cheerful occasion in the village world, where every person enjoyed the festivities. Young boys had permission from their elders to bring out the musical instruments which were owned by the whole clan, to organize a musical band, and to play music day and night. The band sometimes paraded around the village, visiting every house with music and making the people gay and full of cheer. And not least of all the cheer was the constant flow of calls and return calls the different households made on one another so frequently during the period.

But soon the gathering and festivity passed. On the fourth day after New Year, all the shops of Hookow would open for business once more. Fenchow and Dunglin would leave their houses and go back to the store. Life would return to normal in the village and at home.

Once the ordinary round began again, the young men and boys would soon drift off to their own pursuits. Many of them would go to join the village gambling clubs, which were the most popular organizations of the day.

Even Little Brother, though still a young schoolboy, would come to learn gambling by following Fifth *Go* to a farm shed where the village boys gathered to play. There, instead of money, peanuts would serve as stakes. Once when their boyish game was over, Little Brother and Fifth *Go* might go home past the village teashop. They would hear some people quarrelling inside. Attracted into the shop by the noise, they would find many tables of gamblers there. Among them an expert gambler of the village one day quarrelled with Second *Go*, who, it seems, had tried to cheat but had been discovered. Eldest *Go* rushed in to reprimand Second *Go* and drove him home. He succeeded well enough, but once back at home the two brothers, Eldest and Second *Go*, fell to quarrelling again and fought it out by wrestling.

Indeed this was no isolated instance. In the absence of Dunglin, the family head, these two often fought, and they hated one another. Soon they came to avoid speaking to each other unless there was necessity. Their hatred communicated itself to their wives. Alas, the very moment Dunglin thought to be the climax of harmony and happiness in his family, was in fact the moment when the seed of hatred was sown and the foundation of future conflict laid down!

On the fifteenth day after the New Year, which is the Full Moon Festival of the Spring, another village gathering, taking in all the villagers, was held in the ancestral hall of the clan of Hwang, where the oldest ancestral tablets, those common to the villagers as a whole, were kept. Each family of each different lineage offered a table of delicacies together with burning incense, vases of flowers, and a row of red lanterns. The offerings were arranged on several displays, extending from the back of the hall to the front. All the people of the village crowded into the single hall. They pushed in and surged to and fro. Under the bright lantern light the gathering was a bedlam of all sorts of noise, people calling, shouting, greeting, scolding and apologizing.

Suddenly there burst out three successive blasts of gunfire, set off before the main gate. Immediately there was perfect silence. Every person present shut his mouth and held his breath. A silence of ten minutes must be kept, lest calamities befall the village within the coming year. But, unhappily, in the midst of the silence, a dog barked for a while, and then fell quiet. The villagers afterwards spoke gloomily to one another, predicting a hard year to come. Then, after the ten minutes of silence, another blast of the gun was heard and the hubbub began once more.

When the display was over, a feast was held at midnight. The men's tables were arranged in the main hall and in the open yard, and the women's tables were set in the back hall and the rear dining-rooms. Once more the clan elders raised their wine cups and drank each other's health. Again they talked about their ancestors, the events of village history, and told folk-tales. This was the last day of the celebration of the New Year period.

Festivity and work in the village alternate in a cycle. Amid their labour the villagers look forward to the coming of festivals. After these renewals of their energy they go back again to work. Life for them is a single cycle of work and play, but it is very full.

CHAPTER VII
THE AGRICULTURAL SYSTEM

During the New Year period, while the young men of the House of the Golden Wing went off to join the village gambling clubs, Nanmin, the family's employee, silently carried the dung of the pigs and buffaloes, which had been collected day after day by the women of the family, to the space beside the right-hand door of the house. He spread the dung out in order to let it dry under the sunlight. Once the dung was dry, he took a wooden stick and beat it into fine powder. He used a bamboo sieve to sift the fine dung from the coarse. The fine dung was preserved as fertilizer for the farm, but the coarse was put back again into the original dung piles to be dried and sifted again the next time.

The farm work of the year started with the New Year period. Second *Sao* acted then as the family cook. She prepared breakfast for the four farmers of the family. These were Eldest *Go*, Second *Go*, Fourth *Go* and Nanmin. Eldest *Sao* came into the kitchen with a square bamboo basket and put in it some fifteen bowls of rice. Above the rice in the basket she placed side by side several other dishes, consisting of salt fish, salt vegetables, green vegetables, and perhaps a little meat. Four pairs of chopsticks and four empty bowls also went into the basket, which was covered with a woven bamboo lid. This basket of food was to be the lunch of the farmers out in the fields. Besides, there was a large bamboo tube which contained tea.

In addition to their food for the day the four farmers of the family each carried two baskets of dried, fine dung, suspended at the ends of shoulder-poles. They left the house early in the morning and trudged along to a field distant from the village. It was often up high on the mountain. The fields were laid out in terraces, but each terrace might consist of one or several fields. At New Year the soil was dried up after the harvest and the ploughing of the previous year. Eldest *Go*, the leader among the four, climbed up to the top of the terrace and opened a way with his hoe to let water flow from the mountain brook into the fields of the first terrace. The other three farmers each made drains beside the footpaths in each field of the terraces below so that the water could run from the topmost field down to the lowest.

Having filled the fields with water, the farmers took up their hoes. They worked side by side, breaking the wet soil up as fine as possible. Their work proceeded from the topmost terrace downward.

Eldest *Go* was the leader of the group on account of his seniority and his position. He had grown up to be a man of medium size, with a broad face, a big, flat nose, and a dark complexion. Small-pox scars covered his face and together with the odd shape of his head made him very ugly. He had a clever, cunning mind. With only two years of training in the village school, he could write a very beautiful hand and he knew about two thousand characters. He had begun to help manage family affairs in his boyhood, while Dunglin was so often away from home, so that it was he who kept the family's legal documents and its current accounts.

In the fields Eldest *Go* was a serious worker. He was very severe with his fellow-workers and seldom showed a smile. As soon as the sun was straight overhead, he dropped his hoe and curtly ordered his followers to stop work. They went together to the top terrace and sat down in a shady spot on the mountain-side, where they opened the rice basket, spread out all the dishes, and enjoyed their midday meal. When they had finished eating, they each took a turn in drinking their tea by putting their mouths to the opening of the tea tube. Then they sat back lazily for a while. It was at this moment that Nanmin took out his bamboo pipe. The pipe was about a foot and a half in length and he kept it always hanging from his belt against his right side. He filled the pipe with tobacco and, lighting it up, smoked quietly. The smoke whirled from the green mountain-side and blew off into the clear air as if the fatigue of his labours were carried away with it.

As soon as the soil had been worked fine, the farmers applied their fertilizer. If after lunch the soil were not yet fine enough, they probably worked it over once more. They would not stop their labour until sunset. The next day they would repeat the same process in the fields which had not yet been worked. And so the breaking of the soil and the manuring of the fields was carried on until all ten pieces of the family's farm land were done.

On the twenty-ninth day of the first moon, there was a minor celebration known as the Filial Piety Festival. Dunglin bought a big cake and sent for Little Brother to take it home to Grand-mother Pan. Though the farmers got no holiday, they enjoyed the " filial piety gruel " at breakfast. The gruel was made of glutinous rice mixed with red dates, sesame seeds, longans, black sugar and peanuts. Mrs. Chang sent Peimin, the hired man of the house of Chang, to present a box of the " filial piety gruel " to Grandmother Pan. The gift was a token of the reverence a married daughter owes her mother. It is said that the custom originated in memory of a Buddhist saint, the hero of a religious drama. The saint, named Muliin, tried to save his mother, an unbeliever, from her sufferings in hell where she was imprisoned and hungry. The saint first tried to send her rice gruel but it was all eaten up by her ghostly gaolers. He then set to work on a new method of sending the gruel to her. He put into the rice gruel a lot of red dates, sesame seeds, black sugar and other things, so that the ghostly gaolers thought it merely some muddy soil. In this way his mother finally got the gruel and was saved. To-day people present the gruel to their parents as an act of filial piety.

Sometimes the " filial piety gruel " is used to avert the calamities that arise from ill luck. Little Brother, who was nine years of age now, was given this gruel to help him pass his " unlucky ninth ". Those who are aged eighteen, nineteen, twenty-seven, twenty-nine, and so on, are all considered unlucky. They should eat this gruel to ward off evil.

In early spring, at the time of the Pure Brightness Festival, the one hundred and seventh day after the winter solstice, another agricultural process begins : the cultivation of the early rice. The Pure Brightness Festival is actually a spring festival. It is the time for making a spring sacrifice to one's ancestors, which ceremony is as necessary as is the autumn sacrifice in the eighth month of the year at harvest time. The villagers believe their ancestors participate in the production of the crops that make for the welfare of the clan.

For the spring sacrifice, Eldest *Go* and Fifth *Go* were the two representatives chosen from the House of the Golden Wing to officiate in the offerings made before the tablets in the ancestral hall. There was no tomb sacrifice. The sacrificial materials were placed on the tables. Each family had its own cauldron set on the floor of the main hall. Yuhun, who had recently taken over the place of Yumeng as the clan head when the latter died, began to call out orders. The clan head is the man who is highest in generation and oldest in age in the clan. When he dies, he is succeeded by the next oldest of the clan. When Yuhun addressed his ancestors and begged them to come to take the offering, each family representative took some paper money and clothing and burned it in his own cauldron. After the sacrifices the delicacies were carried off by each family to be cooked and eaten.

Although Dunglin was himself engrossed in the store, he never forgot his family's land and its agriculture. He knew that land was the foundation of his family's livelihood and that farming was their fundamental occupation, handed down from his ancestors. Though he was himself constantly absent from his home village, he could entrust the farm work to his eldest nephew, Eldest *Go*, who took charge of the farm work and the festival ceremonies that accompanied it.

The women of the House of the Golden Wing were no less important to the work of the farm than were the four men occupied in farming. At planting time Mrs. Hwang and Aunt Lin, who had charge of the stored grains and rice, gathered up the grain seeds that had been kept from the last harvest and put them in warm water. In four or five days the seeds began to germinate. Then Nanmin took the sprouting seeds and sowed them in the corners of various fields. Nanmin, as the long-term employee of the family, was more than a farmer; he did many chores of all kinds for the family. He saw to agricultural implements, repaired baskets, pails and water casks, cut wood and grew vegetables.

When the green paddy sprouts came up to a height of two feet, Eldest *Go* organized the work of transplanting. He called up Dungheng of the old household, and Peimin, the farmer of the house of Chang, to join in the work. Six farmers working together pulled up the paddy sprouts and tied six or seven of them into a bundle. These bundles were to be transplanted into all the fields. The workers started their planting in the topmost field, where six of them stood side by side in a line. Each bundle of sprouts was pushed down into the muddy soil, planted at a distance of about two feet from the next one on either side or in front or back. Each farmer took care of a space wide enough to accommodate five bundles. He worked from left to right, moving backward step by step. When the transplanting was over, fertilizer was applied to the roots of each bundle, giving food to the new plants. More water was sluiced into the fields. In the evening Eldest *Go* wrote down in his current account the day's work that Dungheng and Peimin had done for the family. This labour was to be paid back later on by an equivalent return of labour.

As soon as the planting of the early rice had been completed, Eldest *Go* and his fellow-farmers started in to sow and plant the late rice. Sprouts of the late rice were set between the bundles of the early rice.

Between transplanting and harvest there is a long period during the hot summer with days of taking care of the plants, of waging warfare upon weeds and tares, of adding more fertilizer, and of managing irrigation. For tearing out the weeds, the Hwang farmers used an iron-toothed harrow with a long handle. The harrow was raked back and forth between the bundles of the rice sprouts. The farmers worked in a line as at the time of transplanting, but instead of going backward, they now worked forward. A second application of the fertilizer was necessary after raking out the weeds. Human dung mixed with water formed this kind of fertilizer. Applying it was a tedious process. Each field had to be worked and irrigated several times before the rice sprouts matured.

In the summer vacation Little Brother came back from his second year of schooling. They set him to care for a flock of ducks that fed in the fields where the soil had been turned over by the farmers, and where there was rich food for the ducks. One day his flock met another and they got mixed up out in the sprouts in the field. Little Brother took a bamboo stick to drive the other ducks off. But unfortunately he struck too hard, and killed one. When he found the dead duck was not his own, he drove his own ducks back to his house.

Half an hour later a loud-voiced woman came out into the field. Finding that one of her ducks was lost, she began to curse the unknown creature that had done harm to her flock. She raised her voice and screamed curses. When her sharp voice penetrated into the House of the Golden Wing, Mrs. Hwang questioned Little Brother and asked if he had done anything to the duck. Thus confronted, the poor little criminal could not help but admit with tears that he had killed it in the field. His mother went out with him, picked up the dead duck and gave it to the loud-voiced woman. Mrs. Hwang begged her pardon on behalf of her son and said it had been killed by accident and promised to pay for it. Thus the loud-voiced woman was satisfied. For with just such fairness did Mrs. Hwang always act in dealing with her neighbours.

The fields were in danger of being dried up during the hot summer days, so the Hwang farmers made arrangements for water to irrigate their land. The lowland fields were watered by means of water-wheels. These were worked by two farmers who, side by side, trod the wheels with their feet in order to pump water upward from streams and drainage canals.

As soon as the crops began to ripen, the Hwang farmers protected them from birds by setting up straw scarecrows in the field. Just before harvest, Eldest *Go* went into the town of Hookow and reported to his uncle the prospects of the harvest. So it was Dunglin who sent notice to the landlords owning the ground rents to come and take their shares on such and such a date.

The fields in front of and below the House of the Golden Wing were the first to be harvested. The Hwang farmers started their work once again from the topmost field. Each farmer used a sickle to cut off the stalks which bore the ears of grain. The stalks were cut down in shocks and piled on the footpaths between the fields. The farmers worked in rows and each took five shocks of rice at a time. To get through the work in a single day, Eldest *Go* asked Dungheng, Mowhun and Peimin to join the harvesters.

Second *Go* and Dungheng went to a nearby plot of level, hard-packed earth and fixed up a threshing frame made of split bamboo set in wood. Each took a shock of rice and threshed it upon the threshing frame. They stood side by side and used the same frame. When one of them lifted his shock from the frame, the other threshed his shock against it. In this way the two men beat their shocks in unison until the grains all fell off the stalks and filled the mats underneath the frame. The continuous noise of the threshing echoed far up the valley.

Fifth *Go* and Little Brother, though young and small, were asked to work during this busy season. They walked back and forth, carrying the shocks from the footpaths to the threshing ground. Little as the boys were, they did a useful job as a link between the cutters and the threshers.

Just before noon the Lin family of Hookow, who owned the ground rents in these fields, sent a steward and five labourers to the village of Hwang. As soon as they had arrived at the threshing ground, Eldest *Go* left his work of cutting and went out to entertain them. It was on the threshing floor itself that the rice was weighed and divided. Two labourers shouldered a shoulder-pole at the middle of which the steelyard beam was placed. Second *Go* and Dungheng put the grain into the bags. A third labourer took a bag filled with grain and fixed it to the hook of the steelyard beam. The steward stood beside the beam and balanced the weights on his left against the bag of grain on his right. Eldest *Go* put down in his account book how much each bag weighed, as the steward reported to him. Division was in the ratio of four to six. The Lin family got forty per cent. as landlords and the Hwang family as leaseholders and tenants got sixty per cent. of the total produce.

The weighing over, the steward sent the labourers back with his bags of grain, but he himself joined Eldest *Go* and other farmers at lunch in the House of the Golden Wing. Then in the afternoon the work of cutting, carrying, threshing, and weighing was continued. The Lin labourers came back again to collect their employer's share.

As the Hwang farmers carried home the new wet grain, the women of the house prepared a clean storeroom in which to store it temporarily. The next morning at sunrise the grain was carried out on to the ground beside the right door of the house to be dried in the sun. Bamboo mats twenty by fifteen feet were spread on the ground and the grain spread on them in the sunlight. This job fell mostly to the women and the boys. Nearly every half-hour the grain had to be turned over on the mats. A wooden " pusher " equipped with a long handle was used for the purpose. The grain had to be dried in strong sunlight for three or four days before it could be stored. Then, on the last day of drying it had to go through two more processes. It had to be sifted through a bamboo sieve in order that weeds and dirt be cleaned out. It had to be blown through a winnowing machine so that the smaller weeds and the chaff could be blown away. The machine was set up on a wooden frame in which a funnel, a winged wheel and a sloping chute through which the grain had to pass were all cunningly arranged. The pure grain dropping through the winnowing machine was then ready to be stored up in the storage loft of the second story of the house.

In these farm operations of the Hwang family, men and women, old and young, all worked together as a unit. The women's share in the farming was equal in importance to that of the men. The family relied on the women to collect the dung fertilizer, to keep the implements, to prepare storage, to get ready food, to preserve seeds and to dry and sift the grain.

Work at harvest-time was heavy for them. Cooking was in the hands of the young women. Second *Sao*, the most recent bride, had to cook for the family for three full years, according to village tradition. After that she could take turns at cooking with Eldest *Sao* month by month. To prepare breakfast was the most difficult job of all the cooking. Second *Sao* had to get up with the first cock's crow. She went upstairs to the kitchen, carrying a lamp with her. She first lighted the dry leaves in the fireplace and put on dry wood. As soon as the water in the main cauldron was warm, she poured in rice, which she had washed. About half an hour later she took a scoop woven of bamboo to sift the boiled rice out and drain off the water. She put the boiled rice into a wooden kettle, which she set to steam in the cauldron. During the time the rice was steaming, she kept wood in the fireplace, washed the various kinds of vegetables, lit up a small stove to warm a pot of tea, and set out the kitchen dishes. At about this time Eldest *Sao* came to help cut vegetables, bring firewood and set the table. The table was placed in the dining-room, next to the kitchen. It was square and large enough for twelve persons to eat together. On the table the women put ten dishes: salt fish, salt vegetables, vegetable soup, beans, green cabbage, pork, and so on, all of them prepared while the rice steamed.

The Hwang farmers were the first to eat breakfast. They then left for work. The women and children then took their turn eating the same kind of food at the same table. Lunch and dinner went off in the same manner except that sometimes the farmers carried their lunch out to the fields. Steamed rice prepared in the morning was eaten at each of the three meals of the day.

After breakfast second *Sao* used the same cauldron to boil chaff mixed with water to form a kind of mash for the two pigs that the family raised. Grandmother Pan set free the ducks, hens, cocks and chickens which had slept cooped in a pit under her bedroom. Rice and meal were given them. The family dog, who acted as gatekeeper and night watcher, was given the steamed rice left over from the previous night's dinner. It very often ate the baby's excreta also.

In mid-morning the older women, Mrs. Hwang and Aunt Lin, each carried a basket of clothing to be washed by the side of the stream below the village. There they would meet a group of the village women who knelt as they did on stone slabs. Above the murmuring of the running water the women gossiped and chatted as they washed. Talking all the while, they washed their clothes by soaking them in the stream, beating and kneading them. Then they carried the clean clothes back to be dried over bamboo poles set up in the open court of the first terrace.

With the exception of the old grandmother, the women of the house all engaged in spinning, weaving, tailoring, embroidery and making shoes. On the seventh day of the seventh moon, there is a festival called " begging for skill in needlework ". The date is said to be the only time of the year when in heaven the cowboy meets the weaving girl. On that day the young women, Eldest *Sao* and Second *Sao*, made an offering in the courtyard below the main hall. The offering consisted of incense, horse beans, peach kernels and coloured flowers. The young women also tried to thread a needle in moonlight on this day. If they succeeded they would be lucky and would become very skilful in needlework. Later the offerings were distributed to the children, who were supposed thus to have good luck in marriage in the future.

For spinning the women used hemp. Hemp was grown on the poorer land. It was first bleached and washed white, and then spun into slender threads. The women spun the threads while sitting on stools with fine bamboo baskets by their sides. After they had spun thread enough they used a wheel to wind it.

The spools were then mounted on a loom. The women had to take turns at weaving, because the family possessed only one loom. But on that loom they produced most of their own cloth.

Then the women cut the cloth to make garments for the whole family. Mrs. Hwang was well known as an expert in cutting out various garments. Many women of the village came to ask her to cut out patterns for them.

The women were also the shoemakers. They made shoes out of the rags they accumulated from day to day. With the exception of Third *Go*, who studied in Foochow, all the other members of the family wore shoes produced at home.

So the women no less than the men did their part in the economic system of the family. Without their preserving and preparing the food, their managing and cleaning the house, and their making and washing the clothes, the men could not have been so free to devote their energies to the fields. At sunset when the farmers trudged homeward the women gladly received them and took from them the green vegetables, frogs and shrimps they had brought in from the fields and ditches.

Then in the evening the House of the Golden Wing became a place of contentment and rest. All the noisy domestic animals except the dog were locked up. Warm water was provided for the tired farmers, to take a bath in or to wash hands and feet. Good simple food with maybe a delicacy or two was served at the dinner-table. When dinner was over, the doors of the house were closed and the lamps lighted. The men sat on long benches in the main hall and the women on small stools. They talked, gossiped, laughed, sighed and argued. Children played about, quarrelling or laughing. In less than an hour everybody dispersed. The house fell silent, dark but full of peace.

In the autumn the late rice was harvested. It was done in the same manner as the early rice. When all the rice had been harvested the Hwang farmers rooted out the stalks with hoes and laid them on the fields to moulder and decay. At home they held a harvest celebration in which the family and their guests—mostly those farmers who had helped with the farm work—all took part. There were sweetmeats and wine and a special kind of glutinous rice was steamed, pounded and kneaded into round cakes and dumplings of different shapes. The farmers raised their wine cups and celebrated their success after a year of hard work.

Then at last the weather grew colder and the farm fields lay barren. It was the season for ploughing. For ploughing the Hwang farmers used water buffaloes. The family possessed a herd of fifteen buffaloes and hired a boy, Suihwa, to feed them and take care of them. The boy drove the animals every day out to pasture upon the hillside. It was the habit of the buffaloes to stand resting in streams for hours in the afternoon. Their value was as work-animals. Consequently they were never butchered for food, nor even milked. In the ploughing season most of the family's buffaloes were rented out save one or two to be used for the Hwang's own ploughing.

Ploughing was a slow business and Eldest *Go* used to do the work alone. When he took a buffalo to the fields he led the animal along by pulling a rope run through the septum of its nose. He put a yoke over the animal's neck, a bent L-shaped piece of wood, the two ends of which were bound with a rope under its neck and attached to long straps running to the plough at its heels. Eldest *Go* held the handle of the plough and whipped the animal forward. As if it were born to be a beast of burden, the buffalo raised its feet and marched on. The ploughshare turned up the soil and set it rolling, wave after wave, as clouds overlap one another in the sky. Thus the earth was prepared for sowing the next season, to produce more of the crops upon which the existence of the Hwang members and the continuance of their family line depended.

CHAPTER VIII

THE RICE TRADE

Before the winter and the long ploughing season, all the men and women of the House of the Golden Wing took part in turning the grain into edible rice. The first process was hulling, by which the grain was passed through a wooden mill. Two persons worked in co-operation. The one who turned the handle of the mill was usually an older man like Eldest *Go* or Fourth *Go*. The other, who poured the grain into the hopper of the mill, was usually a woman, such as Mrs. Hwang or Aunt Lin. Very seldom did two men work together. Occasionally Nanmin did the job of hulling himself.

After the grain had been hulled the husks were blown away by the winnowing machine. Then Eldest *Go* carried the hulled grain to the water-mill to be pounded. The water-mill was located at the side of the village stream. It had been built by the forefathers of the clan of Hwang. Outside, it looked like a house of two stories. The first story was the mill-room; the second story was used for a school, the one where Yuhun once taught. The mill was the common property of the whole village.

When Eldest *Go* put the hulled grain into the stone mortars in the mill-room he moved the great stone pestles down from the hooks where they were suspended from the ceiling. These pestles were connected to the water-wheel turned by running water, and the turning of the wheel moved the pestles pounding up and down in the mortars in a steady rhythm. As soon as the rice in the mortars was pounded white, Eldest *Go* hung the pestles up again and took the rice out with an iron scoop. The women, Aunt Lin and Mrs. Hwang, stood beside him against a big wooden frame. Now they began to sift away the chaff from the rice with their sieves. The rice had to pass once again through the winnowing machine, so that the last remaining chaff could be blown away. After that process the rice had reached its final form. It was ready to be cooked or to be sold. The chaff could be kept for pig food.

As soon as there was more than enough rice for the family's consumption Eldest *Go* made ready to carry the surplus to be sold at the Hookow store. He asked Nanmin and Second *Go* to bring some baskets of rice to the main hall of the house where he placed a big wide-mouthed basket on the ground. When all the rice was poured into this big basket Eldest *Go* filled his mouth with water and squirted the water out on to the rice. Meanwhile, squatting on the ground, he shuffled the rice in the basket with his hands. He repeated the process, squirting water and shuffling rice, until he thought the rice was wet enough. Then he took a measuring vessel to measure the rice. The measured rice, now mixed with water, was poured into a hempen bag. Each bag was filled with ten measures of rice.

Now the three men, Eldest *Go*, Second *Go* and Nanmin, each took up two hempen bags of rice and suspended them at each end of a shoulder-pole balanced over their right shoulders. They used a wooden staff nearly shoulder-tall to distribute the weight of the pole across to their left-side shoulder. In this way their left shoulders helped to carry some of the weight bearing down on their right. As they went along the Western Road to Hookow they met groups of porters coming and going, some of them resting in the shade under the trees and some of them humming as they trotted along.

Nanmin was the first of the three to reach the gate of the store. He could see a crowd of people inside. Dunglin stood up from squatting over a bag of rice he was examining and signalled a welcome to Nanmin.

Nanmin happened to come in at a time when a very characteristic bargain was under way. The stranger was trying to sell his rice to Dunglin. He pressed Dunglin to raise his price. But Dunglin shook his head and said, " Brother, you have put too much water in your rice. I can't raise the price I first offered."

At these words the stranger seized his shoulder-pole which had been leaning against the wall and set about tying his two bags of rice to each end of the pole. While he was tying up the pole he spoke reluctantly to Dunglin, " Your neighbour's store offered me a higher price, but I didn't sell my rice to them. If you can't offer me a tiny rise in price, why shouldn't I go back to your neighbour ? " These words were always used by the rice sellers in the bargaining process.

" Will you let me see your other bag of rice, please ? " asked Dunglin, when the stranger seemed really about to leave his shop for his neighbour's.

" Why, surely," answered the stranger, who undid the bags

from the pole. Then he pulled the other bag over, the one Dunglin had not yet examined.

When the stranger opened the second bag, Dunglin squatted down and pushed his hand into the rice. After a minute's shuffling about with his hand, he grasped a handful of the rice. It formed a damp mass. Then he stretched out his hand and showed the wet rice to the stranger. The store-master said, " Brother, look how much water you have mixed with your rice ! "

" Oh, good heavens ! " retorted the stranger. " Your grip's just like a grip of iron. I'd say even sand from the beach wouldn't fail to form a hard ball in that iron grip of yours ! "

Dunglin stood up from his squatting position, said decisively to the stranger, " I'll add ten cents to the original price I offered. You know your rice won't bring anything higher than that."

" Master, how about adding thirty cents more ? I am anxious to be direct about it and not waste time," asked the stranger earnestly. Dunglin did not answer. He merely shook his head. The stranger once again took up his shoulder-pole to tie his bags of rice to it. As he raised his burden and walked with it slowly to the gate, Dunglin shouted after him, " Brother, wait ! How about this ? " Then as he spoke he raised his hand and held up two fingers, by which he meant of course he would add twenty cents to the original price. The stranger looked back at Dunglin and his fingers, and stood there for a moment seemingly in meditation. " All right, sir," he said, " I'll sell you the rice and not waste more time over it."

In the middle of the hall the chief assistant was busy measuring the rice brought in by Eldest *Go*, Second *Go* and Nanmin. As this rice had come from the House of the Golden Wing and was owned by the master of the store himself, there was no need to subject it to the process of bargaining. The assistant measured out the six bags of rice into a big open-mouthed basket and later poured the rice back again into the bags, working with the help of the three porters. After each measuring he reported the name of the seller of the rice to the accountant, together with the amount and the price agreed upon. In this case, however, no price need be reported because the accountant knew the master was the owner and he knew what price to put upon it.

While the chief assistant was measuring out the rice, a group of people stood in the rear part of the hall waiting for the rice to be weighed. The group consisted of the second assistant and three customers who had gone through the stages of bargaining and measuring. To deal with them, Dunglin went to the rear and took up a great steelyard beam attached by a rope hanging from the ceiling. He placed the beam crosswise in front of him, holding the weights with his left hand and the hook of the steelyard with his right. The second assistant lifted a bag of rice to the hook while Dunglin moved the weights along the left side of the beam to balance the bag of rice and the weights. The balance set, he read off the weight to the accountant, who took it down. There was no need to weigh every bag of the rice of any single seller, for one weighing was quite enough to test how good the rice was. The value of the rice was reckoned by measure, anyway, rather than by weight.

When the weighing was over, the second assistant and the sellers carried all the bags of rice up the stairs into the upper rear story, where they poured the rice into the storage bins. Then they went back into the main hall and the sellers were ready to relax, drinking tea and smoking water-pipes. The second assistant, however, soon left them and went to deal with other rice sellers.

Meanwhile the accountant Kaituan had completed counting up the value of the rice sold by the sellers, using an abacus or counting board. He took out of his cash-drawer the silver dollars and small change he needed, and handed them over to Dunglin, who now stood at the counter. Each silver dollar was stamped with an iron die which bore a Chinese character. A dollar so stamped with this character was issued by the store, and if it turned out later to be counterfeit, it would be redeemed at any time.

Dunglin handed their money to the three sellers who re-counted it and then divided it among themselves. After a while they collected their empty bags and their shoulder-poles and staffs and were ready to leave. They said good-bye to the people of the store and walked out of the gate.

By this time Nanmin and Second *Go* were ready and could be sent back home to the village, but Eldest *Go* remained beside the counter to have a talk with his uncle. None of the men had received any money during the transactions of the day. Dunglin as the head of the family always deposited all money in the store. This selling of the rice from the home farm meant merely another addition to general family funds.

When Little Brother returned from school to take lunch at the store he saw the main gate crowded with rice sellers and their bags of rice. He therefore turned to the entrance of the medicine department. The boy apprentice there was busy weighing different herbs with a miniature steelyard while the customers waited at the counter. The assistant, Yang Ling, came over towards the apprentice and worked an abacus to count the value of the herbs. The customers in turn paid their money, which Yang Ling threw into a funnel through which it dropped into a lower drawer.

In the rear part of the department an old woman took her grandson to Yunseng's table and waited for the doctor to come and examine the little boy. But just now Yunseng was busy bargaining with the rice sellers in the other hall.

Little Brother slipped over into the other hall through the door between the walls. He greeted Eldest *Go*, who only nodded his head. Eldest *Go* never had any affection for his cousins and was becoming more and more dissatisfied that his uncle should send Third *Go* and Little Brother to a modern school and spend the family's money on them. On seeing Little Brother, Dunglin came over and asked him to sweep up the rice which had spilled on the ground.

Seeing Dungdoo come down the stairs from the upper rear story, Dunglin ordered him to set up the table for lunch. Dungdoo was the second son of Dunglin's uncle Yuhun and was now the cook at the store. He was still very young, but Dunglin had promised Yuhun to train him to be a merchant. This plan of the master's grew out of his intention to repay the help his uncle had given him at the time of the lawsuit.

A round table was placed in the middle of the rear hall. As soon as the table was set up, Little Brother called everybody to the meal. Kaituan was the first. He sat on a round high stool at the head of the table. To his left sat Dunglin. Little Brother sat on the left of his father, who picked out of the main dishes specially good pieces of pork for him throughout the meal. Eldest *Go* sat at the lower end of the table and reported to Dunglin on the condition of the Hwang family at home and the management of the House of the Golden Wing. The conversation that uncle and nephew carried on was seldom interrupted by the other people present. Occasionally Yunseng asked a question or two. The lunchers dropped out one by one, and in less than twenty minutes all had finished and gone off back to their jobs, that is, most of them to the bargaining, measuring, weighing, and shipping of the rice.

In these days Dunglin was the sole master of the store, because

Fenchow stayed more and more at home in his new house. The senior brother-in-law had become lazy and quite sad, especially after the death of his eldest son Mowkwei, the fish dealer in Foochow. Mowkwei had got an attack of plague in the city and had died very suddenly. His corpse came back in a coffin to his native place, but it was immediately buried without ever entering the new house where his family lived, because tradition forbids taking the corpse into the house when a person dies outside the house. Mowkwei's wife was a slow, timid but faithful woman. She had given birth to neither son nor daughter in more than ten years of married life. Now that her husband was dead Fenchow adopted a baby to be her son. The widow was to cherish the son and bring him up to continue Mowkwei's line.

Dunglin felt sympathy for Fenchow in this situation and let him retire. Consequently Dunglin carried the whole responsibility of the shop. With a lifetime's experience in business he was an expert appraiser of rice. As head of the firm where he gave out orders to his assistants, accountants, shopmen and apprentices he had got the whole organization working as a co-operative, well-co-ordinated unit.

Next to Dunglin in rank in the shop was Yunseng, the accountant. He was the man who had once been kidnapped. He had succeeded Fenchow as the doctor in charge of the pharmacy department and acted as assistant manager of the whole business. He often came out to bargain with rice sellers. Once a second strange rice seller, seeing Dunglin had settled with a first seller, turned from Yunseng to Dunglin and demanded that he examine the rice. Dunglin did so and asked Yunseng what price he had offered. On being told, Dunglin confirmed it, saying to the stranger that the price offered was a reasonable one for such rice as his, rice that was not only mixed with much water but also poorly pounded. Thus Dunglin backed up his subordinates in their decisions, and so won their loyalty.

Kaituan was the third important member of the store. He devoted his whole attention to the main hall. He was an alert man with a quick eye. He sat in a commanding position at the counter, a foot above the floor of the hall itself, and kept his ears, eyes, and mind open, listening to the prices agreed upon between the master and the rice dealers, and then taking the records of measuring and weighing. He kept the accounts and handled the money. When he closed the cash-drawer, he never failed to lock it. A quick, careful and faithful accountant, he became a favourite of Dunglin's. The assistants and the cook had to do all the tedious tasks of physical labour. Thus the store worked as a co-ordinated whole under the direction of the master.

Towards evening business slowed down and fewer rice sellers came to the store. When it grew dark, only one or two customers who lived in the town appeared, and they came to buy salt fish for their dinners. The people of the store relaxed; some went to wash their face and hands, some sat idly on stools, and some idled the time away beside the gate.

The lamps in the store were lit up. Under the lamp-light, the employees gathered for dinner. Dunglin and Yunseng were the only persons privileged to drink wine, Dunglin being much the heavier drinker. He sometimes poured out half a cup of wine for Little Brother, who refused on the ground that he was now a Christian. The elderly father, who now had grown more fond of this son of his, Sixth *Go*, laughed at him for refusing the wine and argued with him, saying, " That's a poor belief of the foreign devils. They never did understand how to enjoy a drink. Anyway you know, Little Brother, half a cup of wine will ward off evil spirits as well as foreign devils." So he forced his little son to drink, putting the cup to his mouth. Thus the father let fall his cloak of dignity at times and amused himself by joking with his son.

After dinner there was no business of buying and selling to be done. Now and then the people of neighbouring stores spoke to one another as they stood at their respective gates. In a little while, however, they closed up their gates and all retired.

Some of the people of the store had now to set up beds for the night. Little Brother shared a bed with Kaituan, the accountant, a bed they made on the floor behind the counter. They took four stools and put wooden planks over them. Over the planks they put a thickness of rush matting, one of fine grass matting and a cotton blanket. Then they draped the whole bed in curtains, to keep out mosquitoes. It was unfortunate this night that Kaituan found he lacked one stool and asked Little Brother to bring him a stool from the spot where the chief assistant was trying to set up his own bed in the main hall. The assistant himself was off searching in the medicine department for one more stool, which he, too, lacked. When he came back, he found one of his three original stools gone. He swore, " You half-breed you, stealing my stool ! " The oath did not end the matter, and a quarrel began.

Dunglin was lying on his own bed in the room behind the counter. He was well aware of what was going on in the main hall, though he had drunk a little too much that night. He heard Little Brother steal the stool and he heard Kaituan trying to set up his own bed. When he heard the chief assistant call his son a half-breed, a most contemptuous epithet, he got very angry and went to reprimand the assistant. The assistant defended himself. He said he hadn't had the least idea that it was Little Brother who had done the stealing. He had thought it was Kaituan with whom he had been very close friends since childhood. But the altercation between master and shopman only grew greater as the argument flew back and forth. All the people of the store were up now, trying to persuade them to forget their quarrel. Next morning the chief assistant gathered up his belongings, ready to leave. Though all the store people advised him to stay, especially Kaituan who had introduced him at the store, not a single word passed Dunglin's lips. Dunglin might well forgive a little misbehaviour, but a shopman who dared openly quarrel with the master could not be allowed to stay.

This *contretemps* was hardly over when a letter came from Hwang Dungtzu, a former assistant in the store, now successor of Mowkwei in charge of fish purchasing in Foochow. He reported that there was a great demand for rice in the city. On reading the letter, Dunglin ordered a boy apprentice to call Mawoo, the junk owner, to come to arrange for a shipment of rice. Mawoo soon arrived and was invited to sit inside the counter, with a cup of tea and a water-pipe.

The relationship between a merchant and a junk owner was peculiar: if there was a great demand for rice in the city, the junk owner might hold out and refuse to take additional rice for shipment off the hands of the merchant. If there was a scarcity of goods for shipment, the merchant might refuse to ship enough commodities to fill up the junk. Their work bound them to each other.

This time it was Dunglin who begged Mawoo to carry more rice for him. After a long conversation, in which they spoke of their old friendship, Mawoo finally promised to take up thirty sea-bags from the store. A "sea-bag", made of hempen cloth, differs from the ordinary bag in that it is larger and standardized in size.

That evening after dinner all the people of the store, with the exception of Kaituan, who kept the accounts, gathered round the bins for the task of wetting the rice. Dunglin stood beside the bins overseeing the job. The other people, all barefooted, entered the bins and walked on top of the rice. The boy apprentices and Dungdoo each had a waterpot, fitted with a spout to sprinkle the water in a shower. The assistants used scoops to turn over the wet rice, gradually accumulating the wet rice on one side of the bins and leaving the dry rice on the other. The wet rice not only expanded in volume but also carried more weight. Little Brother, who did no work, frolicked about on the rice.

Early next morning Mawoo came with a group of porter coolies to the bins where the assistants began to measure out the wetted rice and put it into the sea-bags, which were sewed up immediately. On the outside of the bags the assistants set seals with the mark of the store. After some talk with Dunglin, Mawoo went off to other stores, but the shopmen and his coolies continued to measure the rice, sew up the bags and get ready for the shipment.

Then the first coolie hoisted a sea-bag of rice to his back, holding it in his hands stretched out behind him, and carried it downstairs. Arriving in the lower hall, he reported his name to the accountant, who took it down, and at the same time directed Little Brother to give him a bamboo tally stick for identification. The bamboo tally stick had both surfaces written over with characters. The mark of the store was on one surface and the number of the stick on the other. The store was going to ship thirty bags, so that it would issue thirty such tally sticks. In the evening the coolies exchanged their tally sticks against their wages, a simple method of checking on their work and on the shipment.

During those days communication on the river between the town and the city still involved great dangers. Shipwrecks were frequent in the rough water. Plundering by bandits was not infrequent either. Powerless to avoid either heaven-sent or man-made disaster, people could only pray to their various gods for protection. Dunglin was no exception in this. He built a shrine to the Dragon King, who was supposed to control the world of water. The shrine stood in the upper back story of the store. On the day that Mawoo's junk sailed, Dunglin went quietly to the shrine, lit candles and incense. He prayed to the god for his rice that was on the river and begged that the powerful influence of the god should protect the junk and let it sail safely to Foochow.

This day the Dragon King seems to have been angry with

Dunglin or on leave from his duties at the water front. An accident overtook Mawoo's junk only fifteen minutes after it set sail. The junk was heavily laden with goods. The news came that it struck a rock in the river. Its back broke, and the whole consignment of rice was lost.

Dunglin was hit hard on hearing the bad news. He immediately went back to the shrine of the god and prayed once more. Walking up and down in front of the shrine for a long while, he waited gloomily for the return of Yang Ling, whom he had sent off at once to get more accurate information.

Yang Ling was in great excitement when at last he returned and told the story of the accident in loud, grief-stricken tones, surrounded by all the people of the store who were eager to hear every detail. The junk had struck against a rock, and was only partly broken up. One-third of the sea-bags of rice had been swept into the water, but the rest were safe. The junk was finally salvaged and anchored against the bank.

Four masters of other stores who also had rice loaded aboard Mawoo's junk came in to visit Dunglin and to discuss the situation. They all agreed the junk should be repaired immediately, and the rest of the rice be transported to the city. As for the missing bags, they would send two men each to form a team to try to fish them out of water. If they were found, or any part of them found, they would divide them equally among the five stores.

Later, when the junk was repaired, it sailed safely on to Foochow, where Mawoo notified Dungtzu of the belated arrival of his ship. Meantime, Dungtzu had learned about the accident from the letters of his master. He scolded Mawoo, who defended himself and said it had not been any fault of his.

Now it was the duty of Dungtzu to sell the rice in the city of Foochow. He went to visit various rice dealers with whom he had frequently done business. The dealers went with him to the junk to see the rice and bargain for it. Once the rice was sold, Dungtzu took the money and deposited it in the native banks. By this time he was now connected with five native banks in the city. The more closely one was connected with the native banks, the greater was one's prosperity in business.

In this way Dunglin exerted his authority over an ever larger and larger range of people. As head of the Hwang family, master of the store and manager of the business, his influence was spread widely. The products from the family land went partly to the support of the family and partly for sale. The income gained from the sale of rice was reinvested in the store in order to produce more money which was lent at interest. Such a store, acting as a link between several villages and the big city, was the centre of economic activities in the whole region. Even in this small world of business, the middleman's world between the city and the villages, a leader was bound to arise, to hold his followers in the ties of a skilful organization dependent upon himself.

CHAPTER IX

THE STORE BUSINESS

News of the shipwreck lost no time in spreading widely among the villagers. When it reached the House of the Golden Wing, Grandmother Pan and Mrs. Hwang were especially worried. They sent Fourth *Go* at once to Hookow to find out what had really happened.

Entering the store Fourth *Go* found his father less energetic than usual. Nevertheless, he was busy. After lunch he said to his son, " Go back and tell your grandmother and your mother not to worry. There has been only a little loss of rice, and even that may still be found." After a pause he continued, " You may go to see Uncle Fenchow and tell him about the accident to the junk and the loss of rice."

When Fourth *Go* went to the house of Fenchow, he found his old uncle in an angry mood. Fenchow pretended to be calm, receiving Fourth *Go* and inviting him in for a talk in the study. But the weeping voice of a young woman could still be heard from the back hall. Soon the aunt, Mrs. Chang, came out to see her nephew and began to tell him what a shrew her daughter-in-law Huilan was !

As a matter of fact Huilan had originally been a happy woman and a good daughter-in-law. She had become a shrew only after the death of her husband, Mowde, who had died from a heart attack two months before. Huilan's parents-in-law wished to keep her a widow for life. Although she had had less than two years of married life, Huilan had had a wonderfully happy time with her husband, who had been overwhelmed by her beauty and her charm on first seeing her. She had been an unconventional girl and used openly to joke and play with Mowde, a form of behaviour traditionally not permitted between husband and wife. She was entirely satisfied with a husband like Mowde, who was a well-educated, pleasant, well-behaved young man. She worked happily at her household tasks : cooking, cleaning, sweeping, spinning, weaving and tailoring. She was industrious, able and clever, so that she soon gained a name as a dutiful and talented daughter-in-law.

But on the day Mowde lay on his death-bed, Huilan threw herself to the ground, and thrashed about on the floor, foaming at the mouth. She wailed and wept day and night and took no food for several days. From that day on she no longer cared about her appearance. She let her hair fall loose upon her shoulders without putting it up into a roll. She often refused to do the housework. When not lying abed, she would often in a tantrum throw something to the floor or break something. Her mother-in-law, Mrs. Chang, first tried to reason with her but later lost her patience and reprimanded her for her wild temper. But reprimands only stirred the young woman up to demand that her mother-in-law send her back home to her own people. This demand was naturally refused. Fenchow talked about finding an adopted baby boy for her, but this only upset her even further because she had seen in the widowhood of Mowkwei's wife her hard life and gloomy future.

Huilan felt herself thwarted by her parents-in-law, hopelessly living a life without future, in endless conflict with her mother-in-law. The two quarrelled bitterly. Fenchow was extremely unhappy at the loss of his favourite son and felt it all the more because of the wild reaction of his daughter-in-law. The family was in constant uproar and Fenchow could not give much thought to the business in town. When Fourth *Go* came with the news, he told the young man that he placed the whole responsibility for the business upon Dunglin.

Fenchow's renunciation of authority only confirmed a *fait accompli*. In fact, the store was growing ever more centralized in Dunglin's hands. Even the Foochow branch now gravitated to his direct control.

Dungtzu, the store agent in Foochow, now lived in the warehouse in which Dunglin had stayed in the early days of his youth. The warehouse was so built that the front part was a stone courtyard, the middle part consisted of a main hall with side rooms, and the rear part was a small courtyard surrounded similarly with side rooms. Except for the rooms of two housekeepers, all the rooms were occupied by fish buyers and agents from the town of Hookow.

By this time Dungtzu had sold all the rice on board Mawoo's junk. It was his duty to keep the traffic in rice and salt fish flowing. Early in the morning he went through chilly air to Pavilion Street, where he bought the several kinds of salt fish : three pails of cuttle-fish, or seven baskets of carp, shark and plaice. Both the pails and the baskets were large in size, about five feet deep and five feet wide.

When Dungtzu went back for breakfast with the other agents in the middle hall of the warehouse, porter coolies carried the baskets and the pails of salt fish which Dungtzu had ordered from Pavilion Street to the front part of the paved courtyard, where they were stored temporarily. The pails and baskets were so heavy that they had to be carried by two coolies, who shared a single big shoulder-pole, shouldering it at each end with the burden in the middle. Each pail or basket was marked with a strip of white cloth on which the mark of the Hookow store and the weight of the load were written.

Having made arrangements with Mawoo, Dungtzu asked the porters to carry all the kinds of salt fish he had bought on board the junk in preparation for shipment upstream to Hookow.

The upstream sailing was a difficult trip. Though it was only a distance of eighty miles between Foochow and Hookow, the junk took seven or eight days for it. Many a time the junk was stranded on the shoals. The sailors then dragged ashore a big rope which was made fast bound to the mast of the junk. Mawoo and his wife poled with long bamboo poles, pushing against rocks in order to get the boat moving. The sailors dragged at the rope on shore. Mawoo stood at the stern steering and the sailors rowed at the port and starboard sides. As they rowed they sang rhythmic river shanties and kept an even pace.

As soon as the junk had arrived at the dock at Hookow Mawoo went ashore to notify the store masters who had shipments in his junk. At once Dunglin ordered the third assistant to go and check the goods. The assistant searched through the holds of Mawoo's junk for the store's goods, checking the white cloth strips. When he had found them all, he called the coolies on shore to carry them to the shore.

The coolies, twenty in number, began the work of unloading. Each two coolies formed a pair to carry a basket or pail of salt fish. Thus the crowd of porters carried the goods up from the shore and up the steep road over the pass of Mt. Hookow to the town which stood at a considerable distance inland from the river landing. Once at the top of the road, they descended into the main street, humming all the way to the store.

In the store there was a new flurry of activity. Each basket or pail of the new goods must be weighed as soon as it came in. The store people compared the weight on their balance with the original weight written on the cloth strip and the records from the letters of Dungtzu, their fish buyer in the city. Often enough they found a discrepancy. The shortage of weight might possibly be accounted for by the shrinking or drying up of the salt fish, but very often the sailors stole some fish for food on the trip up the river.

The new goods were placed in the market side by side with old ones. The market was open to all the people : the town dwellers, the farmers from the villages, rice sellers, travellers, and dealers from the district city of Kutien. From the point of view of the store these last, the dealers, were the best customers because they usually bought goods in large quantity and took them to Kutien where they were once again displayed in the local market there.

One day Wang Hankan, a merchant from Kutien, arrived. His position as the agent for the Kutien store was very similar to that of the fish-purchasing agent Dungtzu in Foochow. The people of the store of course welcomed him warmly. He hardly spoke a word but went directly to the new goods. Examining the carp, he pushed his hand deep down into the basket and turned up several fish from the bottom. Then he smelled them. He did the same thing to the plaice and the cuttle-fish. The sharks were too big to be easily moved but he tested their hardness by using his fingernails. After this careful examination he began to bargain over the price.

The price of salt fish was not fixed. It varied from time to time and from person to person. In selling goods at retail the assistants of their own authority could decide upon the price. But when it came to wholesale lots it was usually Dunglin or Yunseng who bargained with the dealers.

This time it was Dunglin who made a price for carp. Hankan pointed at him derisively with his middle finger. Pointing the middle finger was considered extremely rude in this corner of the world because people took it as the symbol of the penis. Usually the gesture gave rise to a serious quarrel. But it also depended upon the sort of situation or in what context the insult was given. Familiar friends sometimes raised the middle finger as a joke. So it was between Dunglin and Hankan. Dunglin, who was a more polite man, never used the same symbol in response, but he did let loose some dirty banter over this bargain.

The bargain was a long process. Master and dealer argued back and forth, playing tricks on each other. They exchanged words of friendship as well as curses of enmity. They shouted, they laughed, they smiled, they were caustic and sarcastic. The accountant Kaituan, who was also a friend of Hankan's, came out to break into their conversation over the bargain. Naturally he was on the side of the master and poked fun at the dealer. At last, when they had almost come to agree upon the price, Hankan still hesitated but Kaituan asked the second and third assistants to get the goods ready. By this act he forced Hankan to accept his price. Hankan shrugged and silently accepted it.

Now began the task of the assistants. They took bamboo baskets from the loft and filled the baskets with the different kinds of fish. The baskets were of a similar kind, small enough for each bearer to carry two baskets filled with goods at each end of his shoulder-pole. Then each basket was weighed, and the amount and price set down. Finally Hankan hired porters to carry these baskets to his Kutien store.

In the evening Dunglin invited Hankan to have dinner with him in the store. They talked and they drank a great deal. Hankan got drunk and had to pass the night there. In fact he stayed for several days and then went to another store because he had no permanent residence in Hookow. He constantly travelled between the town and the district city where his employer lived.

Besides Hankan, there were seven or eight other dealers from the district city of Kutien. They all bought salt fish from the stores at Hookow for their employers at Kutien. They carried on this wholesale business throughout the year. All goods changed hands on credit in this trade. From the standpoint of the Hookow store it was a lucrative business, so that dealers were well entertained and credit was extended to them. The store sent one of its assistants at least once a season up to Kutien to collect the money owed.

Just then it was nearly the New Year Festival again. The festival was the business period for clearing debts. As usual the second assistant was sent to the district city to collect the amounts which the Kutien stores owed to the Hwang family's Hookow store. But this time the trip took a different turn.

The second assistant brought back to Hookow two bags of black cloth containing silver dollars and banknotes. When he arrived at a turn in the road, two strangers suddenly appeared and demanded his bags. The assistant was a tall and strong man and resisted the strangers. They fought for a while, but the assistant was handicapped by his burden. One of the strangers finally struck him on the head with a stone, so that he fell. The strangers then snatched up the bags and ran into the woods. The assistant struggled to get up and follow the robbers. He shouted after them all the way and begged for mercy. Several times he threw himself to the ground and kowtowed to them as they ran ahead of him. He begged them to remember he was only a shopman and the money did not belong to him. At last the plunderers, whether moved by his pleadings or discomfited by his close pursuit, dropped one of the two bags. The assistant had no better choice than to take up the bag and go back home to give the news.

The news of the robbery disturbed Dunglin greatly, but his experience had trained him to accept patiently any reverse whatever. In his mind he had always kept before him the knowledge that " man proposes but Heaven disposes ". With such a philosophy he was never too greatly disappointed.

In a life of constant economic struggle when a villager rises to prosperity, others always become " red of eye " with jealousy. The store which Dunglin and Fenchow had so successfully established had naturally become an object of envy. That explains why the robbers lay in ambush to snatch the money from the messenger. Thus time after time had Dunglin suffered from his jealous neighbours. But Dunglin felt that such incidents happened as a matter of course in life and in business. He tried to plan for them, to stand ready against them, and to meet them when they came.

So the store stood firmly in the centre of his life, its commodities continually flowing upstream and downstream. Day by day, month by month, year by year, the store never failed to collect rice from villages and send it to the city, and it never failed to bring inland the salt fish of the city and distribute it to the community. The cycle of the year went round and round and the store went on, geared to the complicated business of social life.

Then the New Year came again. It was as great an occasion in the town of Hookow as it was in the Hwang village among the farmers. The people came from different directions to buy things for the festival and the celebrations, so that the whole street was filled with crowds surging like the sea. The assistants were sent to various villages to collect money. The creditors'

THE STORE BUSINESS

pursuit of debts was carried out right up until New Year's Eve, when to the last hour the assistants carried lanterns into every corner of the town and into the villages to search out those customers who still hid from them, trying to avoid their debts.

The store closed up for three days, the only vacation of the year. While Dunglin went home to his family's village, the people of the store organized a gambling party for recreation and entertainment. At home, there was no special ceremony except the usual offering of delicious dishes at the shrine of the Dragon King. But in the main temple of the town there was a great sacrifice in which most of the families of the town participated.

The accountant Kaituan drew up and presented a balance sheet for the total business of the previous year. He counted up assets and liabilities and calculated profits and losses.

Originally the profits went entirely to the partners, Fenchow and Dunglin, who were the masters and had made the original investment. If the store gained they divided the profits equally; if it lost they were equally responsible for its losses and had to contribute equal amounts of capital to cover the operation of the business.

But now in order to encourage active interest in the business, a profit-sharing device had been introduced, an issue of "red shares" had been made. There were altogether twelve shares in the store outstanding, eight ordinary shares and four "red shares". The ordinary shares were equally divided between Fenchow and Dunglin. The four "red shares" were issued to Yunseng, doctor and head of the medicine department, Dungtzu, the fish dealer and agent in Foochow, Dunglin himself, as general manager, and Kaituan, the store accountant, respectively. All profits were now to be equally divided into twelve portions and the four new portions went to the new shareholders.

Those who held the "red shares" had only limited liability; they had the right to take the profits but had no responsibility to contribute capital or cover deficits beyond their shares. That is to say, in case of loss, the deficit would be borne entirely by the ordinary shareholders, not by the "red shareholders". The "red shares" were issued only to those actively working in the store and only as a work incentive. Those "red shareholders" who held no ordinary shares were of course still only store employees who could be dismissed at any time.

The people of the store got their food and lodging at the

store, but this was considered only as an item of general expense. In addition, each member got an annual salary or wage, which varied from three dollars up to one hundred dollars, with the apprentice receiving the lowest figure and the general manager the highest.

When the store opened again after the New Year vacation, there was very little business during the first half of the first moon. The Merchants' Association, of which all the masters of stores in Hookow were members, called their spring meeting. The association had no headquarters and the chairmanship was held in rotation. Every member had the chance of serving as chairman of the association for a year, and during that year his store became the meeting-place.

One day a boy came into the store, with an invitation card in a red envelope which Dunglin opened and read. Then he changed to a clean gown and brushed the dust off his " bowl cap ". Standing before a mirror he surveyed his reflection for a moment and brushed his moustache. Seeing that everything was in order, he left the store for the meeting-place of the association, where some twenty people had already gathered. Everyone stood up to greet Dunglin, who begged their pardon for being late. A chair was offered him and he sat down with the group, who returned to their discussion. They were discussing the celebration of the Full Moon Festival that spring. In past years the celebration had been carried out in different ways : a display of offerings in the town temple or a parade of lanterns and theatrical troupes or a series of feasts. There had to be offerings anyway and the feasting could not be omitted. The only question was whether to hold the parade. Some of the masters moved that the parade be omitted on account of financial difficulty and because of the disturbed atmosphere produced by the banditry that had sprung up in the surrounding countryside.

The storekeepers discussed the matter in a calm, harmonious way. They did not take any decision by vote. They did not argue or debate. All they did was to bring out the reasons for omitting the parade. Since there were no persons who spoke vehemently in favour of keeping the old custom the problem was solved easily and naturally.

The association had no definite times for holding its meetings. Whenever something happened of concern to the town or to business, the head of the association called a meeting. Nevertheless, the functions were wide and various. They regulated the price of commodities, the scale of rents, the fares and even the schedule of junk transport. For all the public affairs of the town the association was the centre of information. The district government was in direct communication with it and held it responsible for assessing and levying taxes from each store and each family of the town. Even the squad of soldiers stationed in the town was partly supported by the association. Besides the festivals and local religious activities, the association dealt also with the problems of building the public roads and bridges and maintaining the temple. Even the missionary school and church were within the scope of discussion in the meetings. If any special emergency arose, the association had to meet that, too.

On his return from the meeting Dunglin was surprised to find his partner Fenchow in the store. Fenchow had grown old and thin. He looked very pale and worried. He told Dunglin that he had come to take up again his duties in operating the store with him, because he could no longer stay at home. Really, of course, he was trying to avoid the gloomy situation of his family since the death of his son Mowde. The constant conflicts between Mrs. Chang and Huilan, the mother-in-law and daughter-in-law, were driving Fenchow to distraction. Unable to stand such an environment where no peace was to be found, Fenchow had lost his temper and reprimanded Huilan loudly in the main hall. Not long afterwards the unfortunate daughter-in-law was discovered hanging from the roof in her room. But she was cut down in time. Of course, all the difficulty Huilan had made came out of her desire to go back to her mother's family. Fenchow knew this well enough, but his stubborn pride would not let him allow her to go, because it would give his family great disgrace to lose a daughter-in-law in such a fashion. So more difficulty came of it and the new troubles only had the effect of forcing Fenchow to leave his once peaceful home.

Back in the store Fenchow soon found he faced a far different situation from the one he had left so long before. Few people came to ask him to feel a patient's pulse. Yunseng now had most of his old customers. The people of the store respected him and spoke to him cordially, but he found himself idle most of the time. The customers seldom consulted him about prices any more. Sometimes he might be asked, but he could not answer and had to turn to Dunglin. All in all the longer he stayed the more he felt his loneliness. He complained to Dunglin that he had grown old, weak and lazy, and his memory had become poor.

Out of all this there grew up the first real difference between the old partners and brothers-in-law. After living an easy life at home for so long, Fenchow was now no longer fit for business. The organization of the store had changed since his first retirement. Dunglin had built up a system of his own. The store functioned perfectly without the presence of Fenchow, who only a few years before had been its general manager. Now he could not help but realize he was out of place. No longer the active manager he was rather a parasite.

So Fenchow did not find himself able to live a happy life in the store. Life in town was no better than his family at home. His mind was in constant conflict and he knew no rest till his brooding nearly drove him mad. But just in time a day came when his second son, Mowhun, rushed into the store, reporting between gasps that his mother, Mrs. Chang, was seriously ill. Fenchow hurried home at once.

CHAPTER X

FENCHOW'S FATE

Mrs. Chang, Fenchow's wife, had been in poor health for years. Now the death of Mowde, her youngest son, and the trouble made by Huilan caused her great worry and affected her health. She lay in bed and knew she was going to die, but wanted to wait for her husband. When Fenchow came into her room she regained her clarity of mind for a few minutes and spoke sadly to him, saying she would not be able to live much longer. Her last words to him were to advise him to send Huilan away, so as to regain peace in the home.

While his wife lay dying, Fenchow called in all the family. There were now beside Fenchow himself, his son Mowhun, his three daughters-in-law including Huilan, his two nephews, Mowyueh and Mowchiao, and the little adopted grandson. Tradition demands that when a person dies all the members of the family should be present to observe the last rites.

As soon as Mrs. Chang had passed away, the three young women began to wail and weep. Huilan had felt no sympathy towards her mother-in-law, yet she could not refrain from tears by her death-bed. The young men, Mowhun and his two cousins, took down the curtains from over the bed and from over the windows. They moved all the furniture to other rooms and opened the windows and the door wide to let in the air.

Mowhun, now the only living son of the deceased, assumed the office of chief mourner. He laid a white paper over the head and face of his dead mother and spread a red blanket to cover her whole body. Then with the help of other persons he set up in front of the bed a "soul table", on which a censer, a lamp and two clay vessels stood. Mourners watched over the corpse in turn by the side of a lamp, which was kept burning continuously. The lamp had an iron stand filled with black oil. It was known as the "netherworld lamp", for it was believed the glow would light the soul of the deceased straight along the way to the underworld. Mowhun used this lamp to set fire to the offerings of imitation money and to burn them in the clay vessels. The belief was that the soul continues to hover about the corpse and that it enjoys such offerings.

Mowhun was a middle-sized young man of dark complexion,

with heavy eyebrows and a receding forehead. Being a farmer who spent his life in the village, he had little contact with the outside world. He was dull and slow, and whenever he spoke, he wrinkled up his eyes several times. He was less highly regarded by his parents and considered less intelligent than either of his brothers, Mowkwei and Mowde. But on an occasion like this he was a faithful performer of the rites.

While praying to the soul of the dead person, and to divine the future, Mowhun took a copper coin called the " soul cash " and tossed it on to the " soul table ". The coin was fastened to a string, which he held while he tossed it. The first throw was the most fateful one. If the coin came heads up the soul was believed to give an affirmative answer to the questions put to it and if it came up tails, a negative answer.

Fenchow mourned deeply for the death of his wife. He sent men to notify the related families. Grandmother Pan, the mother of the deceased, was the first person to come to the house, bringing with her the two daughters-in-law, Aunt Lin and Mrs. Hwang. Mowhun knelt down on his knees to receive the three women, who went directly into the death chamber and began to wail. The wailing was a ceremonial observance done by all the relatives, whether or not it was meant as personal lamentation. All lifted the white paper sheet to have a last look at the dead. Fenchow went in at last to beg his mother-in-law to stop weeping. They talked about his wife's last illness before she died.

At such times a Taoist priest was called in to perform ritual in the main hall. The Taoist set up a ceremonial tree. Its trunk was driven into the ground and branches protruding in the four directions were decked with burning candles. As he recited his prayers, the Taoist led Mowhun around the tree in a circle. The other members of the family, with the exception of Fenchow, were similarly led around in turn. As each person moved around the tree, the others stood back and wailed together. The ritual and the candle-light were believed to help the soul reach the netherworld without losing its way.

Decorations in the main hall were totally different from those of ordinary days. All the usual red curtains, lamps, scrolls and couplets were replaced by white ones. Not a single bit of red colour was allowed to remain. Red is the colour of happiness and white that of mourning.

On the second day the three daughters-in-law of the deceased washed the corpse and dressed it for the funeral. The clothes had to be of an odd number : thus, seven garments for the upper half of the body and five dresses for the lower half. The old lady's outer dress consisted of a long embroidered gown and a beautiful skirt. When dressed, the body was moved to the back hall of the house, and the " soul table " was carried along with it.

The coffin, which had been prepared beforehand, was now moved into the back hall. First, the inside of the coffin was pasted with paper and oil, to prevent moisture getting in. Then a mattress was spread on it. Various kinds of mock money, the so-called coffin paper, were put in the four corners. The hour of coffining was fixed by a soothsayer who read the omens, good or evil, by his calculations.

Before the body of Mrs. Chang was put into the coffin, a niece, the elder sister of Mowyueh, who had married out of the Chang family and had come back now for the occasion, carried out another important rite. She took up a small vessel of water from the stream running in front of the house of Chang. Then she took some paper money and dipped it into the water. She swept the wet paper over the body three times. This was a ceremonial washing ordinarily carried out by a daughter, but now by a niece, as Mrs. Chang had no daughter.

At the moment when the body was to be put into the coffin, Fenchow called all the family to gather in the back hall. Relatives from other families were present, too. Once more the women began to lament.

It was twilight and the atmosphere was gloomy and smoky. The people present in the back hall each took up several of the incense sticks which were burning all the while. They were of a special kind, bigger and longer than ordinary ones, serving not only in the rites but useful also in keeping down the odour of a corpse that had lain there two days in warm weather. The people could hardly see each other in the dark and the smoky air.

Fenchow directed the closing of the coffin. He asked Mowhun to take the head and the three daughters-in-law to take the feet. He himself took the body of the corpse. They lifted it up and moved it into the coffin. Mrs. Chang now slept on a pillow which was made in the form of a cock.

Mowhun called in a carpenter. The lid was put on and the carpenter hammered in the nails. During the nailing all the people knelt on the ground. The Taoist recited prayers all the while and sprinkled holy water all the way from the main hall back to the back hall so as to ward off evil influences.

The relatives of the deceased all put on mourning garments. There were five grades of mourning, based upon relationship to the deceased, with different garments to be worn for different lengths of time. Mowhun, the son and chief mourner, wore the three years' untrimmed mourning. He wore a hat, a gown, a pair of breeches, and a pair of shoes, all made of white linen. In addition he wore another hat of three plaited strings made of hemp, a hempen gown and a square piece of hempen cloth sewn over his white shoes. The garments were all untrimmed. He also had a cord of hemp bound round his waist and a staff. If the dead person had been his father, the staff would have been made of bamboo. In this case the staff was of ordinary wood, painted red and white and bound at the end with three layers of white paper stamens.

The adopted grandson wore the same garments. In ordinary cases a grandson wears trimmed mourning for only one year, sign of the second degree of relationship. But this grandson wore first-degree mourning, taking the place of his adopted father, Mowkwei, who as the eldest son of the family would have been chief mourner if he had lived.

The three daughters-in-law also wore first-degree mourning: hempen garments and skirts, but carried no staffs. The collateral kinsmen, the kinswomen and the relatives belonging to other clans wore the other three degrees of mourning. These degrees also required white linen garments, but they exacted only nine months', five months' and three months' observance, respectively.

Curiously enough Fenchow, who actually grieved most deeply for the loss of his wife, did not wear any kind of mourning. This was contrary to the ancient ritual handed down from the oldest records and interpreted anew with each generation, a system providing obligations of mourning for father and son, husband and wife, and all other kinsmen. But the present practice seems to be to enforce mourning only as a duty of younger to older, juniors to seniors, or inferior to superior, as in the duty of a son to his parents or that of a wife to her husband. For this reason Fenchow was not ritually bound to any other mourning than his own grief.

That grief was great. The luck of "wind and water" seemed to make it Fenchow's turn to suffer. He grew pessimistic and shy in company of any kind. He stayed alone by himself now, growing thinner and thinner.

Smoking and idling did not solve his problem. Fenchow might have felt better if he had gone through all the ceremonies for his dead wife and thus found himself more in accord with his people. But he left all the arrangements to his son Mowhun, who was a devout performer of the rituals, and himself withdrew from his family all the more.

Mowhun performed the worship of the soul twice a day before the " soul table ". The morning worship took place at sunrise and the evening worship in mid-afternoon. The coffin was placed on two benches in the back hall. A " soul shrine " was set up behind the " soul table ". The shrine was made of a framework of bamboo pasted over with paper. Inside the shrine a picture of Mrs. Chang hung in the centre against the paper wall. Under the shrine stood a small bamboo stool, on which stood a pair of her shoes. Upon the stool was a bamboo branch which stretched its green leaves into the interior of the shrine. At the end of the branch a white cloth ribbon hung down in a knot, from which the ribbon fell further in two strands. The ribbon was a symbol standing for the soul, an object of special sanctity. The " soul table " set before the shrine had on it still more objects : a bowl, a pair of chopsticks, a small mirror, a comb, in addition to the original " netherworld lamp " and the " soul cash ".

During the prayers it was Mowhun who knelt before the shrine and tossed the " soul cash ", inquiring what were the wishes of the soul. The three daughters-in-law and the grandson knelt behind him, each holding three burning incense sticks. Such worship was continued up to a hundred days, during which time Mowhun and the grandson did not cut their hair.

About this time the partition between the main hall and the back hall was taken down and a large white curtain hung up to take its place. This was called a mourning curtain and on it different kinds of mourning scrolls and couplets given by friends and relatives were displayed. The things from more important relatives got positions in the middle, while those from less honoured ones appeared on the two side walls.

Mrs. Hwang and Eldest *Go* came over from the House of the Golden Wing nearly every day, helping with the household affairs as well as with the ceremonies. Eldest *Go* was assigned to work as secretary and treasurer, with a table on the front patio. He took charge of receiving gifts and sending out announcements.

On the sixth day after the death a ceremony was held which was known as reporting the death to the netherworld. The villagers believed the dead would never return again after the sixth day and a report should be made to the netherworld. The Taoist priest came again with his two assistants to decorate the main hall in the style of a palace of the netherworld, with ghostly figures placed all round. In the middle of the palace a paper house was set up. In it dwelt a paper woman, the symbolic figure of Mrs. Chang, and her man- and maid-servants. At both sides there was a set of strange things, all framed in bamboo and paper. One was a buffalo, the other a horse, but both had human bodies and limbs. Mowhun, clad in linen and hempen garments and holding a big streamer, followed the Taoist in a symbolic journey through the palace. The performance was accompanied by the playing of drums and cymbals.

On the following day rites for the salvation of the soul began. They were carried out every seventh day, up to the forty-ninth. The main performer was again the Taoist priest, attended by the mourners.

Next, the Chang family printed an obituary notice to be sent to relatives, friends, neighbours, and acquaintances. In the notice a date for public condolences was set so that the recipients could come to condole with the afflicted family.

On this day of public condolence the greatest gathering of all took place in the house of Chang. Dunglin, as a brother of the deceased, came to take his part. He led his own family, who were cordially received at the gate of the house of Chang. The mourners, headed by Mowhun, were all clad in their mourning garments. They knelt to receive the visitors.

As Dunglin entered the gate, he saw a pair of round white lanterns hanging on either side. This was the sign to outsiders that the house was in mourning. Three paper pyramids hung from the door. They were given by the parents of the three daughters-in-law, the *chingchia* of the dead woman. *Chingchia* is a collective reciprocal term used for each other by parents of married children.

As Dunglin crossed the threshold, Peimin, the Chang family's labourer, came out to greet him and offered him a suit of white clothes, which he put on at once. Then he walked under the white awning spread over the open courtyard. Some of the mourning gifts, incense, fire-crackers, paper money and paper ingots, given by friends and neighbours calling to condole with the afflicted family, were placed inside the awning. More mourning scrolls and couplets were hung from the walls. Paper replicas of houses, horses, buffaloes, palanquins, trunks, and so on, and many kinds of mock money were displayed on the floor. They were all destined for sacrifice, to be converted through the sacrificial fire into utensils and currency in the world of darkness. They were material aids sent through the smoke to the soul of the departed.

Dunglin went on into the main hall and saw Yunseng, leader of the ritual. Paying his own respects and carrying out the rites of kneeling and kowtowing demanded of him, Dunglin turned then to Fenchow's room, where the two brothers-in-law at last met again. They talked over family affairs and the business of the store, until Mowkwei's widow came in with bowls of noodles and fried eggs.

Soon the people at the gate announced the arrival of another honoured guest. This time it was Wang Liyang, the father of Huilan, thus a *chingchia* of Fenchow's. He also put on white garments and came up into the main hall, accompanied by Mowyueh, who had gone out to receive him. As Yunseng called out the ritual directions of the ceremony, Liyang knelt down upon a cushion to kowtow. Mowyueh knelt beside the guest to keep him company as a matter of courtesy. The cushions on which they knelt were arranged in three rows. A first row of white cushions, a second row of blue cushions, and a third row of red cushions, signified each of three degrees of relationship. A *chingchia* in mourning was supposed to kneel upon the white cushions. The blue and red cushions were used by less close relatives and friends.

When Liyang got up, the right corner of the mourning curtain was raised and behind it the mourners, headed by Mowhun, knelt and bowed their heads to the ground in response to his ritual act as if to thank him for his condolences.

The rites over, Liyang too was invited to Fenchow's room, where the three old friends greeted each other cordially. Fenchow was pale and sorrowful; Liyang and Dunglin urged him earnestly to take good care of himself and not to suffer too greatly.

In the afternoon more guests came and went through the ceremony, one after another in the main hall of the house.

Finally, towards evening, tables were set up and entertainment began for all the friends and relatives who had come.

This gathering for public condolence was an established ritual, followed thoroughly no matter how the participants felt. Most of the people present enjoyed the feast. There was no more wailing or weeping. This gathering served as a means by which the social ties between people could be renewed. Performance of the ceremonies fulfilled both the duty of the living to the dead and the obligations of all the people associated with them to the afflicted family. Tradition thus carried on from one generation to the next gives scope for a renewal of the integration of the social group.

On the sixth seventh-day remembrance, on the forty-second day after Mrs. Chang's death, a ceremony called " offering the sixth seventh-day rice " was carried out. The offering consisted of a wooden tray of rice, a pot of wine and a bowl of mutton, together with a bonfire of paper money. The belief was that not until this date and the offering of the rice would the dead know of her own death.

In the evening of that day the Taoist priest performed a rite called " a duck crossing a river ". A duck of bamboo sticks and paper was set afloat on the water in a pan. Beside the duck was placed a shell lamp—a broken eggshell filled with lamp oil. The shell lamp was surrounded by bamboo leaves. Reciting prayers to the playing of drums and cymbals, the Taoist slowly pushed the duck across the water of the pan. The rite was associated with a local legend to the effect that a certain woman's soul was saved by the help of ducks when she was crossing a river.

On the forty-ninth day, the last day of the Taoist rites, a final series of ceremonies was carried out in the house of Chang. The first ceremony was called " breaking out of hell ". The replica of the palace of the netherworld was set up, stretching from the main hall to the front patio. In the middle of the main hall the Taoist erected an altar decorated with pieces of variegated embroidered silk and fitted out with lamps, candlesticks and images of wood and metal. He himself was dressed in ceremonial attire, with a hat shaped like a lotus bloom. He sat at the middle of the altar. He held a bell in his right hand and a horn in his left. Two assistants standing on either side of him held musical instruments. One had a wooden fish and the other a copper jar. They carried on a steady recital of prayers, known to possess a special power to redeem souls from hell and to send them up to heaven. They played their musical instruments at intervals, accompanying their recitation of prayers. Several tables, each bearing a complete sacrificial repast of sundry dainties and delicacies, also stood before the altar. The chief mourner, Mowhun, clad in his mourning garments, advanced from time to time to offer incense, and with wailing bowed his head to the ground to urge the soul of the dead to eat and drink its pleasure. In the final rite the Taoist stood up. He took up a knife and broke with it a porcelain bowl which covered a paper figure resting on the floor. This breaking signified that the walls of hell were broken down and the soul was saved.

The second ceremony was a rite involving crossing over a bridge and was performed at midnight. A bridge of wood ten feet long, three and a half wide, and three and a half high, with its floor and sides covered with white cloth, had been erected beforehand in the open courtyard within the gate. A white cloth awning hung over it. First of all the Taoist, carrying a cloth streamer, led Mowhun, who bore a paper figure of the dead woman, across the bridge, leading him step by step in time to music. The other mourners, the three daughters-in-law and the grandson Chenchung, carried figures of the dead woman's male and female servants, and replicas of horse and buffalo across the bridge behind Mowhun. The music during the ceremony, as penetrating and strong as possible, was meant to help the soul across the bridge to the other world against all attempts of malevolent goblins to throw it off into the water.

The third ceremony was a rite in which money and goods were presented to the soul. Paper houses, barns, servants, animals, tools, money, ingots, and other valuable possessions were set on fire as gifts to the dead. The ceremony took place before the front gate.

After all this, life in the house of Chang gradually returned to normal. The long series of ceremonies performed since the death of Mrs. Chang had gone on at a diminishing tempo, providing the survivors with rôles to fill in the period of transition and a new adjustment. Though the dead woman's body lay in the coffin, still kept in the back hall waiting for burial, the members of the family came gradually to pay less attention to its presence. Sometimes Fenchow passed through the hall and looked at the coffin for a while. He always turned away in sorrow. He recalled the days of his prosperity when the house was being built and he had moved in with his wife and three sons. Now he was left alone with only one living son, Mowhun. How he had expected the site of A-Dragon-Vomiting-Pearls to give him luck! But it had turned out differently. He began to think that his " wind and water " had been cursed by some malignant deity.

At the start, much the same pattern of life had been shaped for Fenchow as for Dunglin. But the outcome for each was totally different.

CHAPTER XI
EDUCATIONAL AMBITION

Third *Go* was now a senior at Yinghwa College. Although his father often urged him to get married, he resisted because he did not wish his father to pick a wife for him. A marriage of free choice became his first ambition. And Dunglin, who often went to the city, knew quite well the recent development of so-called free marriage and did not enforce his full authority.

In Foochow, Third *Go* was interested in Chen Shuchen, a student at Hwanan College, a girls' missionary school. Third *Go* had written twice to Shuchen seeking her friendship, but he received no reply. She was not merely keeping her dignity. If she replied to the letter it would mean that she considered herself engaged to him, for such was the general convention of " free " marriage at the moment. When Third *Go* wrote his third letter he sent a message to Shankai, his sworn brother, who was a good friend of Lin Chutung, Shuchen's uncle, the husband of her father's sister. Through this uncle of hers Shuchen got some advice and guidance and she replied to the letter and accepted his proffer of friendship. Immediately following her answer came a letter from Third *Go* proposing to her by post. They exchanged photographs. Shankai and Chutung, in their turn, began to talk the matter over with the heads of the two families.

Arrangements were quickly made between the two families and the boy and girl were betrothed. In the preliminary ceremonies there was an exchange of engagement rings, an innovation in the village.

Third *Go* and Shuchen graduated from their schools that winter, and their parents arranged their wedding. Shuchen was carried in the bridal sedan-chair, escorted by a theatrical troupe. In performing the ceremony of sitting together on a bed where the bridal couple first meet face-to-face, with the bride in her bridal crown and veil, the groom broke the traditional silence by speaking to his betrothed, and the pair talked during the whole performance. This was strange to the bridal maids and to the other spectators, who had never seen a young couple talk easily at their first meeting in the presence of other people.

At the time the couple made their obeisance to the older

relatives of the family, Yuhun, their grand-uncle, was asked to be master of ceremonies. Grandmother Pan was the first one to be honoured. The next were Hwang Dunglin and Mrs. Hwang, who sat side by side, proudly receiving the obeisance of their eldest son and his bride. Then came Aunt Lin, Yuhun, Dungchien, Eldest *Go* and so on. This ceremony was an important one and it lasted a long while.

It was the duty of the new couple to kowtow to those relatives who were senior to the groom in age and generation. These relatives included all the immediate family : the nearer relatives of both his own clan and those outside it, and the elders of his own clan. They were honoured in order from older to younger and from the nearer to the more distant relatives.

But in this ceremony Third *Go* did not honour Second *Go*, though Second *Go* was his senior, his first cousin and one of the family. There was a reason. At Second *Go*'s wedding Dunglin had failed to attend. His absence was very strange to the spectators. As head of the family Dunglin should have been the first man honoured. It was of course a great insult to Second *Go* that he had stayed away.

Later Second *Go* found out his uncle had stayed away on purpose to disgrace him. The insult was the result of a previous incident in which Second *Go* had behaved very badly. Angry about a reprimand from his uncle, which Second *Go* thought unjust, he had seized a wood-cutting knife and chased his uncle with it. Dunglin was not hurt, but the attack with a knife was never forgotten.

The strained relationship of Dunglin and his nephew Second *Go* had affected the feeling between Second *Go* and his cousins, the sons of Dunglin. Later still at the marriages of Fourth *Go* and Fifth *Go*, Second *Go* was again passed over. Almost twenty years had to pass until the marriage of Shoupei, the eldest son of Second *Go*, before the breach was healed. Then Dunglin and his sons were all invited to be honoured and gladly received the kowtows of their young nephew. Everyone forgot the bygone dispute at last and normal relations came into effect again.

The wedding of Third *Go* was the largest gathering the family had ever held. At the wedding feast twenty-four tables were set up. The guests of honour were seated in order. Dunglin's maternal uncle, the one who had helped him long before in the lawsuit, attended the wedding and was asked to sit in the most honoured seat, at the innermost table to the left in the main hall. The next most honoured seat went to Cheng Anchi, an adopted brother of Mrs. Hwang's. He occupied the innermost table on the right in the main hall. A brother of Aunt Lin's was invited to sit in the third most honoured seat at the middle table. Friends like Fenchow, Yiyang, Liyang, Lugo and the other shop owners in Hookow were all seated in places of honour too.

Each family of the village of Hwang sent at least one man and one woman to the party. Each of them acted as hosts or hostesses to entertain friends and relatives from outside clans. The men and women dined separately. Tables for the men were set up in the main hall, the open courtyard and the front patio, while those for the women filled up the back hall and the dining-rooms of the rear terraces.

Third *Go* thus safely married, nothing much happened to disturb the even tenor of village life until an incident took place the following summer.

The wedding had been held during the winter vacation. In the summer the bride had been called home by her mother, and Third *Go*, feeling lonesome after the departure of his wife, had gone with Fifth *Go* to gamble in a neighbouring village. In the evening Mrs. Hwang sent Fourth *Go* to bring them home. The gamblers were in an exciting stage of the game, so that Fourth *Go* stayed on to watch it. When a second messenger, Little Brother, reached the gambling spot the elder brothers kept him too.

It grew dark. Neither messenger had come back. Mrs. Hwang grew more and more concerned about her sons. She then left the house with her little daughter Chumei and walked along the Western Road. They met Yuhun on the way, and the old uncle told the story next day to Dunglin in the Hookow store.

The following day Dunglin came home with a face clouded with anger. No sooner did he arrive in the main hall than he picked up a big wooden stick and beat Third *Go* with it as he sat on a stool waiting to greet his father. Heavy strokes fell upon the shoulders of Third *Go*, but he did not move and merely shed tears in silence.

As Dunglin beat Third *Go* he shouted angrily, " You unfilial son ! You're a man over twenty years of age, a graduate of Yinghwa College, and a newly married man ! Don't you feel ashamed, gambling and gathering with the village toughs ?

What's the use of our educating you? Where is your sense of duty? Don't you care about your mother's feelings? Don't you care that she had to send for you several times? How dare you let her walk out after dark searching for you? How dare you show your shamelessness to the whole village? Why don't you set a good example for your juniors? Shame on you as one of our family! Shame on you as the only educated man in the village!"

Dunglin shouted without a stop, but Third *Go* did not answer a single word. Mrs. Hwang ran in and tried to snatch the wooden stick away. She expostulated with Dunglin, "You are using such a big stick and striking so hard!" Mrs. Hwang was older now and more in a position to interfere with her husband's punishment of their sons.

Dunglin was at the height of his wrath. He turned and scolded his wife, shouting, "It is all your fault. You've spoiled your sons, one by one."

"How is it my fault?" Mrs. Hwang replied. "Sons reaching maturity should be given advice and should be talked to. What's the good of using a big stick and beating them?"

But the father was not satisfied and continued his harangue for a long time. Then suddenly he asked for the "thief-head". He referred to his son Fifth *Go*. An unruly boy, Fifth *Go* did very little work for the family. He spent his time with the village toughs, playing, gambling and running wild. Dunglin used to punish him and called him "thief-head". Hearing his eldest brother being beaten, Fifth *Go* had run to his bed and pulled the blankets over his head. But his father found him and slapped him severely. Mrs. Hwang again rushed in to stop the fracas.

When Dunglin came back to the main hall, Third *Go* had dried his tears but he was still silent. Fourth *Go* and Little Brother, who had not gambled, were not punished. They watched the scene quietly and dared not speak a word. The tension began to fall a little, but Little Brother was still frightened. Fourth *Go* pointed to him and spoke jokingly, "It's now the turn of this little gambler." Little Brother broke into loud wailing. The elder lad only intended to ease the situation by breaking the silence, but the younger boy did not understand. His crying set off the little sister Chumei as well. This turn of the situation made the grown people laugh, and Dunglin came over to soothe Little Brother. Once more the father became tender, and the others gradually felt at ease. So the life of the family returned to its normal course.

Having been educated in modern schools, Third *Go* could not go into farm work or into the store. Hence it was his ambition to find a teaching job. Fortunately he was offered such a position in a high school in the city of Yenping, fifty-five miles up the river from the town of Hookow. This opportunity came shortly after the gambling episode and Third *Go* went off to live two years in that place. He took his wife with him. There they had a child, a boy they named Shouyang. His small family was still only a part of the greater one, even though physically separated from it. Third *Go* did not earn enough money to support himself, his wife and his child, and he still relied upon Dunglin to send him extra money that he needed.

The news of the birth of Shouyang, Dunglin's first grandson, brought good cheer and happiness to the home village. Even though the little fellow was away in Yenping, the Hwang family carried out his Fullness of the Month with a great celebration. Kinsmen, neighbours and friends were invited to the feast. They could compare this feast with that of the birth of Little Brother, when only the members of the household and a few visiting relatives gathered for a bowl of noodles. Times had changed and the family now could afford a big celebration.

In the second year of his stay at Yenping, Third *Go* asked young Sixth *Go* and Chen Chihu, a younger brother of Shuchen's, to join his small family. The two young boys enrolled as students in the high school.

The following summer Third *Go* brought his wife and son back to his native village and left the boys, Little Brother and Chihu, at Yenping. Then he went to Foochow, alone, to get further education in a university. That trip became the occasion of a great event in the family life.

He sailed from Hookow by junk, changing to a steamboat in Shuikow, the terminus of the steamboat line running upstream from the capital city. It grew dark as the boat passed through a narrow channel about twenty miles below Shuikow. Suddenly the report of a gun was heard from the deck. The passengers were greatly alarmed. They rushed here and there. Then there was shooting from both banks and the bullets began to fall like rain.

Third *Go* was sleeping in the cabin at the time. The alarm and shooting woke him with a start. No sooner did he open his eyes than he heard a rush of sound by his right ear. A bullet went through the suitcase he was using as a pillow, missing his head by only an inch. Later he showed the bullet hole to his mother and his wife, who stood horror-stricken with open mouths.

The steamboat came to a stop. Several small boats laden with men in black clothing and bamboo hats drew alongside. Each man carried a gun and a cartridge belt around his waist. They were bandits.

As the band clambered into the steamboat, the chief pointed a pistol at the steersman's head and ordered him to steer toward the left bank. Some of the bandits took up stations at the important points on the boat and others began a search for money and valuables. Rings, watches, earrings, bracelets, and dresses suited them equally well. The passengers were searched and ordered to stand at the sides.

Having gathered up all the money and valuables, the bandits picked out the passengers whom they considered rich men judging by their appearance and clothing. Third *Go* was unfortunately one of the ten. These ten were to be carried off for ransom. Then the chief blew a whistle and the band went off, leaving helpless passengers and several corpses behind them.

Third *Go* was ordered along and forced to climb up the mountains in the darkness. When the band arrived at a steep part of the slope, they stopped to exchange a password between the band who had attacked the boat and the others who lay waiting in the forest. The leader of the first band was calling to the leader of those waiting. As the answer came, Third *Go* thought he heard a familiar voice. He cried out, begging them to release him and pleading he was only a poor student. The leader of the waiting force gave an order, saying, " What is the good of capturing a student ? Release him at once."

Third *Go* heard the order and plucked up courage to ask the leader to give him back the wedding ring, watch and fur coat that had been taken from him in the boat. But the chief curtly advised him to go back without further ado and blandly explained how difficult it would be to find such things in the darkness.

Making his way back to the shore, Third *Go* felt sure the chief who had just saved him from kidnapping and whose voice he had recognized could only be Chen Shankai, his sworn brother. But it seemed to him very strange that Shankai should have become a bandit chief, for he had had a higher ambition. He remembered that not wishing to follow the ordinary paths of education, Shankai had quitted Yinghwa College and entered the Military Academy of North China. After graduation from the academy, he had come back to Foochow and, though he had tried to find a position in the army corps, he had not found one. As Third *Go* stumbled back to the shore, he could not be sure of his impression, but he filed it away in his memory for future use.

Arriving at last in Foochow, Third *Go* enrolled again as a student in Fukien University, where he spent two years more, going home to the village every summer and winter vacation. His wife and son lived in the great family household. Shuchen came thus to the family as a bride and should have been cook for the household during her first three years, later to share cooking by turns with Eldest *Sao* and Second *Sao*. But she had never learned to cook. Her frailty and her education thus made her exempt from cooking. For that reason the cooking for the household had still to be done by Eldest *Sao* and Second *Sao*, and both of them complained a great deal. Finally their husbands spoke of the matter to Dunglin. To solve the problem Dunglin immediately purchased a wife for Fourth *Go*. Fourth *Sao* was a perfect village-style housewife, well able to do the cooking and other household work.

Shuchen thus became Third *Sao* in the family. She found it very hard to adapt herself to the life of the Hwang household. At first Dunglin looked upon her with special favour. He told others proudly that this daughter-in-law of his could write more literary letters than his educated son Third *Go* and he found her attitude towards her elders especially polite and cordial. But Dunglin's favour did not last long when the other women complained about her.

The daily life of the Hwang family started very early in the morning. The farmers were usually up at dawn, ready to go to the fields as soon as they had finished their breakfast. But Shuchen could never get up so early. When she finally came down to have breakfast with her son, the farmers had already worked in the fields for hours, the women had done much of the household work, washing the dishes, feeding the pigs and chickens, cleaning and drying the clothing and the old grandmother had long ago gone off to collect pig-dung. Her daily late-rising made all the others dislike her and she was herself embarrassed over it.

She never went to the stream to wash clothes like the others. To her it seemed a disgrace to do so. She washed clothing instead at home, using much of the water that had to be carried home by the farmers. They too used to complain of her using so much water in that fashion. Shuchen, furthermore, found it hard to grow accustomed to the food. The steamed rice was too hard for her. The people were disgusted with her grumbling at such fastidiousness at her age when the rice was good for the old grandmother every day.

So Shuchen, in her own sphere a perfectly competent young lady, well educated and well behaved, could not fit into the life of the Hwang family. Her different background and training were against her. She had been happy when she and her husband had their little household in Yenping. But in the village a woman of delicate health and considerable education had no place. The village knew only women with strong bodies who could work hard, cook, follow the pattern of traditional life, and bring up many children.

One summer Third *Go* took his wife and son to visit his parents-in-law whose home was in the region of the Eastern Road in the Kutien district. Shuchen's father was a Christian and a preacher, himself brother-in-law to Lin Chutung, another Christian preacher. This Chutung had served as go-between at Third *Go*'s marriage, so that the two men were on good terms. At the home of his wife Third *Go* met other preachers and church-people. They were part of a group enthusiastic in Christian activities.

Shuchen's father suggested that his son-in-law Third *Go* try to be elected as a church representative and be sent to the United States to obtain higher education in that country. Third *Go* was greatly interested in the suggestion because it was his ambition to study abroad. So he began to visit the preachers and important church members in order to obtain their support.

In the autumn a general conference of the Methodist Church was held in Foochow, the capital city of the province. Preachers and lay representatives gathered from the different districts. One of their most important tasks was to elect two preachers and two church members to act as delegates to a conference to be held in the United States. The expenses of these delegates were defrayed by the budget of the Church.

The preachers' delegates were elected by all the preachers, and the members' delegates by all the lay representatives sent from the local churches, two from each. The two members of the conference who got the most votes would go abroad as delegates.

At the time of this conference, Little Brother was a student in the preparatory class at Yinghwa College. He was selected to act as representative from the Hookow church, as an alternative for his elder brother. Actually he was not eligible to vote or even to attend the meeting, as he was much under age. The regulations of the Church required an age of twenty-one as the minimum. Consequently when Little Brother came to the entrance, a blue-eyed missionary asked him his age. With a smile he answered he was just twenty-one and had a son six years old. The blue-eyed missionary laughed dubiously, but he did not keep Little Brother from going in, as he held a certificate from the local church. During the meeting, luckily, Third *Go* was elected to be one of the two delegates. Those who voted for him were entertained in a restaurant and a big feast was held.

The election was certainly great news to the Hwang family. Dunglin sent out invitations once again to his kinsmen, neighbours, and friends, asking them to come to a big celebration in the House of the Golden Wing. The guests came and presented gifts in money and in kind. The corporate clan of Hwang also contributed some money from the rents of the ancestral lands, as an encouragement toward the higher education of their clan brother.

The House of the Golden Wing was now at the height of prosperity and popularity. The success of Third *Go* gave him a reputation as the most educated among the people of the Western Road. His success brought glory to his own family and to the entire clan of Hwang. Going abroad was a great occasion in the village world. Returned students formed a special and privileged class. Third *Go* would certainly become a great man when he returned from the outside world. The Hwang family and the villagers earnestly awaited the triumphant return of their son.

CHAPTER XII

A SPLIT

In the House of the Golden Wing, ever since the lawsuit, Eldest *Go* had gradually emerged as the managing force in the family's affairs, especially in all matters concerning farming. He was, however, not too successful a manager. Unlike his uncle he kept up a stiff attitude towards his fellow-workers. He seldom chatted with them, but often contented himself with giving blunt orders. The man in particular who rebelled against his domination was his brother Second *Go*, a quiet but stupid fellow, the same one who once pursued his uncle with a knife. The conflict between the brothers, Eldest *Go* and Second *Go*, usually began with angry words, but it soon grew to fist fights and wrestling. Their quarrelling, in turn, led to quarrelling between Eldest *Sao* and Second *Sao*, their wives.

Although there was no open conflict between Eldest *Go* and Fourth *Go*, their relations were far from friendly. Eldest *Go* continually pressed Fourth *Go* to do more and more of the farm work. His reason was that since Third *Go* had spent family money in getting an education, it was the duty of Fourth *Go* to do double work to make up the deficit.

Meanwhile Fifth *Go* had also come to the age of beginning farm work. Brought up during the time when the family had been better off he was not immediately pressed to work, so that he used to loaf away his time with a gang of the village youngsters. When Dunglin came home to the village, Fifth *Go* was ordered to join the farming crew. But as soon as his father left the house, he took off his work shoes. Very often Eldest *Go*, seeing Fifth *Go* released from work, took off his work shoes too as an act of protest.

The brothers and cousins in the House of the Golden Wing were all on good terms with their old long-term employee, Nanmin, a hard worker and an experienced farmer. Once when he saw Fourth *Go* and Fifth *Go* wrestling in a field, he tried to separate them and pleaded with them not to fight. But Eldest *Go*, who was also present, said quickly to the labourer, " Granduncle Nanmin, what do you lose by their fighting? Let them fight and we can enjoy looking on." As their senior, Eldest *Go*'s attitude towards his cousins was unjustified. Instead of stopping their fighting, he made fun of them and encouraged their quarrels. But they soon took revenge upon him. When it came to his turn and he was fighting with Second *Go*, his only brother, Nanmin tried again to interfere. But Fourth *Go* prevented him, saying what Eldest *Go* had said, " Grand-uncle Nanmin, what do you lose by their fighting? Let them fight and we can enjoy looking on." So as not to be made fun of, Fourth *Go* resolved never to fight again with Fifth *Go*, but their relations did not improve in other ways.

Dunglin knew little of the dissensions between the brothers and cousins, but he often heard complaints from Eldest *Go*, who disliked the farm work and begged his uncle to give him a position as assistant in the store. In the first few years at the shop, Eldest *Go* had worked diligently there and shown his willingness to follow the directions of his uncle. He had become quite a satisfactory assistant and had sometimes helped to write letters and keep accounts. Thus he was well trained. But Dunglin found him more useful as manager of the farm and kept him on at that task.

Eldest *Go* now could well stand upon his own feet. He began to demand that, instead of following his uncle's desire to build up an ever-larger and stronger family, the family should now be divided, so that he could obtain a large portion of the property and set up for himself. Eldest *Go* was of course the first-born of Dungmin, who was in turn the eldest son. In that division of a family the first-born had a legal right to an extra portion of the joint property as a special recognition of his primogeniture. Furthermore, the education of Third *Go* and Sixth *Go* was proving a great drain on the family income and this frightened Eldest *Go*, who complained of it to his uncle from time to time. Beyond all this, Eldest *Go* had grown more and more attached to his wife Eldest *Sao* and their three children. He wished now to live in a smaller and more peaceful household.

Finally, the demands of Eldest *Go* became so strong that they had to be heeded. He brought in Lin Tienlan, a distant nephew of Aunt Lin's, to act as arbiter in the family division. In strict fact Tienlan was not the right person to act as arbiter, according to customary rules. In any division of a family between brothers, a maternal uncle was usually the most suitable person. The proposed division theoretically took place between Dunglin and his long-dead brother Dungmin. Any arbiter such as Tienlan, chosen from Dungmin's wife's clan, would be considered partial, because he was not related equally to each of the original brothers.

But as Tienlan was a close friend of Eldest *Go*'s, he insisted upon him.

In discussing the division Dunglin tried to be fair, but Eldest *Go* demanded too much, so that there came into being several points of conflict. The first matter of dispute was the land to be dedicated to the memory of Dunglin's parents. It was Dunglin's wish that the land below the House of the Golden Wing be set aside thus as common sacrificial land. However, Eldest *Go*, who intended to possess this piece of land for himself, argued that the land had been bought by his father Dungmin and therefore should be assigned to him by right of primogeniture. As both sides clung to their points, Tienlan found it very difficult to negotiate between them. Dunglin explained to him in reasoned tones that land so near to the house should be common property, so that both branches of the family could make use of it for cultivating rice, vegetables, sugar-cane, beans and taro for table use. If this land were assigned to one line rather than the other, it would cause inconvenience to the other line, who would have no near-by land on which to grow their daily food, especially their green vegetables. Tienlan found this argument very reasonable, so he urged Eldest *Go* to make another demand instead. Eldest *Go* finally asked for a thousand dollars in lieu of his rights of primogeniture and Dunglin was forced to comply. The land was thus set aside as a common or sacrificial plot, but until the death of Grandmother Pan there should be no sacrifice held upon it, and the two lines should take turns cultivating the fields.

A second point of conflict arose over the question of the marriage of Fifth *Go* and Sixth *Go*, the only two males of the younger generation who did not yet have wives. According to tradition two portions of money or other property should be reserved for their marriages. Eldest *Go* demanded that if portions were to be reserved for his two cousins, then one portion should also be reserved for the marriage of his son Shoutai. But this demand was felt to be very unreasonable. Next he argued that Sixth *Go* had already spent his portion on his education and that he had thus no right to an additional portion. Only after considerable mediation by the arbiter did uncle and nephew agree upon the reservation of only one portion for the marriage of Fifth *Go*.

The third point of conflict was concerned with the money savings of the family. Dunglin agreed that the family could well be divided, to live henceforth with "separate hearths" in order to reduce the internal friction of so large a household. But he wished all money savings to be preserved intact so that the business could be carried on more effectively. Fearing his cousins Third *Go* and Sixth *Go* would spend more money on their education, Eldest *Go* insisted on a division of the capital. In the end it was decided to divide up all the money, reserving only a thousand dollars as a common fund for common purposes, such as house repairs, common taxes, the expenses of the future funeral of the old grandmother, and so on.

A fourth point of conflict was the disposition of shares in the Hookow store. We remember that the Hwang family had four ordinary shares in the store. Eldest *Go* demanded an equal division of the shares. But Dunglin, as founder and owner of the store, could insist on reserving more shares for himself. He had already given up one-half of the money and property he had gained from his lifetime of business to the nephews whom he had saved from starvation long ago in the days of the family's first poverty. He kept two and a half shares for himself and let only one and a half shares go to the nephews. Eldest *Go* was far from satisfied with this arrangement, so the seeds of further future conflict were sown by the old man's refusal.

When all the points of conflict were settled the Hwang family chose a day of good omen for carrying out the ceremony of the division of the family. The negotiator, Lin Tienlan, had to be present. Dunglin's uncle Yuhun, who had now become the head of the entire clan of Hwang and was now the oldest survivor of Dunglin's lineage, had also to be present. Besides Yuhun, a few more elders of the various lineages of the clan were invited to attend the ceremony and the feast.

The elders and the arbiter gathered in the main hall at the House of the Golden Wing. Yuhun was asked to draw up a deed for the division of the family. Two names were chosen to differentiate the two new families. The line descended from Dungmin was to be called "the literary lineage" and that from Dunglin "the military lineage". Yuhun wrote out the first part of the deed, a traditional legal instrument. It began by describing a division of the family as an event as natural as the continuous flow of water from a source or the spreading of branches in a tree. Then it gave the historical background of the division.

In the second part of the deed Yuhun recorded the assignment of the ancestral lands and other properties, their values and their locations. Immediately following he listed the farm lands that were to go to " the literary lineage " and those that were to go to " the military lineage ". Many pieces of land were equally divided, and Dunglin and Eldest *Go* drew lots in the presence of the arbiter and the elders. Mountain lands, trees and forests, pools and roads were similarly divided and the portions drawn by lot. Next came a long record of buildings, structures, and rooms. Living quarters and apartments had already been divided at the time the Hwang family moved into the house. Now additional kitchens had been built to set up " the separate hearths ". Kitchens, dining-rooms, barns, stores, and farm sheds were all equally divided. But neither furniture nor actual cash-in-hand were mentioned in the deed.

In the last part, the date of making it and signatures of both parties to it, as well as those of the arbiter and the guarantors of the contract of division, were set down.

Finally, in a separate transaction but still in the presence of the arbiter and the elders, all furniture was taken into the main hall and there divided and assigned by lot. But personal possessions like the dowries of the wives were not included.

The last part of the performance was an offering of two wooden kettles before the ancestral shrine. The kettle was heaped with steaming rice, the symbol of abundance. Dunglin and Eldest *Go*, now equal heads of two equal lineages, bowed down before their ancestors. Then each took a kettle to his respective kitchen. Thus at last the Hwang family was divided, and two " separate hearths " were set up. In the evening a feast was held, in which the arbiter and the guarantors were guests of honour.

The next morning the two new hearths steamed their own rice. The old grandmother took turns eating with each. For the first three days she had her meals with " the literary lineage ", and then went to " the military lineage " for the next three days. Eldest *Sao* and Second *Sao* took turns cooking each month for the family of which Eldest *Go* was now the head, while in Dunglin's own household, Fourth *Sao* became the only cook. Grandmother Pan was very old now and did not work any more. Yet she still enjoyed life. Usually she walked down after lunch with the help of a bamboo staff towards the old house in order to chat with the old women there. She spent many hours there sipping the tea served her by the young women of that house.

But Eldest *Go* was not content with this division. He began to plan another with his brother Second *Go*. Tienlan, a close friend of Eldest *Go*'s, was again invited to be the negotiator. But when they presented their plan to Dunglin for his approval, he looked over the list of things to be assigned to each brother and discovered the plan to be most unfair. According to the plan, three-fourths of the property would go to Eldest *Go* and only one-fourth would be left to Second *Go*. Demands based on the rights of primogeniture were specially large. Furthermore, a portion for the marriage of Shoutai, the eldest son of Eldest *Go*, was figured in the list. Having examined the list in detail, Dunglin grew angry and scolded Eldest *Go*, calling him a man of no conscience. He thrust the list aside and would not consider the matter further.

After a while, therefore, Eldest *Go* went back to the village of Hwang and tried to arrange a division with Second *Go* by himself. But the two brothers were soon in serious conflict over the matter. Second *Go*, who had always been quiet and rather reserved in speech, began to pour out his hidden hatred of his brother aloud. Eldest *Go* refused to make any concession and they soon passed from quarrelling to outright fighting.

One time the two brothers fought in the main hall of the House of the Golden Wing and their wives took up the quarrel. Seeing the fight become really serious, Eldest *Sao* called upon her son Shoutai to help her husband. Eldest *Go* was not so strong as Second *Go*, who though shorter was much the more powerful man. The pummelling and wrestling kept on till the men parted, exhausted.

From then on quarrels between Eldest *Go* and Second *Go* happened more frequently, and their wives kept the conflict alive. Their mother-in-law no longer knew how to stop them. Sometimes, indeed, Aunt Lin found that she herself was the cause of their quarrels. If she helped Eldest *Sao*, Second *Sao* was sure to complain, and *vice versa*. Any interference in the conflict on her part, either in the quarrels between her sons or in those between her daughters-in-law, won her only rebuffs. She was a pitiful old mother, suffering wrangling and rebuffs from both her sons. Thus as the conflict between the brothers grew so bitter some sort of division became more and more necessary, but any adjustment of their irreconcilable claims upon their joint property was exceedingly difficult.

At this time Third *Go* had not yet gone abroad, and it happened that he came home during the winter. Immediately Second *Go* came to him, telling him of the selfishness of Eldest *Go*, and asking him to act as arbiter. As a cousin of the two brothers and a liberal, educated man, Third *Go* was thought to be a good judge, on whose fair play and impartiality Second *Go* could rely. But even he found it very difficult to deal with Eldest *Go*, who obviously intended to gain as much as he could, and so shifted his position endlessly. Thus Third *Go* discussed the situation with the brothers without any result. He left for his trip abroad the following spring without having accomplished anything.

Finally, Eldest *Go* and Second *Go* did succeed in putting into effect a plan of division of their property. Making use of Tienlan again, they proceeded to a division the following autumn, even though some problems remained unsolved. They split their land, the house rooms, the furniture and all other goods except their shares in the stores. The shares were the chief of the problems that lingered on for a long while afterward. In the ceremony Tienlan, Yuhun and Dunglin acted as guarantors and signed the deed. Thus the two brothers also set up " separate hearths " and went to live by themselves, only their mother Aunt Lin remaining the connecting link. " The literary lineage " had split in two.

In the early days of Dunglin's struggles, he had worked hard to carry on the store and to become successful in his circle of society. He had wished to maintain the family in an integral unity. The end he desired was considered by all the local world an eminently laudable and virtuous goal. But the internal conflict between the brothers, between the cousins and between the wives of the younger generation had made family life difficult on the scale he envisioned. Strife and complaint were too much for him and he could not help but let the family divide.

Dunglin could well have foreseen this further splitting of " the literary lineage ", in which break he now acted as one of the guarantors. He thought to himself that family history goes by cycles, for his mind turned back to the days when he and his brother divided the family with their uncles, the brothers of their father. One of the participants in that division was dead long ago now, leaving a line that had gradually declined. The other, his old Uncle Yuhun, still lived and carried on side by side with Dunglin's own family, but he had never emerged from poverty and often relied upon Dunglin for aid. Now perhaps Dunglin's own family might be facing the same sort of division into a rich branch and a poor, if things should go badly with his nephews.

Even though a family divided one might hope the tie of kinship would still unite the branches. Dunglin hoped that the new branches of the Hwang family might hold together as the old branches had held. For, though poor, old Uncle Yuhun, who headed the impoverished branch of his father's family, had been very helpful to Dunglin. It was he who had stood firmly at the side of Dunglin in the days of the lawsuit. It was he who had gone to prison with Dunglin. It was he who had come happily and cheerfully to grace every occasion of ceremony and celebration in the House of the Golden Wing. Only once had uncle and nephew fallen out. At one time when Yuhun was in the Hookow store, Dunglin reprimanded Dungdoo the cook, the old man's second son, in the presence of the old man. Yuhun had got angry then and ordered his son to go back home and quit his job. But even that incident was to be forgiven and forgotten. Years afterwards, when Yuhun's first son Dungheng was to suffer a sudden death and his third son was to be shot by bandits, tired old Yuhun, lying on his death-bed, would gasp out a last request: that Dunglin look after his only remaining son, this same Dungdoo.

Dunglin thus had seen the gradual decline of the families of his uncles go on side by side with the emerging prosperity of his own line. The division of " the literary lineage " and the aggressive attitude of Eldest *Go* made him fear for the future of Second *Go*. His fear was shared by Grandmother Pan, who kept watch even more keenly than he over the development of the generations.

Grandmother Pan was by this time well over eighty years of age. Originally she had been very fond of Eldest *Go* because he was her first grandson and she had brought him up. But lately she had turned her sympathy toward Second *Go* whose incapacity made her fear for his future. The attitude of Aunt Lin was quite opposite. She had at first been entirely impartial in the constant conflict between her sons. Sometimes indeed, as the elder son was much more aggressive, her sympathy had gone out to her younger boy. Nevertheless, from the time of the division of Dunglin's great household, Aunt Lin began to look with great favour upon Eldest *Go*, especially after he had proved his ability to get the larger share of the property for his own line. He convinced her that without him Second *Go* would never be able to wrest any property at all out of the hands of Dunglin. Indeed this partiality Grandmother Pan felt showed itself in the next great event of the family's life.

The old woman fell ill. She was certain that the end of her life was near. She called Second *Go* in secretly and directed him to carry away for himself all her meagre hoard of secret savings. Unfortunately, while he was groping about for the money in the dark corner where she had hidden it, he was discovered by Chumei, who happened to bring in tea for her old grandmother, so that Second *Go*'s secret inheritance was revealed.

But Grandmother Pan's sickness was of much more importance than any question of a special inheritance for Second *Go*. Dunglin came home to find his old mother seriously ill. As he talked with her, she coughed continuously and painfully and Dunglin had to wipe the phlegm from her mouth. As she grew worse Dunglin called all the family to her room, all except Third *Go* and Sixth *Go* who were away studying. But even as they assembled Eldest *Go*, jealous of Second *Go*'s inheritance of his grandmother's money, picked a quarrel with him at the very foot of her death-bed. Dunglin intervened. But Eldest *Go*, in great anger, pushed violently against a wooden case, which toppled to the floor with a thundering crash. At that very moment the old grandmother's breath stopped and she died. In deep grief Dunglin bowed his head. He had wished his mother to die in peace, but he could not find it in his heart to rebuke his nephews then.

With the news of Grandmother Pan's death, the women wailed and the men set about their errands. The House of the Golden Wing prepared once more for mourning. On the following day all the daughters married out of the family were returning home one by one, and all the relatives and neighbours came from far and near to condole with the bereaved.

Grandmother Pan had had two daughters. Her elder daughter, Chang Fenchow's wife, was already dead. Only her younger daughter, who had married into the clan of Wang, came back to join the mourning. But her first act on her arrival was to inquire about the division of the family and its property. She asked Dunglin point-blank why she had not been assigned a portion of the family goods. Dunglin reminded her of the circumstances under which she had left the family, when their father was just recently dead and their mother was a poor, young widow. She answered him, her tiny bound feet stamping upon the floor, saying that she was equally descended from her parents and should be given a share of their property. Dunglin asked her why she had not come forward for her share of the family property when he was languishing in gaol. The question expressed an old resentment, for he had always thought his sister had been unreasonably selfish at the time of his lawsuit, for she had never come back to the village or sent him any message, and her sons had stood aloof, fearing to be associated with the matter.

As Dunglin quarrelled with his sister over her unreasonable demand, announcement was made of the arrival of a group of mourners from the clan of Pan. All the family rushed out of the house to receive them. Dressed in linen and hempen mourning, headed by Dunglin, the chief mourner, the family knelt down in rows by the side of the road leading to the House of the Golden Wing.

The newcomers consisted of eleven people, seven women and four men, all descended from the father of Grandmother Pan. Each represented one of the present families of the Pan connections. Six persons of the eleven had never seen Grandmother Pan and had as yet no association with the Hwang family, yet they came to fulfil their obligations in the ceremony demanded by the bond of kinship. As the newcomers met the kowtowing mourners, they too dropped down one by one to their knees facing the bereaved family. The two groups remained thus for a little while, wailing in concert. Then the newcomers rose and went over to assist the others to their feet. It was worthy of note that even Chen Shuchen, the wife of Third *Go*, called back from Kutien city where she had held a job as a teacher in a girls' school since her husband had left for abroad, took her place among the mourners. As the daughter of a preacher and herself a devout Christian she had never worshipped other gods. But this time she closely followed all the mourning rules. Otherwise she would have been ridiculed or even punished. By following them she tried to adapt herself to the family's life.

Once in the house the newcomers from the Pan clan found the bitter wailing and weeping of Dunglin's second sister highly filial. They would never have known from her conduct that there was a bitter conflict about the family property.

Like Dunglin's sister, Dungmin's eldest daughter had come back and complained before Aunt Lin that she had been given nothing at the time of the division between Eldest *Go* and Second *Go*, her younger brothers. She was cordially hated by Eldest *Go* and his wife, who blamed her husband for the scandal at their wedding long ago. But she also cried bitterly before the coffin of Grandmother Pan, the very model of a filial granddaughter.

Among the mourning daughters Dungmin's second daughter was the happiest. She came back without any demands. She had never forgotten how, long ago, she had been a betrothed daughter in the Hsu family, faced with starvation there, and how her Uncle Dunglin had saved her. She cried before the coffin according to the custom, but not without sincerity.

So in the mourning for Grandmother Pan the House of the Golden Wing was totally different from what it was in ordinary daily life. The ceremonies continued for a considerable time and the mourners and their visitors renewed the old ties of relationship. Once again the rites served as an integrative force, rebuilding a common unity of feeling among them after the disturbance of normal life which the crisis of death had brought.

But although the mourning in the House of the Golden Wing brought such a temporary truce among the family, the forces of contention and division could not be crushed entirely. They could be found even in the ceremonies themselves. The quarrel between the two brothers at the very moment when their grandmother was dying, the demands of the married daughters and their complaints all indicated that the house was far from united.

CHAPTER XIII

DIVISION IN THE STORE

In the house of Chang, Fenchow had been most unhappy during the last few years. He had acquired money and property, but it had availed him nothing. He felt alone and out of place both in the store and at home. When he had joined the farewell celebration for Third *Go*, who went abroad to study, he thought once again of his favourite son. Mowde had been no worse than Third *Go*. Mowde might have gone thus. But Mowde was dead. The old man's memory carried him back to the days of prosperity when he had been the manager, to the building of his house and the gatherings of his own wife and his own sons. Now the house was quiet once again, except for the young widow Huilan who was still murmuring against her fate. But day after day Fenchow grew worse, until finally he lay flat on his bed. Worry and unhappiness at last carried his life away.

Fenchow's death was certainly the turning point in the fate of the house of Chang. His only remaining son, Mowhun, inherited all that his father had left and succeeded him as head of the family. Strong and young, Mowhun wished to follow the footsteps of his father and to rebuild the family's fortunes into a more happy and prosperous state. As soon as the mourning was over, he set about his desires.

Unlike his father, Mowhun did not want to hold the young widow Huilan. After the death of the old man, Huilan became worse and openly declared that if she were not allowed to leave the family she would commit suicide. So Mowhun sent for her father to come to take her back to the family of Wang. The beautiful Huilan dreamt of a new life after her years of widowhood and once more she became happy. Her parents discussed a new marriage for her.

Mowyueh and Mowchiao, two nephews of Fenchow, were less fortunate than Eldest *Go* and Second *Go*, the two nephews of Dunglin. The nephews in the house of Chang were ordered to work, with no possibility of inheriting any property from their uncle. Mowyueh, of the same age as Fifth *Go*, was his close friend. The two of them had been brought up among the village toughs, the gambling clubs and the hooligans of the place. They both intended to join the army. But the traditional attitude was that a good son never became a soldier, so that both family heads refused to allow them to enlist. Now Mowyueh insisted on leaving the family since his old uncle was gone. His cousin Mowhun could not keep him at home. Mowchiao, the younger cousin, remained and carried on the farm work with the labourer Peimin.

In time Mowhun became less and less interested in his farm work and more and more interested in the town of Hookow. As a large shareholder in the store, he went to town often to discuss its affairs with his Uncle Dunglin. There he met his former companion and close friend, Eldest *Go*, who now at last was an assistant in the store. Dissatisfied with the allotment of shares that had been given him, Eldest *Go* set to work to persuade Mowhun to be his partner in a new store of their own, free from the control of Dunglin. He stirred up trouble between Dunglin and Mowhun. He demanded that Mowhun withdraw his capital from the store for the new investment. The two young men discussed their plans secretly from time to time and encouraged each other toward the new step.

Finally, the two young men found another able young man, by name of Chu Fangyang, to join them. Together the three of them decided to start a store dealing in fish and rice after the fashion of the original store of Dunglin's. So the two cousins withdrew their capital from the old store and Fangyang added a share of his own.

In this way a new store came into being. The three partners arranged their work so that Eldest *Go* and Fangyang were actual managers, Mowhun preferring to be nominal supervisor. Fangyang acted at the same time as accountant. They employed some shopmen and apprentices. The new store went successfully enough from the outset.

Mowhun was happy in his new life. He became an important man of affairs, going to and fro between the village and the town. After a time his wife died without leaving him any children and he immediately started to discuss getting a new wife. As he was now nicknamed Millionaire Chang, many people thought him a good match, so that go-betweens came continually to discuss his marriage. One charming lady even changed her surname of Chang, intending to marry him, because clan surname exogamy was the rule and no people of the same surname might be married. Yet when Mowhun discovered her real name he dared not break the traditional rule of exogamy even though he appreciated her beauty very much.

When Mowhun finally took a young wife, his wedding was an occasion for a great celebration in which neighbours, relatives, kinsmen, and friends in the town all participated. But his new marriage did not keep him long at home. As his associations broadened, he went out constantly and spent his time away from home.

The house of Chang once again knew prosperity. The death of Fenchow made it possible for the young man to solve the lingering troubles of the household, sending away the widow Huilan and allowing the rowdy cousin Mowyueh to join the army. The Chang family lived in happiness and peace once again, though fewer people by far filled the big house which Fenchow had built than the House of the Golden Wing.

With his family problems settled Mowhun had time and energy for his interests in town and a chance for development there. His association with Eldest *Go* brought him business and signs of promise could already be seen. This sudden success in town was soon reflected in his home village, especially in his second wedding. Now opportunity was open to him, and if he could make use of it his success would be easier than that of Dunglin after the death of his brother Dungmin.

Business in the town of Hookow had developed into a new and different stage. The introduction of steamboats at the port shaped the town's life. Formerly junks had spent three or four days sailing downstream from the town to the coastal city of Foochow and a whole week sailing upstream. Now the steamboat took a day, or less than two days, for a single trip either way between the river port and the capital. The new technique shortened the time for both transport and communication. It meant not only a quicker circulation of commodities but a more rapid spread of news and business information.

As steamboats were very expensive, it was impossible for a single store to buy a boat for itself. The store masters thus organized as shareholders in a single steamboat.

The stores which had shares in a steamboat had an immediate and an immense advantage in transporting their merchandise. The steamboats were five or six times as fast as the junks. Those stores which had no shares in a steamboat at once found themselves at a disadvantage. Two old stores in Hookow were thus forced to close because of the keen competition that arose after the introduction of the steamboats. Their bankruptcy, as always, was announced very suddenly, so that creditors and the native banks got no time to ask for payment.

The new store, in which Mowhun, Fangyang and Eldest *Go* were partners, had a chance to exist because the partners had become joint shareholders in a steamboat bought and managed by the old store of which Dunglin was still the master. With the help of their steamboat transport, both the old and new stores were able to carry on their business as usual and keep pace with the keen competition.

A slow but amiable man, Mowhun had no experience and took little interest in operating the store. As merely nominal supervisor he left the management completely in the hands of Fangyang and Eldest *Go*. He spent his time travelling from village to town and from town to city and back again. He was an important shareholder in the steamboat, so that there was no need for him to pay any fare.

Once when Mowhun was on board the steamboat he found that the Chang woman, who had changed her name to win him in vain at the time of his second marriage, was a fellow-traveller bound for the city of Foochow. She had since become his " aunt ", having married his mother's cousin, Dungchin, a poor little farmer who lived in Dunglin's old house. As Mowhun was a nephew of the clan of Hwang, he had come to visit them fairly often. So his acquaintance with the Chang woman had progressed and by now he constantly cast sheep's eyes at her. Hearing that she was going to Foochow by steamboat on a visit, Mowhun had seized this opportunity to follow her.

In Foochow Mowhun spent his time with the Chang woman. They visited the city parks, the White and Black Pagodas, the Long Life Bridge, and Nantai Island, on which the modern buildings, banks, schools, churches and other edifices now stand. They went together to shows and plays, and Mowhun bought her many gifts. City life was such that nobody cared about other people's business. Acquaintances took it for granted that they were merely an " aunt " and a " nephew ".

Vacation ended. Mowhun and the Chang woman had to go back. They took the steamboat together again. The boats' schedule was controlled somewhat by the tide of the Min River, as it had been with the junks. At low tide some stretches in the river were practically unnavigable. There were six hours of flood tide and six hours of ebb tide. Usually the flood tide was used for the upstream passage, while the ebb tide aided the passage downstream. The turning of the tide varied from day to day, and fifteen days formed a complete cycle, there being two cycles in a lunar month. The lunar system of time reckoning has thus been followed by the merchants and sailors no less than by the farmers, who rely on the twenty-four festivals of the lunar year for the turning points in their agricultural calendar. The system reflects the importance of the tides in the daily life and habits of the people, and their determination of the hours for loading and unloading merchandise, for scheduling transport, and for computing the speed of travel and commerce.

On the day Mowhun and the Chang woman sailed upstream, the tide came in mid-afternoon, so that the steamboat started in the evening. When the boat arrived at the port of the Hungsan Bridge, a point of entry for inland towns and villages, it had to stop to report at the customs house there. The captain submitted his ship's papers, in which passengers and cargo were listed and went to the customs office to pay the tolls. The customs official took his time with the papers. He was typically proud, avaricious and easily angered. The captain had to speak to him in a low and obsequious voice, as a slave to a master. The official examined the papers thoroughly and ordered the captain to wait quietly. By the time he was ready to board the boat for inspection, the captain had passed already more than an hour in the office. The inspection of the steamboat and its cargo sometimes took as long as several hours. And the steamboat had to undergo three or four such inspections at each of the customs houses on the way from the coastal city of Foochow to the inland town of Hookow. So the time for the actual passage was hardly more than the total of the hours the boat was detained by the customs officers at the different ports.

It had grown very dark when the captain finally led the customs official of the port of the Hungsan Bridge to the steamboat. The official, escorted by two armed guards, searched for contraband and went carefully from hold to hold, from baggage to baggage, and from passenger to passenger. In the course of his inspection of the passengers, he flashed his flashlight into a cabin where a couple slept together in close embrace. He woke them up and confiscated a camera, forbidden by military regulations.

But the couple was not a respectable married pair as the official thought. They were Mowhun and the Chang woman, an " aunt " and " nephew " caught in clan incest. The news immediately became an open secret and circulated rapidly. Dungchin heard about it, but he was poor and could do nothing. He was secretly dubbed by the people " the living turtle ", their contemptuous word for a cuckold. The Chang woman was disgraced and gained the reputation of a lewd woman.

" Millionaire Chang " was not disgraced at all. He was ridiculed mildly by his friends and companions, but suffered no other damage to his reputation. But because of his amour he neglected both his family and his business so that the episode did not leave him entirely unscathed.

His neglect of the store came at an inopportune time. A conflict had arisen between the other two partners, Eldest *Go* and Fangyang. Mowhun did not know which side to take. Eldest *Go* and Fangyang were equal partners and had equal rights in the managing of the store, but Fangyang was the accountant and took advantage of his knowledge of the accounts. When Eldest *Go* made a check-up on the accounts, he discovered some jugglings by Fangyang and demanded that Fangyang keep the accounts according to the forms of the old store. This the accountant refused to do. The two partners began to quarrel, and there seemed no chance for compromise as both of them rushed to extremes. Mowhun, just back from his philandering, did not at once realize the critical character of the dispute.

As an old chum and cousin of Mowhun, Eldest *Go* tried first to persuade him to make new arrangements in the store. He suggested that the two of them should either force out Fangyang or withdraw from the business and let him operate it alone. They well knew Fangyang had not enough capital, and if they should stand together he could eventually be forced out. Eldest *Go* warned Mowhun that Fangyang would continue his peculations and was not a reliable man.

Fangyang on the other hand tried to win Mowhun as the wealthiest of the three partners to his side. He invited Mowhun home to dinner and prepared a table fit for a gourmet. The two men drank and talked till midnight. They vowed friendship and confidence in one another and then went to sleep in the same bed. Fangyang was a clever, eloquent person. He explained convincingly how faithful he would be and how much better their business could be operated without Eldest *Go*.

Mowhun was won over by Fangyang. So when the three partners got together again, Eldest *Go* announced his withdrawal from the partnership, but Mowhun decided to continue the business with Fangyang. Eldest *Go* asked him as an old friend why he had changed his mind. Mowhun could only reply that he believed Fangyang was a reliable person and had sworn never to betray his partner.

So Eldest *Go* withdrew all his original capital and reinvested it in the old store which he again joined as an assistant. Lacking capital for the new store, Mowhun was obliged to withdraw more of his money that was still invested in the old store. Dunglin warned him against such a move and asked him to reconsider, but to no avail. Mowhun persisted, and Eldest *Go* was sent to the village to notify Mowkwei's widow of the transaction. Her son Chenchung was involved as he had a claim to the property of the Chang family.

Mowkwei's widow was now a middle-aged woman, an honest, quiet person. She did not agree with the course her brother-in-law Mowhun had taken. She felt he had spent money like a spendthrift since the death of her father-in-law, Fenchow. Hearing from Eldest *Go* that Mowhun was withdrawing more money from the old store to make up the deficit of the new one, she rushed to town and begged Dunglin not to allow Mowhun to make the withdrawal. Dunglin told her he had done what he could. Mowhun was the owner of the shares and he had the right to withdraw them. Dunglin advised her to speak directly with her brother-in-law and to plead with him to think about Chenchung's future.

If Mowkwei's widow had been a stronger and abler woman she might have prevented the withdrawal. But, tame and obedient, she let Mowhun, the family head, overcome her protests. Mowhun thus got a free hand to do as he wished. He placed full confidence in Fangyang, now his only partner. The new store continued to operate without Eldest *Go*.

The move led to a drastic shift in all the associations that Mowhun had hitherto made. It soon turned his life in a different direction. Till now he had been close to the members of his family, to his partners, to the old store and to Dunglin. The change immediately affected the whole circle of his relationships. But for a time the new store was fortunate, and the effect of the change was not immediately apparent.

At home Mowhun had now to find a propitious site in which to bury his parents. He was a devout believer in " wind and water ". Since a series of misfortunes had overtaken his family, his house site, A-Dragon-Vomiting-Pearls, now came to appear in a different light. The geomancers began to explain that the seemingly propitious site was marred by the Western Road which runs across the Dragon Mountain. To them the road resembled a sword which cut through the rump of the dragon. The dragon was thus dead, they said, and the site had become one of bad omen.

After a search Mowhun finally found a beautiful burial site. Unfortunately the land belonged to a certain strong clan not his own. To make use of it, he had to make a secret burial. But once again misfortune dogged him. During the midnight of the secret burial, in the midst of heavy rain, the funeral party was discovered by the landowners who sent out their men to prevent the burial. In the struggle the coffins of Mowhun's parents lay on the side of the mountain battered by heavy rain and menaced by lightning. The villagers criticized Mowhun severely for this fiasco. They held him up to scorn now as an unfilial son who topped his immoral act of incest with a desecration of the remains of his dead parents.

Returning to the town of Hookow after this failure, Mowhun found his store in a state of bankruptcy. His partner Fangyang had secretly embezzled all the money of the store. Mowhun had previously withdrawn all his capital from the old store and had nothing more with which to make up the loss. Fangyang escaped to join bandits in the mountains, leaving Mowhun to bear all the debts alone. Faced with ruin, Mowhun had to sell out his land and woods in order to pay off his debts. Soon all that was left to him were the house and the small plot dedicated to his ancestors. To lose them would be extinction, and he managed to stop just short of that. How deeply he regretted his decision!

Thus at last, borne down by his disappointments, Mowhun lived on idly at home, bewailing his bad luck. But he found it very difficult ever to do farming. Gradually he drifted into the habit of smoking opium and sank into dejection.

The people of the old store, particularly Dunglin, had worried about Mowhun's ill-starred partnership with Fangyang but had never expected such a tragic end for Mowhun. When Mowhun withdrew all his capital, the old store underwent a radical change. With none of his money left in the old store Mowhun was no longer considered as a shareholder. The store re-allotted its shares. In those years, after a term of prosperity, the business was again in a state of depression. Even the old store suffered a deficit. To give each shareholder an equal right in the profits and an equal obligation in the deficit, Dunglin decided to abolish the distinction between ordinary shares and " red shares ". There were henceforward to be only ten shares. Dunglin took five for himself and gave his nephew Eldest *Go* two. One each of the other three was allotted to the doctor Yunseng, the fish dealer Dungtzu, and the accountant Kaituan. Eldest *Go*, as always, however, was dissatisfied with the redistribution and contended that he had got too few. So the arrangement was not very stable and bade fair to lead to future trouble.

Building up and operating a store was not an easy matter. Nevertheless, the effort revealed a great deal about the character of those who attempted it. The villagers were not slow to read the character of individuals in the record of their success or failure. The failure of Mowhun gave them ample evidence of his weakness and incapacity. Likewise it set off the contrast with Dunglin's experience and judgment. People compared the two men the more readily, too, because their families were so closely related in blood and in partnership and because they had risen at the same time to the same eminence.

Thus the further ascent of the Hwang family and the swift decline of the Changs were discussed as vivid evidences of the truth of old maxims concerning human adjustment. From a lifetime's experience, won by trial and error and constant effort, Dunglin had learned to fit himself to fate and to keep abreast of all his associates, so that he remained completely successful in the management of his business. Mowhun, on the other hand, young and inexperienced, had failed in a similar adjustment that might eventually have had the same success.

CHAPTER XIV
THE BANDITS

One summer vacation, Sixth *Go*, now a student of Yinghwa College, set out to go back home from the city with six of his schoolmates. Their steamboat stopped first at the port of Shuikow. There they transferred to a small boat they had hired specially for the trip and continued upstream.

Less than two miles from the port a sudden clap of rifle-fire brought the boat to a stop. Thirty or forty shots from the cover of bushes on a steep bank overhead pierced the sails. The students looked at each other in fear, not knowing what to do.

Another " piah " crashed out and more shots came. This time the bullets made a hole only a foot from where they sat. Water rushed in and threatened to sink the boat and drown the eleven persons in it.

Little Brother, dizzy with fright, clapped his hand over the hole. But he could not stop the water. One of the other students made a wad of his handkerchief. Frantically they managed to stop the leak. But the boat was no longer under control, as the terrified boatmen left it helpless to the mercy of the wind. The breeze, blowing in favour of the attackers on the shore, sent the boat toward them.

In no time bandits came aboard. There were five or six of them, wearing bamboo hats, short black shirts and long grey trousers, and carrying guns. They drove the students out of the boat and ordered them to climb up the bank to the bushes that had concealed them. There the boys met more than thirty more, dressed and armed like their captors.

The bandits prodded them and the students stumbled ahead. They were forced to march at great speed. Five miles, ten miles, fifteen miles and even twenty miles they marched without any stop to rest. At last they came to an old house far away from the spot where they had been captured.

Here the bandits took off their straw sandals and piled them into a great heap at the door. Soon they had all scattered, leaving four men to guard the wretched students. Tired and sore, the hungry students sank to rest. They had not eaten all day, though they had marched for nine hours.

After only a few moments' rest, with only a cup of tea to

sustain them, the students were ordered to march again. Two of the four guards went in front and two behind. They carried their guns with bullets ready, covering the students step by step as if they had a great responsibility.

The students did not stop until they had reached the top of a high, steep mountain where there was a hut among the bushes, a hut which was to be their prison. There the students' hands were bound with rope, and their feet were fastened in stocks so tight as to make it impossible for them to stand up or turn round. Innumerable mosquitoes stung them, leaving not an inch of their hands, feet and face unmarked. The guards did not take very much care of them and fell asleep.

Early next morning the guarding bandits found one of the students missing. Excited, two of them shouldered their guns and rushed about searching for him. But after a while they returned without finding anything. The upshot of the escape was that the remaining six students were ordered to march at once to another hut, because the bandits feared the escaped student would lead soldiers to the place.

Little Brother and his five friends were held prisoners by the bandits for a considerable time. At first the prisoners tried to communicate with each other only in Mandarin, in order to fool the bandits into thinking they were not natives of Fukien. In the end the bandits were not fooled because the students spoke with the native accent of the province and because the bandits' spies soon found out the home and family of each prisoner. One of the bandits' petty chieftains, a former sailor between the inland ports and the capital city, came to visit prisoners one night. He recognized the prisoners and named their families. He knew four of the six students were sons of merchants in Hookow. The fifth one he recognized as a son of Lei Wuyun, the district counsellor, who had figured in Dunglin's lawsuit. But the petty chieftain could not identify the sixth and last student, the eldest and tallest of them all. This student, Lin Chuhsien by name, was a native of the Eastern Road and spoke excellent Mandarin. Consequently he was the only one who had kept on fooling the bandits. The other students pretended to act as interpreters between Lin and the bandits.

Wuyun's son Hsiwen was Little Brother's most intimate friend. The two boys had become sworn brothers at school. Hearing now of the capture of his son, Wuyun at once wrote a letter to Dunglin. He addressed him as brother because their sons were now sworn brothers. We remember how Wuyun had been bribed by Eldest *Go* at the time of the lawsuit. He had taken very little interest in Dunglin till this day. But now, through the relationship of their sons the two men began to see a good deal of each other. Learning of his son's whereabouts, Wuyun sent men to speak with the chiefs. Those worthies gave orders to release Hsiwen at once, for they feared Wuyun. He was an influential man in the district yamen, who could well do something disastrous to them. Releasing his son, they sent words of apology back with him to Wuyun.

An old man brought to the prisoners' hut the message of the release of Hsiwen. The students had met the same old man in the cottage where they had stopped for a few moments on the first day of capture. The man had been fierce-looking then, but now he smiled at Hsiwen and wanted to know why he had not told him the first day that he was the son of the great counsellor Lei. If he had said so he would not have been treated as a prisoner.

Several days later two other students were ransomed by their parents. One of them was Wei Chenchin, a friend of Little Brother's since their days at the primary school in the town of Hookow. That left only three prisoners in the hut, Chuhsien, Cheng Seng and Little Brother.

The guards were changed from time to time so that bandits and prisoners did not have enough time to make friends with one another. But finally a new guard came who turned out to be Suihwa, a former herd boy in the House of the Golden Wing. Before he came, moreover, he had happened to meet Fifth *Go*, who had invited him home and offered privately a substantial reward if he could release Little Brother. Suihwa was only a minor bandit. He dared not try what he was asked to do. He did not tell Little Brother that he had met his brother. But he treated the prisoners very well and regaled them with all sorts of experiences of the bandits' life. In his stories he revealed his strongest ambition to be a bandit chief.

The main camp of the bandits often sent minor officers to inspect the guards as well as the prisoners. As long as Suihwa was in the hut the prisoners enjoyed considerable freedom. They were not tied up with rope and stocks. Yet they were warned to be ready for inspection at any moment. If the chiefs found the prisoners free, the guards would be punished.

One day the sudden arrival of the bandit chief was announced.

In the hut the usual life was immediately turned upside down. The three prisoners jumped into their wooden bed and tightly tied their hands with ropes. They tied their feet to the blocks. The guards set things in order and hastily arranged the hut to look more like a prison.

No sooner did the chief, escorted by guards, come into the hut than the whole atmosphere changed to one of severity and seriousness. The chief scowled very fiercely and the guard bandits stood at attention before him with concerned expressions. The prisoners lay motionless on the bed. Their hearts beat rapidly. The chief specially questioned Chuhsien, who pretended not to understand him. Thus Little Brother became translator between Chuhsien and the chief. The fierce-looking chief became all the more fierce when he ordered Chuhsien to communicate with his family or be shot, but Chuhsien's pretence was so well done that even the chief was fooled. In fact the bandits' tactics indicated they never had discovered who Chuhsien was and where his home was.

The bandits carried the prisoners again and again from one prison hut to another. They never kept the prisoners in the same hut for more than a week, lest it be discovered by spies sent from the prisoners' families or from the military. Among the lofty mountains where the bandits carried out their activities there were some seventy huts used as prisons.

When Suihwa was called back to the main camp, a fellow named Kwanmin came to take his place. In talking with Kwanmin, Little Brother discovered he had formerly been employed as a long-term labourer in the house of Liu Fengwan, one of Little Brother's intimate friends when he was studying in the primary school at Hookow. So friendly had the master and the labourer been that Kwanmin and Fengwan had become sworn brothers. As a result, Kwanmin carried messages from Little Brother to Fengwan, whose house was not far from the prison. On the day of the Dragon Boat Festival, Kwanmin arranged for Fengwan to come to visit Little Brother. He brought with him many presents, such as three-cornered dumplings, peanuts, wine and other home-made delicacies. A party was held and the prisoners and guards enjoyed their happiest day. They drank, talked, and made merry.

Some time later another new man, Tsunching by name, came to join the guards. By this time the guarding force was reduced to three who watched over the three remaining prisoners.

F

Besides Kwanmin and Tsunching, the third guard was a young man under twenty who had only recently joined the band and was a sort of probationer so that he had not been issued a gun or other weapon.

Little Brother spent two days talking with Tsunching. He found him to be a neighbour of his uncle, Cheng Anchi, the adopted brother of his mother. Having established this relationship, Little Brother and Tsunching talked as familiarly as old friends. They recalled the associations between the Hwang family and the Cheng family. Tsunching mentioned specially the marriage of Third *Go*, in which the whole Cheng family had taken part. Little Brother told him that Third *Go*, his eldest brother, was now studying abroad in the United States.

The talks between Little Brother and Tsunching went further and further. At last Tsunching told the student how hard the life of being a bandit was and how deeply he regretted having left his farm. Little Brother suggested that he return home and reform. Finally the two newly-made friends made a plan of escape from the prison hut. Little Brother told the plan secretly to his schoolmates, Chuhsien and Cheng Seng, who were only too glad to hear it. Tsunching won over Kwanmin, who was friendly to Little Brother and who accepted Tsunching's suggestion at once. That left only the third bandit. But he had no weapons, so that they were not much afraid of him.

It had been raining for several days. Communication between the main camp and the hut was blocked by a flooded ravine and conditions were favourable to their plan. On the night set for their attempt they waited eagerly for the third bandit to fall asleep. When they heard him snoring, they all got up quietly and equipped themselves to start their journey. Kwanmin and Tsunching took their guns and bullets. Little Brother carried a candle and matches. They descended the mountain and Chuhsien and Cheng Seng followed them.

It was the thirty-fifth day after the capture of the students. Their long confinement made walking difficult, especially on such a rainy night. It was blowing hard, and the rain soaked all their clothing. In the total darkness they could see nothing. Little Brother tried to light his candle, but the matches were all wet. Once he fell into a pit and could not move for many minutes. As the road was shut off from them by the darkness they were guided only by the sound of a flowing stream as they descended the steep mountain. The dim flickering of occasional fireflies, the mingled noise of wind, rain, stream and their muffled footsteps, hope of reaching home and fear of waking the third bandit to give the alarm, all conspired to work on their excited minds.

After a sharp and choppy descent of about four hours they arrived at the village of Liucheng, only three miles down the Min River from the town of Hookow. A mountain torrent flows through the village into the river beyond and the people had built a bridge on which their main street crossed the ravine. When the ravine is without water or with only a little water, the people can cross under the bridge. As the fugitives reached the village, intending to cross under the bridge so as not to be noticed by the villagers, they doubted very much whether the crossing could be made in the flood season. Kwanmin offered to go first to explore their chances and asked the rest to wait for him. Five minutes, ten minutes, fifteen minutes and even twenty minutes passed. Kwanmin did not return, and Tsunching grew frightened and suspicious. He knew well one of the petty chiefs of the bandits was a native of this village and often stayed in a house there with some of his subordinates. He suspected Kwanmin might have gone to report their escape to the petty chief. If this happened Tsunching would doubtless be shot, and the prisoners either shot or recaptured. Tsunching and the three prisoners, cold and frightened, whispered to each other without knowing what to do. Finally Tsunching, instead of entering the village, turned downstream along the bank of the river. The prisoners followed him and begged him not to desert them. After a hasty rush in the darkness for half an hour more they paused. Then, and only then, did Tsunching dare open his mouth. He told Little Brother they would go to the village of Chaotien where his family and the family of Little Brother's uncle still lived.

They went on and on in the darkness and the rain. They struggled among the thickets and bushes, forcing a way through. Once in the mist Cheng Seng, who was young and had never experienced such hardship, became too tired and lay down on the ground. He declared he would rather die than struggle on. But Little Brother and Chuhsien helped him to get up and advised him to walk on, but slowly. Tsunching, walking at the head of the procession, used his gun to beat a way through. Little Brother followed him closely, carrying one end of an impromptu litter of which Chuhsien carried the other end. Between them they bore nearly the whole weight of Cheng Seng. Thus they continued for more than ten miles until they arrived at the village of Chaotien just before dawn. There they called the old uncle Anchi out of his bed. After tea and gruel the wanderers still could not rest but were sent on to hide in a mountain shrine, so that the secret of their escape might not be discovered.

The flight was typical of the way in which bandits suspect each other. Their distrust of one another was illustrated even in the separation of Kwanmin and Tsunching at the edge of Liucheng. Nevertheless, their power was very great. Although the bandits had their camp deep in the mountains, where they had built their huts, yet their influence extended not only into the villages in the mountains but even into the villages and towns where military garrisons were stationed. They lived by sudden forays, appearing by surprise now and then, plundering here and there, and bringing trouble and terror to the people.

The bandits were not without an organization. Farming people in the mountain villages carried on life as usual without any disturbance from them. They might often see the bands pass and might trade with them in the normal way. The bandits had their "ears and eyes" in the surrounding towns in the whole region. For instance, one petty chief had his home at Liucheng, the village situated along the river which served as an important station on the great trading road. There the escaped prisoners had shivered in hiding beside the bridge.

Since the day of Little Brother's kidnapping by the bandits, his father Dunglin had shut himself away from the outside world in the upper inside room of the store. Dunglin gave himself up to working out a plan of rescue or ransom. He lost both appetite and sleep over it, but he could not hit upon a scheme whereby his son might be restored to him and his worries relieved. The more he planned, the more he became confused, so sometimes he abandoned himself to smoking opium.

There were many difficulties. First, Dunglin sent a middleman to ask for the conditions of ransoming Little Brother. The chiefs set a big price which the middleman did not dare meet. The preacher of the Hookow church had acted as middleman between the prisoner Chenchin's family and the bandits. He volunteered next to take up the case of Little Brother. He offered the chief of the bandits one thousand dollars ransom for Little Brother. But he did this without first consulting Dunglin, who seemed unable to raise such a large sum so soon after the division of the family property. Later Dunglin sent the original middleman back again, who argued hard with the captors to get them to reduce the ransom figure. That was why Little Brother waited in vain day after day for his ransom.

At dawn of the thirty-sixth day of Little Brother's captivity, as Dunglin lay still abed, someone knocked at the main door of the store. After a while Kaituan opened the door and was startled to find a stranger there speaking of Little Brother. He brought him in at once to Dunglin. This stranger was Kwanmin, who related the story of the escape from the prison hut. When he had returned to the spot where he had left the fugitives after investigating the flooding of the ravine he had found nobody. He thought naturally they had gone on to the store and so here he was expecting to meet them. Upon hearing this report, Dunglin became very much excited. He did not know whether his son was saved or not. The fugitives might still be pursued by the bandits or might have been recaptured.

Dunglin became more and more concerned as the day wore on and there was no news of Little Brother. All through the morning suspicious-looking strangers came to the store or passed the main gate seemingly looking for someone. For example, Fifth *Go*, who had come in to town from home and was staying at the store to get some information about his brother, was questioned by a fellow who used to loaf about the town and who was suspected of being a spy for the bandits. The townspeople had never dared report him to the military for fear of retaliation. One can see what the influence of the bandits was!

The bandits' spies were eager to learn whether Little Brother had already come back or not. If not, they could still send men out in pursuit. Later it was learned a group of bandits searched as far as the village of Chaotien, for they knew that was the home of Tsunching. Fortunately they had not found him, for he and the students were hidden safely in a mountain shrine.

At noon a boy came into the Hookow store and asked to see Dunglin, the master. He had been hired, he said, by two women, strangers to the town, who now were standing at the bridge reluctant to enter the town. They asked the store master to go to meet them at once. Dunglin sent Eldest *Go* in his place. When Eldest *Go* came to the spot, he recognized them. The younger woman was his "aunt", the wife of Anchi, Dunglin's brother-in-law, but she did not recognize him. The woman hesitated for a moment. Eldest *Go* then introduced himself, telling them he was sent by his Uncle Dunglin to welcome them to the store. The younger woman pointed to the older one and explained she was her neighbour, the mother of the Tsunching who had taken Little Brother home. She told him the fugitives were now hidden in her village and begged him to get Dunglin to send men to fetch them as soon as possible. The women refused to come to the store but hurried back to their own village at once.

The next day Dunglin and the father of Cheng Seng sent several men to Chaotien to meet Tsunching and the three students and to take them first to the town of Shuikow, where they hired a group of soldiers to escort them back to Hookow. When at last Little Brother was restored to his father he was greatly startled at seeing how much the old man had changed. His once-grey hair and moustache had turned almost entirely white. He smiled now, but his face was pale, his eyes sunken, and many new wrinkles creased his forehead. When they all met, Kwanmin came out from the upper room where he had been hidden for two days, glad to see his companions unhurt. Tsunching and Kwanmin were greatly surprised to learn for the first time that Chuhsien also spoke the native dialect.

Later on a clerk of the store, named Li Kwan, who had once been associated with some bandits, took a great interest in Kwanmin. He induced Kwanmin one dark night to dig up the gun and the bullets that he had buried before he came to knock at the door of the store. Li Kwan did so and took the gun to hide in the house of an unlicensed prostitute he knew. But Dunglin pressed him to give up the gun; so this gun and the one that Tsunching had brought from his house at Chaotien were presented to the military corps at Hookow, where the two reformed bandits were now registered again among the respectable citizens. They received a certificate and reward money.

However, some time later a junk sailing upstream from Foochow was plundered near Liucheng and two sailors were killed, and the case coming into the hands of the military corps at Hookow, Li Kwan was accused of the crime. They picked him up at midnight at the house of the unlicensed prostitute. Taken to the town temple, where the military corps was quartered, Li Kwan was rigorously questioned and severely beaten. They demanded that he confess the facts set forth in his deposition. The prostitute, who was attached to him and who had followed him to the temple, begged him not to " confess " at whatever hardship, for she knew he had not committed the crime. In those days even the most innocent persons, forced to confess under severe torture, were shot right away.

To save her lover the prostitute visited the concubine of the corps leader. The concubine was her close friend and told her the secrets of the case. The charge had been brought by Chenchin's father, a store-master, to do injury to Dunglin. This last case in fact grew out of the kidnapping. Chenchin had had to be ransomed with a large sum of money, but Little Brother had come home without any expense. Chenchin's father thus nourished the suspicion that Dunglin or his store was in some way associated with the bandits. He thought his assistant Li Kwan was one of the group. Naturally, in bringing the accusation, the rival store-master was not disinterested, and he brought his charge for purposes of his own.

When Dunglin heard of this mean attack upon him by his business competitors he grew angry. But he was equal to the challenge. He immediately sent Fifth *Go* to see Shankai, the officer who had become Third *Go*'s sworn brother long before. Shankai was now a lieutenant-colonel in the army, stationed in the district city of Kutien. Hearing thus of the case, Shankai wrote to his colleague and friend, the lieutenant-colonel at Shuikow, the officer who was the immediate superior of the corps leader at Hookow. An order came from Shuikow that Li Kwan be released at once. Both the local corps leader and Chenchin's father were taken by surprise. They were astounded at the influence that Dunglin wielded. As a result he gained much " face " from the case. Far from doing him injury, the incident redounded greatly to his credit.

In order to exist in such a world a man had to have many associations with many different circles of people. In the case of the Hwangs, Dunglin had not only his relatives and business friends but he also had to cultivate such officials as Wuyun, such soldiers as Shankai and even such bandits as Suihwa. Although the incident of the kidnapping threatened almost to destroy the life of Dunglin and his family, yet once he survived it he strengthened his position all the more by his manipulation of many wide circles of people in the region. And in this survival the man and his family rose to an even higher level of influence and power.

CHAPTER XV

THE FRATERNAL CONFLICT

The new eminence of the Hwangs was not without its dangers, internal and external. One day the leader of the military corps at Hookow came unannounced to pay Dunglin a visit. It was merely a social call. But on the second day the leader sent soldiers to the village of Hwang and searched some of the houses under the pretext of looking for bandits. The soldiers took away four village elders, all of them living in houses below Dunglin's old original house. The leader artfully displayed a pretended secret charge by Dunglin himself that some bandits were hidden in the houses of the village. The knowledge of such a charge gave rise among the Hwang villagers, except the nearest kinsmen of Dunglin, to a suspicion that their most influential citizen was betraying his own village. Thus the leader set off all too easily the latent conflict between the two main groups of families in the village.

One group, the distant kinsmen of Dunglin, whose elders had been taken by the military corps, set about organizing their able-bodied men at once. Several of them formed a band armed with long knives and attacked the old house, threatening the people there with further trouble. But they dared not invade the House of the Golden Wing because it was fortified with two corner towers. In defence then, Dunglin's nearer kinsmen also began to take protective measures as the other party grew more and more hostile.

In reality the leader of the military corps had played a dirty trick. He hated Dunglin because of the case of the assistant, Li Kwan. He managed thus to raid the villagers supposedly in line of duty, and to avenge himself at the expense of Dunglin at the same time, for he knew quite well that one of the four elders he seized did in fact have a son among the bandits. His scheme had other advantages, too. For by arresting the four elders, the leader also planned to get some money in bribes, if not in outright ransom, before he must release them.

Once set in motion the effects of the leader's schemes did not soon stop. The son in the bandits' camp begged his bandit superiors to avenge him. He too laid the blame on Dunglin, his distant " uncle ". Late one evening, seizing the opportunity of the opening of a side door, bandits broke into the House of the Golden Wing, captured two men and took away what guns and valuables they could seize. They were in such a hurry and left the village only after a few minutes' plundering because the military corps was stationed only two miles away and they feared discovery by the soldiers.

The two men the bandits carried away, however, were not really members of the Hwang household, and because that was the case the raid was fruitless. One of the captives was released immediately because he spoke the brogue of a neighbouring district and swore he was only a labourer. The other one was indeed a native of the district but he was only a herd boy, a creature poorer even than the labourer. The bandits did not release him but he escaped from the prison some days later. They were glad to see him go.

Nevertheless, even after the plundering of his house Dunglin was only the more eager to make peace with his fellow-villagers. He tried hard to make them believe in him. He even swore to some of the elders that he was ready to undergo an ordeal before the ancestral tablets to prove his innocence. Little by little the remaining elders were convinced. They gathered together again round Dunglin to lay plans to save the imprisoned members of their village. Finally, money was collected from all the clan, bribes were paid, and the elders were released.

One must bear in mind that in those days the bandits and the military were really not very different. The military were in fact recruited from the bandits. The difference was only that the latter were obvious outlaws, while the former preyed on the people surreptitiously. Otherwise one could only distinguish them by the fact that the soldiers had uniforms and lived in the cities and towns, while the bandits wore rags and hid in the fastnesses of the mountains.

But the troubles of the village were not over. Immediately after the village got its taste of military corruption and banditry it suffered another calamity. Buffalo plague struck for the first time in the history of the region. As a first warning, the herd boy discovered a female buffalo with a tumour in her neck. The tumour grew bigger and bigger and the infected animal became too weak to move. The next day she lay dead in the cattle yard. The occurrence alarmed all the owners of cattle in the area. They tried to drive their buffaloes away as far as possible to avoid the plague. But the disease was discovered in one animal after another. In the end Dunglin's best herd of fifteen buffaloes dwindled away to the last animal. Three other herds of cattle in the village were infected and practically none of the animals survived.

As the plague spread the buffaloes that were found to be ill were segregated from those still in good health. At the time Little Brother was at home for a summer vacation. In the emergency he was put to work to look after two male buffaoes on a hillside. There a sudden rainstorm caught him unprotected and drenched him, giving him a bad cold and sending him to bed with a fever that increased from day to day.

On top of that, news came that serious illness had overtaken Fifth *Sao*, Fifth *Go*'s wife. She had married into the family less than a year before and had recently gone back home to see her mother. Tired from helping his brother and cousins bury the buffaloes one after another, yet Fifth *Go* could not be kept from going off to see his wife at the house of his mother-in-law. But it was not these illnesses so much as what grew out of them that tried the house of Hwang the most.

On his way Fifth *Go* reminisced to himself about his life before his marriage. He fell to thinking especially of his attachment to the girl named Redflower. She was a daughter of Dungchien's eldest girl, and thus a "niece" to Fifth *Go*. Redflower had once come to the village of Hwang with her mother when the older woman returned to visit her own parents. She had been only sixteen then, three years younger than Fifth *Go*. But she had grown up into a very alert and precocious young woman. She was charming. Her eyes were large and brilliant, her bound feet let her make only the most graceful movements. The people of the village confessed that they had never seen such a pretty girl and many young men were attracted to her.

Fifth *Go* was one of the young men who greatly admired Redflower. He went every day to the old house where Dungchien and his children lived in order to get a chance to meet Redflower. But Redflower was not accustomed to seeing strangers. She hid herself when visitors appeared. This was in vain, for the more frequently she hid herself the more eager was Fifth *Go* to see her.

His chance came when Redflower's mother was called back home. Redflower continued to live with her grandparents. One day Fifth *Go* brought them a letter written by Redflower's brother and addressed to their mother in care of the Hookow store because there was no post office in the village. Armed thus with the letter, Fifth *Go* made his entry into the old house. He presented the letter to Dungchien. The old man took it, but as he did not know how to read he asked Fifth *Go* into a side hall where Redflower sat alone on the lower step of a wooden staircase, spinning her hempen threads. Dungchien asked Fifth *Go* to open and read the letter in the presence of the girl, for she also was illiterate. Fifth *Go* was only too glad to do so and he read the letter off in the lengthiest way he could devise. All the time his heart beat rapidly. Once satisfied about the contents of the letter Dungchien went away and left the two young people together. Thus they began to talk together for the first time. They talked formally, as relatives, as " uncle " and " niece ".

In the days following, Fifth *Go* came more often to the old house. Redflower did not hide from him any longer. In fact they were very happy to see each other. Handsome and distinguished in his new-fashioned clothing, Fifth *Go* was certainly a very attractive young man. In the old poor village Fifth *Go* and Redflower looked like a prince and princess together.

Situated half-way between the old house and the House of the Golden Wing, there was a small house built by the three younger brothers of Dungchien. Redflower often went there to visit Yingmei, her grandfather's niece, and her aunt, and also to see a friend of Chumei, Fifth *Go*'s little sister. When Fifth *Go* went with his sister to the small house he met Redflower there too. For nearly a month every afternoon the three girls, Yingmei, Chumei and Redflower, gathered to spin in the back kitchen of the small house to avoid the hot weather outside. Nearly every afternoon the young man turned up and took great delight in chatting with the girls.

Thus Redflower and Fifth *Go* fell in love. All these frequent meetings increased their attachment but gave no scope for any closer contact, for tradition forbade it. But there was no secrecy in this village world. Even these harmless meetings between Fifth *Go* and Redflower gave rise to rumours of a love-affair. Other young men were jealous. They began to ridicule Fifth *Go*, saying that he had got the degree of Doctor of Philosophy. The term was a new one and, not knowing its meaning, they used it jokingly to suggest that he had possessed Redflower, the beauty of their small world.

Frightened by such gossip, Fifth *Go* stayed away, though

Redflower waited for him at the same spot day after day. A few days later Fifth *Go* was walking across the hillside above the kitchen of the small house. Redflower saw him and shouted to him, " Uncle, uncle." Standing at the top of the hill looking down at his pretty " niece ", Fifth *Go* stared spellbound at the little round face, bright as the moon, below him. She perched her slender form on the railing and looked up towards him eagerly. " Why don't you come any more, Uncle ? " she called in a low, soft voice, love and tenderness in her expression. The heart of her " uncle " melted before this vision, and he hated himself for not being a poet able to translate the scene into golden words.

But gossip about the love-affair of Fifth *Go* and Redflower kept on spreading. Redflower's grandmother, Dungchien's wife, warned her. Mrs. Hwang asked everyone about the affair, at the same time denying the rumours and swearing that her son Fifth *Go* had never slept outside the House of the Golden Wing. So the affair had become serious indeed. Finally, Dunglin heard of it. Fearing that his son might break the tradition of endogamy among those of the same generation he decided to end the possibility of further mischief. He sent off a go-between to discuss Fifth *Go*'s engagement with another girl, who later became Fifth *Sao*. Thus Fifth *Go* was married against his will and lost his first love, Redflower, for ever. It was this memory that filled his mind as he made his way to his sick wife, leaving behind him the household where the buffalo plague had struck.

When Fifth *Go* reached the house of his mother-in-law and entered the bedroom, he found his wife at her last gasp and unable to speak. He arrived in fact only in time to order a brief ceremony for her to be carried out. A few days later after consultation with his father he hired bearers to carry the remains in the coffin back to his native village, there to be buried practically without any ceremony. The life of a young daughter-in-law was as cheap as that of a buffalo.

Dunglin always believed in the old adage that misfortunes never come alone. A continuous series of calamities had struck the family. To Dunglin there was no distinction between any different forms of misfortune. The cattle plague and the death of Fifth *Sao* were only further calamities of the series. He was frightened lest his favourite son, Little Brother, lying ill of fever, should be the next victim. Delirious, the boy spoke wildly and without meaning and tossed restlessly all the time. Dunglin hung over the bedside of his sick son and left his business unattended to.

To believe in the " luck " of a person does not mean one lets a sick man go without treatment. Doctors were called from near and far, and every means of cure was employed. Fourth *Go* thought Little Brother might have been frightened on the spot where he cared for the two buffaloes to the extent that his soul was lost. Accordingly he went to pray on the hillside. He knelt down on the spot and recited incantations. He picked up a round stone and called out the name of his sick brother, calling for his soul to return. All the way home he kept calling out the name and holding fast to the stone, to which he believed the lost soul adhered. Then at home he put the stone in the bed in which the sick boy lay. Fortunately, Little Brother recovered at last, but he was very weak after two months of lying in bed. His recovery seemed to call a halt to the calamities overtaking the house of Hwang.

Soon after this the family received a cablegram from Third *Go*. That young man was now returning from the United States where he had stayed for the last four years. The news of his coming stirred up the villagers. They expected the newcomer to be no less glorious than an old-time prefect returning from the examinations for the mandarinate.

To the disappointment of the villagers, however, the young man came home alone, without any attendants and without any retinue of guards and musicians, as the old mandarins had come. He was even less impressive than the chief of the local garrison who used at least to be escorted by his guards. The returned student brought nothing back but a gramophone to cheer up the crowds in the evening. Thus in this hidden corner of the world, American songs and band music, sounding like the croaking of crows, were first heard amid the laughter of the villagers.

But Third *Go* had not long been home when a new dispute arose. A petty quarrel led Little Brother to speak against his sister-in-law Shuchen, Third *Go*'s wife. Her retorts only drove him to pour out all his hidden animosity toward her in the presence of her husband and Mrs. Hwang. He reviewed bitterly the life he had led when he had lived with Shuchen and Third *Go* in Yenping. He accused Shuchen of selfishness, and asserted she had treated him as her cook, her coolie and her child's nurse. Once, when he had broken a bottle by accident, she had slapped him and he still thought her most unjust and unfeeling.

Furthermore Little Brother had a particular instance of her injustice to recite. Shuchen once found a wet umbrella on one of her tables and began to reprimand Little Brother. But her brother Chihu, who then lived with the family, confessed he had done it. Shuchen immediately changed her tone. She put on a happy smile for her brother, asking pleasantly when he had bought such a beautiful umbrella. This sudden change of attitude struck deeply into the heart of Little Brother. He had never dreamt his so-called " educated " sister-in-law could be so mean. Hearing the accusation made by Little Brother in the presence of her husband and mother-in-law, Shuchen grew very excited. She began to cry and ran back to her room, refusing to eat her meal. Mrs. Hwang stroked the hair of Little Brother, who sobbed out his story. Third *Go* was silent.

Because of his quarrel Little Brother went to the store. He wanted to see his father and to meet his brother, Fifth *Go*, who had become recently most intimate with him. Learning that open conflict had broken out between Shuchen and Little Brother, Fifth *Go* immediately sided with Little Brother. He had been sympathetic about the love-affair between Redflower and Fifth *Go*. While the younger brother stayed on with their father, the elder brother went back to the House of the Golden Wing.

After the departure of Little Brother the house was in great agitation. Third *Go* now became the centre of trouble. He gathered up all the complaints against Little Brother. Those who disliked the boy felt free now to complain to the returned student who had become a man of weight in the family. The three persons who complained against Little Brother were Shuchen, Aunt Lin and Fourth *Go*. Shuchen was hurt and her bitterness was very natural. Aunt Lin charged that she too had once been offended ; also that her second daughter-in-law had been cursed, and her eldest grandson Shoutai slapped by Little Brother. Fourth *Go*, who used to be friendly towards Little Brother, changed his attitude completely, because Little Brother had also dared to criticize his wife, Fourth *Sao*, before Dunglin.

Thus a division between the brothers began to take shape. Fifth *Go* came home defending his young brother completely, even though the boy was now considered the cause of all the woe in the house. Fortunately Mrs. Hwang remained a placating and good-natured mother. She took no sides in the fraternal conflict, and her attitude counted a great deal when the case was presented to Dunglin, who heard about the conflict for the first time. The father was a little indulgent toward his young son. He took the case lightly and decreed no punishment. Soon Little Brother left the village for his school and the conflict blew over. Afterwards he proved himself a good brother and grew to appreciate better the indulgence of his elders.

As Dunglin grew older his authority in the family took another form. He had usually been strict and severe toward his sons. But he now became more tender, and never again beat his sons or punished them in any other way. His experience had matured him into a managerial, well-rounded personality. The kidnapping of Little Brother and the series of misfortunes following it had disturbed Dunglin and his family greatly. Although the sources of difficulty had been removed one after another, yet Dunglin had really been left exhausted. He began now more and more to lay his hopes in his sons. Especially did he like Little Brother, who was still young enough to be cheerful before his old parents.

Nevertheless Dunglin never asserted his authority sufficiently to establish a command over his two nephews, Eldest *Go* and Second *Go*. He never settled the problem of the division of their property, which lingered on for years. So when Third *Go* had come home, a scholar and a man with a voice in family affairs, Second *Go* seized the chance to enlist his authority. Second *Go* asked him to act as judge on the questions of money and business still unsettled between Eldest *Go* and Second *Go*. The reluctance of Eldest *Go* to face the problem had given rise again to a serious quarrel and the two brothers repelled one another like fire and water.

The open quarrel between the brothers Eldest *Go* and Second *Go* created a perpetual antagonism between their wives and children. The two brothers never spoke to each other. Poor Aunt Lin had a hard time, mediating between her sons and her daughters-in-law.

Once Second *Go* needed some dung for fertilizer on his lands. He scooped up some dung from one of Eldest *Go*'s barrels, an act observed by Shoutai's sister. The little girl had been trained by her mother to spy out such things. She ran to tell her mother, Eldest *Sao*, who in turn called upon Shoutai to confront Second *Go*. When Shoutai came to the spot his poor uncle was still scooping. The nephew instantly shouted, "Thief!" Rushing over he pushed his uncle violently aside, so that he fell flat on the ground and one of his hands was badly hurt. Second *Go* showed his wounded hand to his Uncle Dunglin. Dunglin in turn told the story to Eldest *Go*, but Shoutai was not punished.

The unfilial act of Shoutai gave rise to much criticism in the House of the Golden Wing. But if Eldest *Go* did not intend to punish his son, no other man could take the responsibility. Second *Sao* was especially disturbed. She went to see Kaituan, the accountant at the store, and asked him for advice. She knew very well that Kaituan was a rival of Eldest *Go* in the store and would be favourably disposed. Kaituan secretly told her to take her revenge by striking Eldest *Sao*, who was more delicate than she. But she felt dubious whether such an action would be fair. Kaituan, however, insisted. He swore that to strike a sister-in-law was not nearly so bad as to strike an uncle.

Second *Sao* returned home and privately cherished her plans for revenge. Soon an opportunity came. One day she found her own daughter fighting with Shoutai's sister on a wooden staircase. She saw Eldest *Sao* come down from the upper story and slap the face of her own daughter. Second *Sao* rushed up, caught Eldest *Sao* and beat her with her fists. The two sisters-in-law hated each other. They set to work with all their force to beat each other. They wrestled till the elder woman, weaker and more delicate, was pushed rolling down the stairs. Thus Second *Sao* was privately satisfied and got her revenge. Eldest *Sao* shed tears of shame as well as of pain from this treatment. The two sisters-in-law, like their husbands, disliked each other and now their antagonism was all the greater.

Dunglin heard of the fight between Eldest *Sao* and Second *Sao*, but it was certainly beyond his power to interfere if he could not stop the conflict between the two nephews, Eldest *Go* and Second *Go*. Thus his continued absence from the House of the Golden Wing was partly a cause of the fraternal squabbling. But his change of temper, like the tenderness he developed in his old age, also contributed. So the house became the scene of frequent bitterness, of complaints and of muttered imprecations. Though these internal disturbances were hardly noticed by outsiders, the time seemed not far off when the disintegration of the household itself after the two divisions should become evident to all the world.

Even Eldest *Go*'s small family, broken off from the main

stem, was still a scene of conflict and disturbance. The troubles
there were of course connected with those of the larger household
group. The trouble began with Chimei, the wife of Shoutai,
who had come in as a very young daughter-in-law. She was
the only child of Tienlan, an intimate friend of Eldest *Go*. Spoilt
at the hands of her own family, Chimei found it very hard to
change her temper and habits in marriage. Eldest *Sao* attempted
to enforce her authority as mother-in-law, but that led only to
disobedience and rebellion on the part of Chimei. Yet Eldest
Go favoured his young daughter-in-law very considerably. Thus
Shoutai's mother nagged him continually to beat his young
wife, and Eldest *Go*, defending his daughter-in-law, was in turn
nagged by his own wife.

Into this situation came Chinma, and her intervention
precipitated a crisis. Chinma was the wife of the eldest brother
of Eldest *Sao*. She came to live in the House of the Golden
Wing as a guest. She was an aged woman, respected by everybody. One day when she heard Shoutai and his wife quarrelling
in their room she rushed in to make peace. As she entered the
door she found Chimei pursuing her husband round the room
brandishing a heavy knife. Greatly alarmed, Chinma called
to Shoutai and pushed him out of the room. She stood by the
threshold and spread her arms to prevent Chimei from going
out after him. Thus halted, and unable to get hold of her husband, Chimei grew enraged. In an instant she raised her knife
and slashed the wrist of Chinma's right hand. Chinma fell to
the floor bleeding. The incident at once became deadly serious.
The women and children of the house all gathered about,
terrified at the sight of Chinma, who lay gasping and pale. As
the attack had taken place in her house, Eldest *Sao* had to notify
her own family. Next day Chinma's son, a nephew of Eldest
Sao's, came to the House of the Golden Wing with two strangers.
Chimei peeped out from her room and saw her mother-in-law
entertaining the three strangers in the main hall, all of them
whispering together. Knowing the strangers had come to deal
with her case, Chimei slipped out, clucking along on her way to
the side-gate as if she were searching for the chickens. Once
out of the house she ran as fast as she could to the house of her
mother's father, Yuchung, who was then the headman of the
Hwang clan and a distant uncle of Dunglin's. When the
strangers and Eldest *Sao* became conscious that Chimei had fled
the house it was too late to act immediately.

The strangers discussed the matter with Eldest *Sao*. They wanted to refer the case to the district yamen and charge both Shoutai and Chimei, the young couple, with unfilial conduct and let the prefect punish them. To discuss the charge further Chinma's son went to get the opinion of Fourth *Go* and Dunglin, for once the lawsuit was begun Dunglin and Fourth *Go* would be called to be witnesses.

Chinma's son was discouraged by the opinion expressed by Fourth *Go*. That man, though hostile all the time to Eldest *Go*, saw danger in the lawsuit. He advised Chinma's son not to throw away the money of both families. Unconvinced, Chinma's son went again to Hookow, this time to get Dunglin's opinion. Dunglin, opposed to the lawsuit, questioned the wisdom of bringing the charge. Furthermore, he told Chinma's son the story of Eldest *Sao*'s daily conflicts with other members of the household and pointed out in particular the incident when she had commanded her son to strike Second *Go*. He concluded that a woman like Eldest *Sao*, who urged her son to do an unfilial act towards an uncle, was no better than a woman like Chimei who had committed an unfilial crime against her mother-in-law. Faced with all this opposition, then, Chinma's son felt there was no chance of winning the case, as all the potential witnesses were unfavourably disposed. Consequently he reluctantly abandoned the idea of bringing the charge.

Thus the opposition put up by Fourth *Go* and Dunglin to bringing legal charges indirectly helped Eldest *Go* and Shoutai to escape from the consequences of their troubles. Chimei had hidden herself in her grandfather's house. Now she was called home, but only after much consultation and giving of guarantees. Although Eldest *Sao* ordered Shoutai to bind Chimei and punish her with a whipping, yet Eldest *Sao* and her own maternal family lost much face. Their ill-considered plans, so dangerous to the family, perhaps threatening its eventual ruin, were squashed, and much of their reputation for good sense was lost too. The House of the Golden Wing was thus saved once again from its continued crises. No open dissension came to the view of outsiders.

Nevertheless the situation of the family was now amazingly different from what it had been in the early days when the Hwang people were gradually building up its future and position. Then co-operation among the family members, spurred on by hardship, had created a very efficient household management, in which each individual took his part and did his respective work without dissension. But since then, as the family divided up, three separate groups now lived side by side, conflict raged between individuals within each group and set the individuals of the different groups in the house against one another. All of them now had well emerged from poverty, and there was no need any longer to struggle for a minimum livelihood. But there was time and energy instead to quarrel and to fight.

Yet Dunglin, old and feeble as he was, still represented the final source of authority in the house. His control, weaker now, still remained, and it was his voice that decided in the case of Chimei. Without him, legal charges might have been brought and the household managed and controlled from without. As long as he remained alive the break-up of the Hwang could never be complete.

CHAPTER XVI

THE EXPANSION OF THE STORE

The life of the Hookow store was closely bound to that of the House of the Golden Wing and dependent upon it. After the reorganization of the store, when Mowhun withdrew all his capital, the disturbances like the bandit attack and conflict among the brothers affected it too. In addition, all this time Eldest *Go* was still dissatisfied with the reorganization and kept on demanding more shares for himself. Crises and business depressions silenced him for the time being.

Now at last there were signs of returning prosperity Eldest *Go* began to grow eager to make money again. Thwarted in his desire to obtain more of the profits of the store he once again thought of opening a new store. Though the store which he had operated with Mowhun and Fangyang had been closed in bankruptcy, he had not suffered loss of his own capital, as he had withdrawn it in mid-course. So he still hoped to make another attempt.

Using his old tactics—setting up dissension among the people at the store—Eldest *Go* began to consult in private with Yao Kaituan, now the most important of the personnel after Dunglin. He tried to get him to operate the proposed new store. But the two men could not reach a satisfactory agreement. They had been rivals too long to make such co-operation easy. In fact Kaituan did not trust his colleague. He thought him an unstable man. Moreover, Kaituan did not want to rebel against Dunglin who had nourished him like a father. Likewise, close friendship between Kaituan and Third *Go* since boyhood made it all the more difficult for him to do any harm to the store Third *Go*'s father owned.

Failing to convince Kaituan, Eldest *Go* tried the next one. He approached Yang Ling, the newly promoted accountant, who had been the manager of the medicine department. Yang Ling was not an honest man, though clever and cunning. He once stole twenty silver dollars from the till and hid it in his suitcase, where Dunglin found it. Although Dunglin never told anybody of Yang Ling's theft, Yang Ling was very much frightened. He feared his master would not trust him further and that his position as accountant would not be permanent.

It was for this reason that he promised to go in with Eldest *Go* in opening a new store.

But Yang Ling was still only a young man and not very experienced in business. So Eldest *Go* wanted also to induce Yunseng, Dunglin's old associate, now head of the medicine department, to leave. Yunseng had been a faithful friend, but his position in the store had grown less and less important. The selling of medicines was only an appendage to the rice and fish trade. He had won no additional favour in all these years. Thinking that the new shop might open up a better prospect, Yunseng yielded to Eldest *Go*.

Once they were agreed, the three of them went together to put their plans before Dunglin. Dunglin was worried at losing three people at the same time. While he was hesitating Dungtzu, the fish dealer, came back from the city. Eldest *Go* took the opportunity to tell Dungtzu of his plan and to promise him the fish agency for the new organization at a double salary. Attracted by the prospect of profit, Dungtzu recommended the plan to Dunglin and advised him to help finance it.

Moved by the arguments of Dungtzu, Dunglin finally let the three people organize the new store and took up some shares himself. He did not worry about the withdrawal of capital from the store, because the store had plenty of money at the time, especially since Shankai, the sworn brother of Third *Go* and the lieutenant-colonel, invested his money in it.

After the withdrawal of Eldest *Go*, Yunseng and Yang Ling, Dunglin called in Fourth *Go*, who had long wished to go into the business. An intelligent, diligent and frugal young man, Fourth *Go* soon proved himself to be a good merchant. Before this change he had been a hard-working farmer. He had gone out to the fields every day with other farmers, but he differed from them in the fact that he spent two or more hours reading in the evenings. He read well and wrote beautifully. Besides classical books and histories, he often picked up the modern textbooks left at home by his brothers. In this way he became interested in science, arithmetic, geography and the world outside.

Farming in the daytime and studying at night kept Fourth *Go* busy. He was tall and thin, so that Mrs. Hwang worried about his health. She kept begging him to go to sleep earlier and not to study. Studying, she said, was the business of his elder brother Third *Go* and of his younger brother Sixth *Go*.

She never understood why Fourth *Go* took the trouble to read and write. But he ignored the constant admonitions of his mother and kept on at his learning. His judgment certainly was better than hers, for he was now well equipped for a career as a shrewd and able business man.

With capital more than sufficient and a reorganized personnel, the store continued to operate in the usual efficient way. Dunglin was still the manager. He had faithful helpers in the able accountant Kaituan, the shrewd fish dealer Dungtzu, and the intelligent clerks Fourth *Go* and Fifth *Go*. The master and his assistants worked together with a single aim. Once again the business became very prosperous.

During this time the revolutionary forces that had started from Canton were successfully fighting their way northward. They had overthrown the northern government in Peking and established the new National Government in Nanking. Working with the Central Government, the provincial government of Fukien effected a considerable reorganization. As the salt tax was an important source of revenue, the provincial government set up a special office to deal with the trade in salt.

The salt office did not totally monopolize the salt trade, but it set up several regulations and published them so that the people could follow the new orders. At that time Third *Go*, who was teaching both at Hwanan Girls' College and at Yinghwa College, went over one day to talk over the matter of the salt trade with one of his friends who had become the general secretary of the salt office. The result of the consultation was that Third *Go* became a wholesale dealer, buying salt from the government office and transporting it to Hookow, whence it was distributed to different stores for retail sale.

Third *Go* acted in this on behalf of his father's store, which now had complete control of the salt trade for the whole town. There was a salt warehouse situated on the peak of Hookow Hill, from where the main street of the town gradually descends. Kaituan, as the intimate friend of Third *Go*, was given the appointment of manager of the salt warehouse. He thus divided his time between the store and the warehouse and got a double salary.

The salt was a necessary staple among the common people and the selling of salt was a profitable trade. As Dunglin and Kaituan had control of the salt warehouse, the merchants of all the other stores were forced to come to them for their supplies.

Thus the two of them became very important personages in the town of Hookow. The store of which Dunglin was the master gained complete ascendancy over the other stores of the town.

One incident was enough to show the raised status of the store. Hung Heng, a new prefect and a former classmate of Third *Go*'s, came to town. Usually officials were entertained by the Merchants' Association, but this time the salt warehouse was selected as the place in which to receive the prefect. Kaituan and Fifth *Go* prepared a banquet in honour of the prefect. With this event the warehouse took over the function of the Merchants' Association.

Dunglin, old and happy now, was glad to see his business prosper, to know that his assistants were competent, and to see his sons grown up to be successful men. Now, surrounded by faithful employees and filial sons, he no longer worked so hard and began to rely more and more upon the young people.

Human life takes its course like a current in the sea, sometimes peaceful and sometimes rough. No one can live a smooth, monotonous life. Life changes all the time. Even the most balanced life shifts under new stimuli or in a new environment. Crises come and go. They are simple or prolonged. And each must be surmounted to establish once again a relatively stable state. The story of Dunglin's life is the story of the rise and fall of the waves, the succession of the peaceful and the rough stages of his life.

The monopoly enjoyed by the salt warehouse did not last long. A change in government policy toward the salt trade soon rendered the warehouse organization useless. Every store got the right to buy salt directly from the salt office. Once more every store became an equal competitor for the salt business.

Soon another horizon of business began to appear. One day Dungfei, a foreman of Dunglin's in charge of lumbering, came into the store. He tried to persuade Dunglin to buy a pine forest. From the forest he had in mind the pines could be cut down and turned into logs, which in turn could be transported to the city to be sold as fuel. Such trade in timber was quite profitable.

As there was considerable capital on hand in the store Dunglin promised Dungfei he would try out the wood trade and appointed him chief agent to deal with the purchase and cutting of the timber.

The trade in wood was a long process. When he had bought the forest Dungfei organized a group of labourers and took them to the mountain to do the lumbering. The crew was made up mostly of farmers who took to lumbering during their slack season on the farm. It was a job at which they could earn some additional money away from their farms. A few of them were men who did not farm at all but were specialists in lumbering.

The first job was to fell the trees. Using axes the labourers cut deeply into the body of the trunk. They chopped from opposite sides at once. When the trunk was cut almost through and barely supported the tree, by pulling on a rope which had been bound beforehand round the top of the trunk, the woodsmen felled the tree in the desired direction.

The felled tree was sawed up into small logs, each about one and a half feet long. The logs were piled up to form a tower with a big hollow centre. Such towers were built up as high as twenty to thirty feet. Whenever the skies were clear one could see from a distance the towers of piled wood placed together upon the gently sloping mountains, looking like the watch-towers of mediæval castles.

The towers of wood were left to dry and to wait till the rainy season made transport possible. When at last the rains came and the streams swelled enough to float the logs the labourers dismantled the towers and pushed the logs into the streams. The flowing water carried the logs down toward the town of Hookow. All the while the labourers, directed by Dungfei, followed the floating logs along both banks. They carried iron hooks fixed on long bamboo shafts. With these hooks they pulled or pushed the logs caught or jammed in the stream.

At the mouth of the stream which joins the Min River just outside the town of Hookow the labourers fixed a heavy line of ropes across the surface of the water to hold up the logs carried by the stream. The line served as a dyke, preventing the logs from floating farther out into the river. There the logs were collected and loaded on board river junks or left there to wait for the next loading.

The danger occasionally arose that the dyke, strained by further heavy rains or a sudden rush of water from upstream, might break. If a break took place, the logs drifted out into the river and scattered, so that often it became impossible to collect them again. Consequently Dunglin ordered his assistants to keep watch over the condition of the rope dyke and the logs stored there.

The logs on board the junks were transported to the city of Foochow where Dungtzu sold them to woodyards. The money earned was then used to buy more fish and salt to be brought inland.

While wood and salt were still transported by means of junks, rice and fish were now carried entirely by steamboat. By that time the store and its associates owned a steamboat of their own. Third *Go* was now the largest shareholder, as he had taken over all the shares left over after the bankruptcy of Fangyang and Mowhun. Fifth *Go* had become captain of the steamboat at first, but later, on account of the demands of business activity in the town and the work in the store, he had appointed his friend Weikuo to act as his representative and to serve as captain of the steamboat.

All this spelled further change in the life of Dunglin and in that of his family and store. The fates now carried him on to a new expansion. The stimulus for it came from the growth of business brought about by the wider contacts he had made. Out of the temporary salt monopoly made possible by the efforts of his son Third *Go*, the returned student and teacher in well-known colleges, Dunglin had acquired a higher status. More and more the people of all the town came to him when they needed help or advice. His new trade in wood, leading to the employment of more men, added still more to his local prestige.

It was a very big year when Dunglin became chairman of the Merchants' Association of the town of Hookow. The association had been founded long before and the chairmanship was held in turn by the masters of the various stores. To help in directing all the affairs concerning the town—those of the business men as well as those of ordinary citizens—the association invited the local gentry to take part in their meetings. The chairman called the meetings of the association and the meeting-place was his store. Dunglin, old and tired of meetings, frequently asked Kaituan to take his place as the chairman during the year of his incumbency.

Once during his term a problem of grave significance for the town arose and Dunglin was obliged to call a meeting of the association. The problem was whether to organize militia for the protection of the town. Bandits had been increasing in number in the district and the government was encouraging people to organize their own militia corps. Wang Chihsiang, a retired prefect, took the initiative in the matter of organization. He set up a central camp for the militia at his own village of Wang and sent out letters to all the other towns and villages urging them to organize subdivisions of their own. Several places had already responded and followed his example.

In the meeting of the Merchants' Association, of which Dunglin was chairman, the members adopted unanimously a motion to organize a local subdivision of the district militia. Every store contributed a man and a gun. Thus there were about twenty men in the subdivision. Fifth *Go* was appointed division commander. Having once been something of an organizer among the village boys and having grown up among the local toughs and in the gambling clubs, Fifth *Go* was a very suitable man.

Not long after this, another problem arose for the consideration of the association. This concerned the appointment of a representative of the town to join in a petition from the district to save the life of Shankai, who was then imprisoned at Yenping. Dunglin cast round to find the right man to act as representative. Just at this juncture Little Brother, now a graduate of Yinghwa College and grown up, came back from the city. When he entered the store Dunglin smiled at seeing his young son. Immediately he ordered him to leave for Hwangkow, two miles up the river, to join the petitioners. Little Brother was amazed at this command from his father as he knew nothing about the case. But he followed his instructions and left the store at once.

Shankai was held in prison by one Wu Anban, a military commander-in-chief stationed at Yenping. Anban had originally been a bandit chief, but later he had joined the army and risen to become the head of a military corps. His forces garrisoned several districts covering the whole upper Min valley, including the district of Kutien. When Shankai incorporated his force with those under the command of Anban, he too was promoted to a colonelcy and was ordered to garrison a frontier region north of Yenping.

Recently Anban had sent troops to overcome Shankai's force, and had captured him. The attack was made because of a rumour that Shankai was about to rebel against Anban. Later Anban found out that the rumour had no foundation. Shankai's friend, Chao Meng, a colonel who was a favourite of Anban's, investigated the matter and explained the situation to the commander. Shankai had had no plan of rebellion, but he had on various occasions made complaints about his commander. Learning the true state of affairs, Anban did not intend to kill Shankai. He merely suggested that Shankai might be released if the Kutien gentry could be induced to come forward and act as guarantors for him.

Chao Meng communicated Anban's suggestion to Chi Yakwei, a colonel stationed at Kutien city who had formerly been a subordinate of Shankai's. At the suggestion of Yakwei the gentry of Kutien gathered to send a petition to Yenping to ransom Shankai from prison. The group consisted of the important men of the district. They were Wang Chihsiang—the retired prefect and present commander of militia; Lei Wuyun —the district counsellor; Chen Tachuan—the chairman of the Merchants' Association of Kutien city; and Ma Nanshao— the richest merchant of the district. All the petitioners gathered at the house of Nanshao in the town of Hwangkow, from where they intended to sail upstream to Yenping.

Little Brother, as representative from the town of Hookow, arrived to join the petitioners. Among them he knew only Wang Chihsiang who had once taught him at Yinghwa College. Thus he met for the first time the father of his sworn brother Hsiwen, for Hsiwen's father was Wuyun. He was taken before Colonel Chi and introduced as the youngest brother of Third *Go*. That day the colonel received a telegram from Anban, ordering him not to leave his post, but welcoming the group of Kutien gentry. So Colonel Chi went back to Kutien city while the petitioners, about fifty in number, sailed upstream.

When the petitioners arrived in Yenping they marched in parade to the office of Commander Wu. Many of them carried streamers, scrolls, and placards, all made of vari-coloured silks. On the streamers and scrolls slogans and inscriptions praised the Commander's sterling virtues and lauded his beneficent administration of the Kutien district. But the petitioners were kept waiting at the gate for about an hour, until finally word was sent out that the Commander appreciated the gifts very much but that he was sorry he would not be able to see them at present.

Then the group went to see the senior major-general, an immediate subordinate and cousin of Anban's. When they arrived, that worthy's assistant came out and took in ten persons from the group to act as representatives of the whole. These ten were brought to the major-general's bedroom, which was his office. No sooner did they enter the room than they smelt the odour of opium. The major-general looked like a man of fifty, though his actual age was nearer forty. He was thin, pale and ghostly. He stammered when he spoke. Indeed he spoke very little, letting his assistant talk all the time. His patent vulgarity showed clearly his former life as a bandit in the mountains.

Finally, Anban sent an officer to arrange an agreement with the gentry of Kutien. The document related the story of Shankai and provided for his release upon a guarantee from the gentry of Kutien. Little Brother signed and sealed the contract as one of the ten special representatives. He was amused to recognize the officer who brought the document as a former preacher in a Methodist church whom he had known when he was studying in Yenping. The officer was as eloquent as ever, but now he talked administration instead of the Gospel. His gestures and manner of speaking were practically the same, except that he was clothed in an army uniform instead of a preacher's gown.

Thus Shankai won his release from prison. He was delighted to meet his old friends from his home district and he was pleasantly surprised to see Little Brother who had grown up so tall. But the incident had cost him his commission, and he was now a mere civilian.

To show his hospitality Anban arranged a banquet of about ten tables. The gentry of Kutien were invited and Anban's staff were summoned to entertain the guests. Anban and his next in command, the major-general, did not talk much but they nodded affably when the company paid them compliments. The preacher-officer was very eloquent and comparatively well behaved. Chao Meng, Anban's favourite, though illiterate, was a shrewd and cunning man. He talked fairly well and was the only man in the corps who seemed to have a little intelligence. All the other colonels and lieutenants were of dark complexion and powerful physique. They spoke coarsely and boldly recounted their feats of banditry to make a great show of their bravery.

In fact there were banquets for several days because each of the lower officers had to show his sense of hospitality. Finally,

Shankai gave a party to thank the people of his district who had come to save his life.

When the petitioners returned home at last to their native district Little Brother went straight home to the town of Hookow and reported his successful trip to his father. Dunglin received the news with great pleasure. He felt happy that this youngest son of his was able and promising like all his older ones.

In all these events fate carried Dunglin once more to further economic and political success. In a small town like Hookow business could not long be separated from other phases of life. The Merchants' Association habitually took charge of the public affairs of the town, levied its taxes, and kept its connections with the government and the military. The organization of a militia extended the power of the association, and as chairman Dunglin came to deal directly with persons influential in military and political circles. Under his protection Fifth *Go* became commander of the local militia and Little Brother a representative of the town among the gentry of the district. Their ability in turn added to the prestige of their father. So Dunglin gladly listened to the gossip of the villagers and the townspeople and liked to think that his four sons were ideally fitted to make progress along different lines, in business, in politics, and in intellectual and military spheres.

CHAPTER XVII
THE CHANG VERSUS THE HWANG

The height of prosperity and influence that Dunglin and his sons now shared coincided, strangely enough, with the very period when the Chang family, with whom Dunglin's household had started out on its life's course upon a basis of equality and partnership, sank to a disastrous end. Indeed as the Hwangs had risen in the world the Changs had fallen. Their final destruction touched the lives of the Hwang sons, but by now the connection between the familes was strained and remote. In fact, when the end came for the Changs, the Hwangs were hardly affected at all, except sentimentally, and even sentiment was not enough to bring them to active support of their former allies.

Of Dunglin's four sons, only two remained at home when the events that finally destroyed the Changs took place. The eldest, Third *Go*, lived with his wife and children in Foochow, where he taught in the colleges. But although he had set up a separate household he was not yet economically independent of his father. Little Brother too had now gone away. He was studying at a university in Peiping, the former national capital.

Fourth *Go* and Fifth *Go* stayed on with their father. They hired labourers to work the farm lands and went home often to inspect the work. Fourth *Go*, who had been well schooled as a farmer, now became a diligent and hard-working helper in the shop. Fifth *Go*, rather differently, became an active participant in public affairs and as popular a figure among the townspeople as he had been among the villagers. Many incidents contributed to his popularity.

During this time the district government, supported by the rich merchants, organized a company to build a public road for motor buses from the district city of Kutien to the town of Hookow. But when the construction work reached the village of Hwang, the road workers treated the villagers harshly. Arrogantly, as befitted their quasi-governmental authority, the road workers pressed the villagers to supply tools and food and threatened them with seizure of their lands for the construction of the road. Many complaints were made to Fifth *Go*. He finally went to the spot to see for himself how the road workers were conducting themselves. He came upon an inspector of the construction work beating a Hwang villager. The farmer ran over to Fifth *Go*, begging his help. Angry at the sight, Fifth *Go* demanded of the inspector what law he thought gave him the privilege of beating villagers. Thus interrupted the inspector furiously turned on Fifth *Go*. He in turn demanded of Fifth *Go* what his business was and how he dared interfere with government work. They quarrelled violently though they separated without blows. The case was eventually submitted to higher authority in the company. Fifth *Go* went to the district city and recited the incident to the manager of the company, a former student of Third *Go*'s. The manager immediately issued an order discharging the inspector. He took that action, not only because he had once been associated with Third *Go*, but also because Dunglin was one of the chief shareholders in the company. After that the Hwang villagers did not suffer any further damage from the road workers, and the people thought highly of Fifth *Go* and his ability to deal with such a situation.

Another incident crowded fast on the heels of this one. No sooner did he return from his triumph than Fifth *Go* found a rent collector quarrelling with his father at the store. The quarrel had begun over the matter of an increase in the rent. The collector asserted that his master the landlord demanded additional payment. But Dunglin argued that he had received no formal statement from the landlord so no increase could be made. The two men quarrelled. The collector got angry and pounded with his right hand upon the table. Thinking that a threat of force could overcome a mere rent-payer, the collector tried to intimidate Dunglin by seizing his coat collar. Such offensive behaviour usually heralded a fight, but how could old Dunglin fight with a strong and healthy man?

Just at this juncture Fifth *Go* entered the store. Seeing the attack on his father, Fifth *Go* rushed across the room and seized hold of the collector. About the same time Fourth *Go*, back from an errand, ran in to join Fifth *Go*. Together they tied up the collector with rope. Greatly surprised at this turn of events, the collector began to fear the consequences of his former bravado. His arrogant and aggressive attitude quickly changed to a humble one.

Fourth *Go* and Fifth *Go* jerked their prisoner to his feet, each holding an end of the rope that bound him, and marched him through the street to the town temple where the militia corps was quartered. There the brothers handed him over to the militia for safe keeping. The head of the militia was Mowyueh, Fifth *Go*'s old friend, who had had many years of experience in soldiery by now and had been appointed through the influence of Fifth *Go* to head the local militia.

But this manner of treating a rent collector was a little too much. Only a thief could be taken bound to be thrown into prison in the camp. Some few of the townspeople thought the Hwang brothers two bullies for daring to ill-treat a rent collector, even though he was the type of man who was harsh with the common people.

So the next day when the rent collector begged to be allowed to send for men to come to negotiate his release, Dunglin intervened. He did not wish the incident to grow any larger. He demanded only that a public apology be made by the rent collector. It was the custom that a public apology was made by exploding fire-crackers before the town temple. The rite indicated an acknowledgment of the misdeed before the public and saved the face of the injured party. So after that apology Mowyueh released the rent collector and the incident came to an end.

These incidents in which Fifth *Go* figured were not isolated ones, however. For the connection between Fifth *Go* and his old friend Chang Mowyueh, now the militia commander of the town, soon swept him into the rush of events that destroyed the house of Chang.

As militiaman in chief over the town, Mowyueh had the responsibility of protecting it. But he had it in mind to do more than just that. He dearly wanted to track down one Chu Fangyang, a notorious local bandit, the same man who had once cheated his cousin Mowhun in the matter of the abortive store Mowhun tried to set up long ago when the men were all younger. Fangyang had become the chief of a local gang that terrorized the region.

Fangyang during the ensuing years had become quite a famous bandit chief. His men ranged through the whole countryside along the Western Road. He led them boldly from one village to another. Recently he had become more cruel and bold than any of the bandit chiefs previous to his time. At that time, because of general political disturbances, the military often moved away from their regular posts to take part in local political feuds of their own so that towns were left open to the attack of bandits. Only the few places guarded by their own militia escaped such attentions.

In those days the Flower Bridge above the Hwang village was a necessary means by which the bandits crossed from one side of the water to the other. It was also a necessary crossing for the traders and travellers who went between the district city and the river port. Consequently people were often robbed, wounded or even killed near the bridge.

Ambitious to carry on his work as militia commander and also to win his revenge, Mowyueh once lay in ambush with his militiamen in the forest above the Flower Bridge. When a group of more than ten bandits passed over the bridge Mowyueh ordered his men to fire upon them. Four of the bandits were killed outright and the others fled in disorder back to their camp. It was a clever coup, but it was also the beginning of open conflict between the militia and the bandits of which Fangyang was the chief.

Another militia corps soon became involved in this feud. In the village of Chenyang, the native place of Chang Fenchow, another subdivision of militia had been organized under the leadership of Mowheng, who had been long ago a shopkeeper in Hookow and who had moved his family back to his own village. Mowheng had formerly been a student of the retired prefect Wang Chihsiang, and got his appointment to organize the militia through him. Mowheng and Mowyueh, themselves cousins, both hated Fangyang, who had done so much to damage their cousin Mowhun. Fearing Fangyang, the two militiamen had once combined their two subdivisions to form a bigger force. They had pursued Fangyang so closely as to compel his men to flee their main camp. Thus the hostility between the militia and the bandits grew deeper.

Consequently the stage was set for a greater struggle. It happened that Mowyueh and four of his men were hired by a group of traders to escort a shipment of their goods from Hookow to Kutien city. News of the shipment was carried by a spy back to Fangyang. The chief immediately mobilized his men and set an ambush at the half-way point on the road. When the traders reached the Flower Bridge the bandits opened fire. Mowyueh and his men responded. They stood their ground until, seeing more men run out of the bush, Mowyueh called a retreat. But the retreat became a rout and all too soon Mowyueh found himself running alone in the fields. Several of the bandits pursued him at a run along the footpaths. Finally one shot got him through the back. He fell headlong into the growing rice. Then one of the bandits overtook him and put another bullet through his head. His blood spurted out to mix with the muddy water and his body lay still.

This was by no means the end of the feud which soon was to sweep Fifth *Go* in its course. Fangyang was destined to get still more victims from the family of the Chang. Mowchiao, Mowyueh's younger brother, had become a soldier in the militia. He took up the feud, vowing to avenge his brother. But he was killed in the next battle. Then, still not satisfied by the successive killing of Mowyueh and his brother, Fangyang planned a secret attack on the village of Chenyang, where Mowheng was the head of the militia.

One evening at twilight Mowheng was called out to meet some visitors. As he stepped out on to the threshold a stranger whipped a pistol out of his shirt and shot him dead. The stranger was Fangyang. The raid of the bandits was swift and complete. They surrounded the house where Mowheng lived and captured the whole village. Before they withdrew, the village was plundered, the house of Mowheng completely looted, and the militia disarmed.

After the murder Yuehying, Mowheng's daughter, fled to the district city and sought help from her godfather Wuyun, the district counsellor. Under the constant entreaties of Yuehying, Wuyun could not help but turn the case over to the prefect. The yamen sent out secret police.

The events that swept the house of Hwang into the feud between Fangyang the bandit and the house of Chang grew out of the murder of Mowheng. Shortly afterwards, Fifth *Go*, wishing to go on an errand to the district city, innocently asked a friend, one Chang Mowsui, to go with him. Chang Mowsui was a farmer, a native of Chenyang village, and a clansman of the murdered man. There was nothing to implicate him in the murder. He was merely a harmless small farmer.

Fifth *Go* and Mowsui arrived at the city in the evening. But no sooner had they come up to the gate of a local inn than policemen suddenly appeared. They seized Mowsui, and when Fifth *Go* tried to remonstrate or inquire into the reason for his arrest, they drove him off and took Mowsui away, without letting him learn why.

Lost in the mist, Fifth *Go* did not know what would happen

to his friend. When at last he got some information, it was to the effect that Mowsui was charged with banditry and the killing of Mowheng. But he knew the accusation was not true. Mowsui had never been a bandit in his life. Mowheng had obviously been killed by Fangyang, the bandit chief.

Before the case came up in court, Fifth *Go* learned that Yuehying was the accuser. He decided to go and see her in order to explain the situation. As he did not know her he presented himself as the brother of Sixth *Go*, who had been her classmate in primary school and whose betrothal to her had once been discussed. A proposal to betroth Little Brother and Yuehying had long before been made by Third *Go*, but was refused by Mowheng, Yuehying's father. But the refusal had not ended the matter. When Mowheng later moved back to his native village he sent his daughter to study at a school in the district city. Seeing his daughter grow up into an accomplished and beautiful young lady, Mowheng tried once again to find a young man of good family as a match for her. At that moment Little Brother was studying at Yinghwa College and was credited with being intelligent and able. So Mowheng went to speak first with Mrs. Hwang. But that lady had been too embarrassed to give an answer because tradition did not encourage a direct discussion of the betrothal of one's children. But when Mowheng went to Dunglin the two men discussed the matter openly, as both of them had become relatively modern. Dunglin told Mowheng that Little Brother had been educated in the modern fashion and intended to make a free marriage, that is, to find a wife for himself without the interference of his parents. Dunglin's statement was not without foundation. After the death of Fifth *Sao*, it had been Little Brother's turn to get married, but he had insisted on letting Fifth *Go* have a second marriage instead and asked his parents not to bother about a betrothal for himself. However, Mowheng and Yuehying still thought there might be a possibility of getting Little Brother and they thought Yuehying was the very lady for Sixth *Go* to marry.

With this background then, Yuehying seemed happy to hear the news of Little Brother and to learn about his advanced studies in Peiping. But when Fifth *Go* turned the conversation to the case of Mowsui and denied his guilt, Yuehying changed countenance and became very angry. She said she had learned from her father that Mowsui was his enemy and cursed him bitterly. She insisted there was no doubt that Mowsui had induced the bandits to come to the village to kill her father. The young lady broke off the interview in the bluntest possible fashion, asserting she was interested only in getting revenge for her father's death.

Mowsui was thus accused, tried, and sentenced to death. Fifth *Go*, to his great sorrow, was unable to help him. Before Mowsui was executed in the public square he was paraded through the streets. As he was dragged through the streets he bewailed the injustice of his punishment, but to no avail. As a matter of fact he had once been a friend of Fangyang's, but their association had never been close enough to give cause for his execution as a bandit. Thousands of bandits became soldiers and officers after they had lived for years as outlaws, but this innocent farmer had to be killed in the name of a banditry he had never committed.

After the execution, Fifth *Go* went back home alone, depressed and frustrated by his inability to save his friend. He went to see Mowhun, who lay ill at home and had been bedridden for several months. The report Fifth *Go* gave him only increased Mowhun's dejection. Mowhun knew his life was being ruined by Fangyang, his former partner. The present bandit chief had killed all his three cousins : Mowyueh, Mowchiao and Mowheng. Mowhun could hardly bear to listen to the story of the feud between his family and the bandit chief. For now it was turning into a feud among his own kinsmen, for Mowsui was a distant cousin, one of the Chang. Sick and weak as he was, Mowhun could only lie in bed. How could he get up to do heroic deeds of revenge ?

In Mowhun's dejection one could read the fate of the house of Chang. This big family had dwindled. The propitious site, A-Dragon-Vomiting-Pearls, on which old Chang Fenchow had so hopefully built his magnificent new house, had not helped. Rather, it had hastened the decline of the family. Lying in his bed, Mowhun, tired, old, and lonely, could only curse Fangyang, whom he had once treated as a partner and a friend. He cursed him as the devil who had destroyed his life, his property, and his kin.

But perhaps the reasons Mowhun gave for the decline of his family were too simple. He was certainly wrong to put all the blame upon Fangyang. He made a personal devil out of the turns of " wind and water ". He did not see that the personal devil, the mere human agent of a larger fate, also was a product of his environment, his time, and his place, operating in a larger web of human emotions and human reactions to circumstances that neither he nor Mowhun could understand. Fangyang had not been born a bandit chief. He had begun among the toiling farmers just as Fenchow and Dunglin, and many others in South China had begun. The cheating, the dishonesty, the violence, and the hatred that were his character had taken him along one road, as other qualities had taken the others along different roads that lay open. The Changs had taken a path where Fangyang's acts had been the momentary catalysts that had spurred them to take one fateful turning rather than another. The turning they took led them through catastrophe, back to the obscurity and the poverty out of which they had originally come. The Hwangs had taken a similar path of their own, but the catalysts of events in human relations and material circumstances which spurred them on had turned them differently toward still higher paths.

Thus the downward road of the Changs, along which the acts of Fangyang served as such fateful deflecting forces, contrasted now all the more strongly with the still rising road the Hwangs pursued. No greater contrast could there be than the difference the two family heads now presented. As Mowhun lay sick upon his death-bed, weakly cursing the personal devil of his clan, Dunglin became the centre of the pride, solidarity, and filial piety which marked another high-water mark for the house of Hwang. The family soon gathered to honour in the old man the seat and symbol of their power and unity.

In order to parade the merits of a *paterfamilias*, the district had a custom of celebrating the important birthdays of a family head. These celebrations were long-life feasts. The fiftieth birthday is the first long-life feast, the sixtieth birthday the second, the seventieth birthday the third, and so on. As Dunglin was now sixty years of age, his birthday had been planned by his sons as the occasion for a great feast.

The celebration of the day was to be held in the city of Foochow, where more friends and relatives could be expected to participate than in the country. The Kutien Guild Building was chosen as the place. Within the city of Foochow all the country districts had erected special buildings of their own for their merchants associations. The Kutien District's building was situated in the section where people from Kutien congregated to trade, not far from the warehouse where Dungtzu, the agent of the Hwang stores, now dwelt. It was a building of two stories, roughly divided into three parts. The front part contained a theatre for plays, with actors' dressing-rooms at the side. Every guild building served also as a place of recreation, and old-fashioned plays were still the most popular form of entertainment. The middle part was an open courtyard and the back part contained a big main hall with smaller chambers opening off it. These chambers were used for holding conferences, for storage, and for living quarters.

To announce the date set for the celebration, a notice printed on red paper was sent out to friends, relatives, colleagues, associates, fellow-merchants and acquaintances. The notice for such a celebration differed from that announcing marriages, as it was signed by the children, not their parents. While marriages were considered a responsibility of parents towards their children, the long-life feast was the duty of the children, who were affected to celebrate the merits and the achievements of their parents. Third *Go* signed the notice first. After his name came those of his three younger brothers, his younger sister, his two sons, two daughters, and his three nephews and three nieces, all of whom made up the direct descendants of Dunglin. It was not strange that the wives, Third *Sao* Shuchen, Fourth *Sao* and second Fifth *Sao* were not on the list, for young women by custom were left out on such occasions.

The Kutien Guild Building was decorated from top to bottom. On the walls around the main hall there hung all sorts of scrolls and banners made of embroidery and vari-coloured silks. These had all been given by friends and relatives as congratulatory presents. Of the presents the most precious was a series of silk scrolls, each one ten feet long and six feet wide. They had been given by the colleagues of Third *Go*, who was now acting-president of Yinghwa College. A biography of Dunglin, beautifully inscribed on these scrolls, was ready to be displayed to the public. It related how Dunglin began his business, expanded his shop and made a great deal of money. It related again how Dunglin established his family, his house, and his farms. Dunglin's interest in public service, in local administration and in business was described. His merits as a filial son and as a benefactor of society were emphasized. His wife, Mrs. Hwang, was described as a faithful wife and a virtuous mother, who helped her husband and children in every possible way. Even the work of Dunglin's sons and the merits of his children and grandchildren in school were described and said to be due to his good teaching at home.

It was a longer than usual but typical public eulogy, glorifying the Hwang family.

On the first day of the celebration the guests were mostly merchants and their families. These were old associates and friends of Dunglin, the people of the fish, rice and wood trades. Some of them were fellow-merchants from the district of Kutien. As the guests gathered, they were invited to sit in the main hall. Tables for women and girls were placed in the main hall side by side with tables for men, for contact between men and women in the city was freer than in the villages.

On the stage in the front part of the building a theatrical troupe started up a wonderful concert. This was followed by a play called "Heaven-Sent Felicity", designed for such occasions. The guests of the main hall enjoyed their sumptuous food and as they ate took delight in watching the actors.

The troupe had a large repertory of historical and dramatic plays. The plays they presented were selected from a list from which the guests had chosen. While hosts and guests enjoyed themselves in the main hall, outsiders and strangers were allowed to stand in the open court and in the patios to watch the play, so that the whole building was filled with crowds of merrymakers.

The crowds and the celebration in the Kutien Guild Building continued into the evening, when larger and better plays were presented. At midnight Third *Go* led his brothers and the other junior members of the family to every guest table, thanking them for their pains in coming to so humble a celebration of a birthday.

On the second day a similar celebration was held, but the guests were different. Now they were civic officers and college colleagues, teachers and schoolmates of Third *Go* and Sixth *Go*. Even some friends of Little Brother in Peiping mailed presents for the occasion, as an indication of their friendship with the family.

The guests of the third day were the more intimate friends and kinsmen of the younger generation of the family. The ceremony was not so formal as on the first two days, but it was still a hearty and joyous occasion.

The celebration both broadened the associations of the family and raised the popularity of Dunglin still further, a fact which made it easier for him to do business in the city and to deal with its public affairs. Now at last he was not only a great man in the district but also a popular figure in the city. Never in the history of the clan Hwang had any member held so important a position.

By contrast, on the very occasion of the festivity and glory of the celebration of Dunglin's birthday, the tragic end of Mowhun came about. The long illness that Mowhun suffered had carried him from worse to worse. Finally he fainted away. His wife had to send for help, and Peimin, the faithful hired man, set out from the house.

Going first to the House of the Golden Wing, Peimin knocked at the gate. Second *Go* came out. He was the only grown man present in the house, because all the others had gone to Foochow to attend the birthday feast. But even though Peimin notified him that Mowhun was very ill, Second *Go*, who remembered that Mowhun had done nothing for him, coldly refused to go and see him. He excused himself on the ground that he had the responsibility of looking after the empty house. A mere labourer, Peimin could not persuade him, so he turned sadly away, hearing the gate close after him.

Going next to Hookow, Peimin called on the doctor Yunseng, who now worked in the new store established by him in partnership with Eldest *Go* and Yang Ling. But Yunseng too refused his help. His partners had gone to Foochow to attend the feast, and Yunseng said he could not leave the store to go out to attend Mowhun. It was very late. Yunseng said that he might visit the man the next day. Yunseng heartlessly forgot that he owed his knowledge of medicine to Fenchow, the father of the sick man Mowhun.

Mowhun was gasping when Peimin came back empty-handed and alone. The master's young wife sat beside the bed. She shed silent tears, knowing full well what was going to happen. Mowhun sighed very weakly. He opened his eyes once, only to close them again. After sadly viewing the tragic scene Peimin retired to his own room, cursing the people who had come between the glorious days of the household and its bitter present state.

Soon Peimin heard the noise of wailing and knew his master was dying. He went out and breathed the biting air and the ghostly atmosphere of the night. Through the door of Mowhun's room, he could see Mowkwei's widow and Mowhun's wife wailing by the bedside. Mowkwei's adopted son, now in his teens, also was there, crying in company with the two lonely women.

Early the next morning Peimin took the news to the Hwangs.

Second *Go*, though unwilling, had to help now. The two men quickly put the corpse in a coffin. Hardly any ceremony was observed. The head of the house of Chang was no more.

It was indeed the end. With no more work to do, Peimin had to leave the house. Mowhun's young wife soon remarried under the promptings of her parents. Of all the brave company who had known it in the days of its prosperity, only Mowkwei's widow and her adopted son were left in the house A-Dragon-Vomiting-Pearls.

CHAPTER XVIII
LOCAL POLITICS

High as their road had taken them, the Hwangs were no more immune to sudden turns of fate than the Changs had been. The rushing events of the next few years, when the whole province, like China itself, was to be torn asunder in war, were soon to teach them that. But there was a difference, for even through the losses and the flights forced upon civilians in bloody civil war Dunglin survived, and the family of sons and their interests and properties he had built round him clung together and outlived the dangers of disruption.

However, before the full force of civil war struck the district, it looked for a moment as if peace and security might reign. It was a false hope, but the destruction of the local bandits, which raised that hope, bade fair to bring a new day. The end of Fangyang, quick upon the heels of his victory over the Chang, came very suddenly. But its effects faded just as suddenly before new events.

Fangyang, Mowhun's former partner and his successful enemy, was really a very prosperous chief of bandits. The number of his men had increased to more than a hundred. They were still plundering and killing ruthlessly among the villages here and there in the district of Kutien. Indeed, until a new lieutenant came to garrison the town of Hookow, they were almost unopposed.

On his arrival to take up his new duties the lieutenant planned a treacherous stratagem. He sent agents to recruit Fangyang and his men into the regular army.

As soon as the discussion between the army representatives and the chief had taken definite shape and solemn promises of both parties had been exchanged, Fangyang brought his men in several boats to Hookow. When they arrived at the port, representatives of the lieutenant received them warmly on the shore. Leaving the boats, Fangyang walked at the head of his men from the shore up towards the camp of the lieutenant. About half-way up, the lieutenant appeared ostensibly to welcome Fangyang. But suddenly the line of Fangyang's men was broken, and an ambush of troops rushed out to seize them. The bandits were disarmed and captured. Only about a score of the bandits at the end of the line escaped by jumping into the water and swimming across the river. Others who fled, but could not swim, were captured, and some of them shot dead.

Among the captured bandits there was a lad only twelve years old. The boy was the son of Fangyang, so the bandit chief threw himself on his knees before the lieutenant to beg for the life of his son. Fangyang had no complaint over the punishment by death that he should receive as chief of the bandits, but he pleaded that his son had done no wrong and had merely come to visit him. Touched by the plea the lieutenant promised to save the lad, but ordered all the other bandits to be killed. Thus the great massacre, terrible as it was, brought some rest and peace to the people of the region. The whole district cheered up at the news. Those families who had suffered from plundering and destruction of property took especial delight in their revenge. Mowhun, however, did not live long enough to see Fangyang, his friend and enemy, lie dead in the public street.

In such a time of trouble as the province was passing through the people had little chance to enjoy the peace which, they hoped, the end of the bandits might bring. The military soon proved more terrible than any bandits. Commander Anban, the man who had degraded Shankai, soon created a more terrible disturbance than ever. The military forces led by Anban now occupied the whole region of the upper Min valley. They had gradually extended their zone of occupation downstream as far as the important river port of Shuikow. The district of Kutien, situated between the city of Yenping and the city of Foochow, was thus also under their military control.

Though Anban was a member of the provincial council, he was not satisfied with his position. His advisers pushed him to take the city of Foochow, the capital of the province. He resolved to do so and attempted it first by trickery. He called a conference at Yenping, which many provincial administrators and council members attended. Once they were assembled in conference, he summoned his soldiers, seized the provincial administrators and threw them into prison. At the same time he dispatched several divisions of his soldiers downstream along the course of the Min River and laid siege to the capital city. After doing so he announced to the governor of the province, a former admiral of the navy, that if the city of Foochow attempted to resist he would kill the captured administrators. But the governor disregarded the threat and took defensive measures, so that

Anban was forced to move the rest of his troops to the attack on the city.

The city of Foochow was garrisoned by marines, some of the divisions being manned by soldiers from North China. They were without any local ties and could not be either intimidated or bought. Consequently, even though Anban mobilized all his best troops, he found it hard to capture the city. Foochow was not taken.

In this civil war the district of Kutien suddenly became very important for strategic reasons. An event took place there which was to affect materially the success of Anban's venture. In view of the growing importance of the district Anban sent his favourite colonel, Chao Meng, there. Chao Meng, recently promoted to major-general, was to garrison the district and to watch over the actions of Chi Yakwei, the colonel who was a native of Kutien and who had long garrisoned the district city. Chao Meng spread his soldiers along the Western Road and stationed one division in the city of Kutien itself.

When Chao Meng arrived in Kutien he was very warmly received by Colonel Chi, who had now become Chao Meng's subordinate, at least nominally. The two officers seemed on good terms and often invited each other to dinner.

One of the ornaments of these dinners was Chi's concubine, a woman who had originally been a prostitute and who had long been a wise adviser in planning military measures. The woman made a practice of cultivating the local schoolgirls of good family and often made friends with them. These dinners, with their added attraction of schoolgirl company, were to have important consequences. Learning soon that Chao Meng wished to get himself a literate wife, Chi's concubine was only too glad to introduce some of these schoolgirls at one of these dinners for him. Chao Meng wanted such a girl because he himself was illiterate; he hoped to get a literate wife to help him keep secret messages and documents, as well as to ornament his new rank.

Upon receiving an invitation from Colonel Chi with an attached message saying that he would be introduced to several schoolgirls, Chao Meng accepted gladly. He gave little thought to any treachery. On the night appointed he left his camp with four guards and presented himself at the house of Chi. The guests were warmly received and were offered tea and tobacco. A banquet was set up in the upper story of the inner house. The party was to consist of girls only, except for Colonel Chi and Major-General Chao Meng, and the four guards were entertained in the outer part of the house. Drinking and eating, the party proceeded merrily. Chi had an aide, Lieutenant Tan, a big and tall man, well known as a ruthless killer. Tan came in late and joined the party, too. He apologized politely for his lateness.

In the heat of drinking Lieutenant Tan leaned over with a cup of wine at Chao Meng. As Chao Meng took the wine cup Lieutenant Tan, who stood behind him, seized his neck tightly in both hands. Chao Meng cried out, "Don't tease me, Lieutenant Tan." The answer was, "This time it's no joke." Suddenly conscious of his peril Chao Meng convulsively thrust his hand into his trousers pocket and drew out his pistol. But just as quickly Chi's concubine snatched it away. With a movement like lightning, Chi's concubine pulled the pistol downward against his head and pulled the trigger. The new majorgeneral stiffened and died instantly.

In the midst of the scuffle all the girls scrambled under the table or into the corners of the room. Colonel Chi, afraid of the noise of guns and even of fire-crackers, stood aside trembling. The banquet table was upset and the cups and dishes fell broken and scattered to the floor.

As soon as the shot in the room was heard, soldiers in the outer part of the house sprang into action. Three of Chao Meng's bodyguards were captured and killed, but one escaped and reported to the main force. But it was already too late. The forces of Colonel Chi surrounded the camp and commanded Chao Meng's division to surrender their guns and munitions. A few of Chao Meng's soldiers resisted for a while, but it was not difficult to overcome them.

The murder took place in the dark of night. The next morning marines entered the city of Kutien to join Chi's forces. Colonel Chi had of course secretly communicated with the marines beforehand and had killed Chao Meng in order to go over to the provincial forces. For his night's work he was immediately promoted to the rank of major-general. His forces combined with the marines and advanced westward along the Western Road to attack the few remaining troops of Chao Meng still commanded by his subordinates.

Learning of the treachery to Chao Meng, Anban rushed troops of his own from Yenping to reinforce the garrison at

Hookow and to effect an advance toward the district city of Kutien. His troops rounded up the common people to act as bearers of munitions, and they treated them brutally. Very soon, when Anban's troops arrived in a town or village, all the inhabitants fled, leaving only one or two old persons to watch over the houses and stores.

An incident that took place in the street before Dunglin's store may suffice to show the cruelty of Anban's soldiers. A labourer, captured and forced to carry heavy munitions, was driven along bound with rope and whipped with a horsewhip. Tired and sick, he fell down on the roadway and lay there, despite a severe whipping. He closed his eyes and gasped as though dying. Unable to whip him to his feet, a soldier poured a pail of cold water over his head, but still the labourer did not move at all. Finally they left him for dead. After the troops had passed, Dunglin came out to move the corpse, but feeling warmth in the body moved the labourer into the store and put him on a comfortable bed, where he made him swallow some warm soup. The labourer gradually regained consciousness and thanked Dunglin for saving him.

Anban's troops retreated along the Western Road to the village of Hwang. They occupied the House of the Golden Wing, using it as the headquarters of their camp because the house had fortifications. By this time all the family had fled except Fifth *Go* and Aunt Lin, who had to stay on for the sake of the property and furniture.

At the time Mrs. Hwang and her daughter Chumei were in Foochow living with Third *Go*. Fourth *Go* had taken up the job of fish dealer and was now also in Foochow. As communication between the capital city and the upper Min valley was cut off, the Hwangs in Foochow worried very much about conditions at home, especially as they read in the newspaper that fighting was raging back and forth round their native village and the town of Hookow.

The severe fighting forced Dunglin and Kaituan, the last two men in the store, to flee the town. They withdrew into the deep mountains, where they met Fourth *Sao* and second Fifth *Sao* and their young children. The families of Eldest *Go* and Second *Go* were also fugitives in the mountains. The villagers made a temporary abode in the deep mountains, stationing the women and children at the centre, with the adult men surrounding them.

All during the fighting between the rival military forces there was little the villagers could do except hide. They had little interest in, and even little understanding of, this warfare or the reasons for it. Once, for example, an illiterate native of the Hwang village carried a letter from the marines, who were stationed at the top of the mountains opposite the village, over to the enemy troops of Anban. He got two dollars for this trip and was exceedingly happy over his good fortune. But the next day, when he took a letter from the enemy troops to the marines, they shot him without giving any reason. The event alarmed all the villagers, and not a soul dared to appear before either army thereafter.

During these terrible times it was Fifth *Go* who kept watch over the House of the Golden Wing and who kept open the secret communications between the villagers' temporary refuge in the mountains and the house and the town. It was he who kept the fugitives informed of outside news concerning the movement of troops, the progress of battles and the general conditions of the people. On the darkest day of all, Fifth *Go* failed to come to the mountains where the villagers were hiding, and the Hwangs feared they had lost him. He had been forced by a retreating band of Anban's men to transport munitions for them, but he escaped when they reached the town of Hwangkow.

After this escape Fifth *Go* came again to the mountains and he advised his father and the others to move eastward toward the district city because he had seen Anban's reinforcements coming up and had heard rumours of an immediate counter-attack. The proposal gave rise to much dissension among the remaining Hwangs. Dunglin, hating to move farther, hesitated. Eldest *Go* decidedly did not wish to go any farther and strongly urged his Uncle Dunglin to stay on.

Most of the arguments centred round the protection of the house and the family property. Fifth *Go* strongly advised his father to give up the idea of watching over the house. Not only was there danger of destruction to the house and property, but peril of life itself in staying on. He argued that they could at least go to Foochow and join Third *Go* there should the house be lost. Eldest *Go* thought differently. He had a family of his own, and he had no other refuge to take them to, so that the destruction of the house would mean the permanent loss of their home. Moreover, he hated the idea of his uncle's family moving to Foochow. Without his uncle Eldest *Go* knew he would certainly become hopelessly involved in difficulties, political and social as well as economic. He saw clearly now that in the years he had become prosperous he had been under the constant protection of Dunglin, who had much the wider associations and whose sons were associated locally with officials and gentry of the district.

Luckily, before the decision to abandon the district had to be made the counter-attack of Anban's forces came and went. Anban's men were at first successful, but soon were again repulsed by the combined troops of Colonel Chi and the marines from the capital city. Finally the insurgents retreated northward. Failure to hold the district of Kutien cut Anban's troops into two parts; one part besieging the city of Foochow, and the other remaining in the upper Min valley with Yenping as their centre. The besieging troops were next driven out and forced to retreat northward along mountain roads, many of them being captured, pursued and killed in the end. Anban was confined to a restricted region in the upper Min valley.

When Dunglin and the members of his household came back from their mountain refuge they found that their house still stood, though much of their property had vanished. Anban's men, who hated the villagers and townspeople for favouring the governor's side, had stolen all the money in the stores. Dunglin's store and that of Eldest *Go* and his partners had each lost about twenty thousand dollars and were now almost bankrupt.

Dunglin and his family could do nothing about the loss but complain of it. As a matter of fact, these disturbances of local politics and civil wars had a far wider effect. They ravaged the whole province, though the district of Kutien suffered most. The village of Hwang and the town of Hookow had been a battleground several times and suffered great damage and destruction. Imagine the total disruption of the placid, ordinary life of the small village world! Two antagonistic groups of fierce strangers had suddenly thrust themselves into the local scene, seized whatever they pleased, destroyed what they could not take, and fired on one another. Killing, bloodshed and wounds became the order of the day. The peaceful green mountain slopes and the carefully-tended terraced fields suddenly were transformed into burning, bloody earth.

Daily life came to a complete halt. No living creature appeared in the towns or in the villages. The houses and stores were deserted, the animals killed for food for the soldiers and all the valuables looted. No business could be carried on. The farms lay barren. The river flowed on its usual course, but no trace of humankind floated upon it except the corpses killed in battle. The road lay bright under the sunlight as usual, but no human footprints marked its surface.

In the village of Hwang such a disaster had never occurred since the days of the first ancestor. The House of the Golden Wing as the richest house had suffered most from looting. Still the loss was temporary and as soon as the fighting was over normal conditions could gradually return and all the people could begin to take up their normal round again.

At this period Dunglin took a special interest in the timber business. Before the civil war he had made some money from it. Now his trade in wood grew bigger and he changed from selling pine logs to selling cypress, a material used in building houses in the cities.

When the civil war was over Dungfei once again led labourers to work in the forest. They felled the trees and stripped off the bark. Then they sawed up each log into beams about fifteen feet in length. The beams were floated downstream in the rainy season to the town of Hookow. There, instead of being loaded in junks as had been the pine drums, the cypress beams were bound together to form rafts. Four or five rivermen were hired to pole each raft from the town downstream to Foochow. They drifted only during the daytime and anchored along the bank at night. A round tent of bamboo covered the sailors when they slept. They cooked and ate alongside it. The trip to Foochow took some ten days. There the cypress beams were sold to wholesale dealers, who loaded them on board ocean steamships for Manchuria, to be sold in the market there. The trade was a lucrative one and gave considerable promise.

Because of this a big forest of cypresses was bought with the combined capital of Dunglin's store and that of Eldest *Go* and his partners. During that summer the rafts were floated to the port of Foochow, where they were held for a better price. Some dealers came to discuss the price but did not settle, and Dunglin and his associates waited confidently for better prices in the autumn. But this time the local merchants reckoned without the larger developments of the world of international trade and politics outside.

Suddenly, on September the eighteenth, 1931, the Japanese

invaded Manchuria, China's three north-eastern provinces, and stopped communications between Manchuria and the rest of China. The cypresses in which Dunglin and his associates had invested after the civil war were valuable only for shipment to Manchuria, where they were used in the mines. Now the Manchurian occupation by the Japanese blocked the transport and the price of cypresses fell to nothing. This complete failure meant a great loss. The store run by Eldest *Go* and his partners, which had been operated only for a few years, had already gone through several setbacks. It could no longer continue.

Dunglin's store, though it too suffered a great loss, was saved from bankruptcy, as it could fall back on its greater capital and its stable personnel. The partners Yang Ling and Yunseng became poor and unemployed, and Eldest *Go* went back to work again as an assistant to his uncle. Having twice failed in operating a store, Eldest *Go* was now thoroughly frightened of any new adventure and was satisfied at last to remain under the protection of his old uncle. Dunglin could have refused to reinstate his recalcitrant nephew, but did not because of their blood relationship and from family sentiment.

So Dunglin dropped the lumber business and concentrated once again on the old lines of fish, rice and salt. As Fourth *Go* was able and diligent he became practically an assistant manager, and Dunglin relied more and more upon him. Fifth *Go* was sent to Foochow to be a fish dealer there. The important figures in the store were now Dunglin, his sons and his old friend Kaituan the accountant. The reorganization gave the store a more efficient management, and for a considerable period the business was carried on very profitably. Some of the old prosperity returned and the store regained a little of the money that was lost.

Yet during all this time after the rout of Anban, local disturbances had occurred from time to time. The Nineteenth Route Army, after their courageous resistance against the Japanese invasion of Shanghai, was ordered to garrison Fukien. The declaration of an independent government in Foochow, supported by this army, forced the Central Government to send troops to subdue them. One of the major battles of the rebellion was fought in the district of Kutien, and the people again suffered a great deal.

Likewise the communists, who had their centre in southern Kiangsi, gradually spread toward western Fukien. The principles of communism were widely diffused, both by the communists themselves and by those who attacked them with counter-propaganda. Tightly surrounded by regular government troops, the communists broke through the lines blocking them and spread out in different directions. One branch came into the upper Min valley, where they mixed with local bandits, who gladly joined them.

Soon rumours about the coming of the communists through the Min valley were current. Third *Go*, who was concerned about conditions at home, came back to see his parents. No sooner had he arrived at the town of Hookow than communication between the upper Min and the capital city became difficult. He seriously advised his parents to go to Foochow to avoid the coming disasters. But old Dunglin, who had never fled except at the last moment during all the past troubles, did not want to leave the store and refused, even at the continual suggestion of his sons, Third *Go* and Fourth *Go*. But their old mother, who hated to leave their native village and who had been persuaded to go to Foochow several times before, was again forced to move. Chumei had married and gone off. Finally, Shoutai and his wife Chimei, Fourth *Go*'s two sons and several others followed Third *Go* in fleeing their native village once more.

When Third *Go* brought the fugitives to the shore at Hookow he found many people crowded there waiting for the steamboat. After three hours had passed a steamboat came in and stopped for a moment. Only a part of the prospective passengers got any chance to go aboard the boat. Fortunately Third *Go* and his group managed to get on. Fourth *Go* went along with them in order to see them off at Shuikow.

When the steamboat arrived at the port of Shuikow the passengers had to transfer to another steamboat for the rest of the trip downstream. The transference of passengers and baggage was made as quickly as possible because everyone wanted to be sure to get aboard the steamboat. In the mad scramble Shoutai lost his baggage in the river and his wife Chimei nearly fell in the water as she tried to cross from one boat to the other without help. No sooner had the passengers clambered aboard the new steamboat than the first boat cast off. Fourth *Go*, who had not intended to go to Foochow, was caught in the new boat. Seeing the first boat already six or seven feet away from the one he was on, he did not dare jump. But after a quick decision he dived into the water. Mrs. Hwang and Third *Go* got excited and shouted anxiously after him, but Fourth *Go* slowly and safely swam ashore.

On the very evening that Third *Go* gathered up his group of fugitives and left Hookow, the townspeople celebrated a festival in the town temple. A theatrical troupe played music and gave dramatic acts. Dunglin, released by the sending away of his wife and children, went to the temple to enjoy the celebration and plays. He did not go back to his store until midnight.

At dawn the following morning a cook apprentice opened the gate of the store to find a group of strangers stationed in the street. They were in uniform and each of them had a red band tied round his right arm. They carried guns and knives. The apprentice slammed the gate shut again and hurried to tell Dunglin what he had seen. Terrified by the news, Dunglin immediately jumped out of his bed. He collected all the silver dollars and banknotes of the store and hastily divided them into three parts. He gave Kaituan and Eldest *Go* each a part. All three of them then hid themselves in a dark entrance to the cellar, which communicated with a passageway under the town street. They blocked up the entrance again very carefully with pails and baskets of the kind usually used for fish and other commodities, so that no one might learn how they had left the store.

When the strangers knocked at the gate and the apprentice came out to open it they rushed into the store. They paid no attention to the apprentice because he was poorly dressed and was obviously a mere labourer. One of the strangers asked the apprentice where the manager was. The answer was that the manager had fled the store long ago. But the inquisitor did not believe him, because he said he had seen the manager, whom he knew by his broad round face and white moustache and beard, standing among the spectators at the play in the temple the night before.

The strangers were the long-feared communists. They had seized the town before dawn, while the townspeople were still abed. As there were no regular army troops in the town, they easily disarmed the militia, who were overcome by surprise and made no resistance. The communists used their well-known hit-and-hide tactics, sending ahead their spies under the guise of merchants, farmers and even beggars. That was the reason no one knew of their occupation of the town until daybreak.

About midday a band of communists captured all the women

and children of the House of the Golden Wing. There were no men present. The women, headed by old Aunt Lin, led the children, all under ten years of age. They wept as they were driven past the store, which was now guarded only by the cook apprentice. Unlike the usual military disturbance this incursion caused the so-called rich men, the middle-class merchants, to flee. The labourers and the farmers were " free " and some of them took part in the search for the fleeing " bourgeois ".

Fourth *Go* heard of the incident at Hookow on his way back from Shuikow. He went directly to his native village, where he found the house vacant. From there he sent out to discover the whereabouts of the captives and to negotiate their ransom. Deceived by the poor clothing and the mean appearance of the captives, the communists did not demand much. A ransom of several hundred dollars was paid for the release of all the women and children from the House of the Golden Wing. But among the other captives there were three store-masters and a municipal officer of the town. The officer and one of the masters were killed because of their connection with the government. The second master was ransomed for a great amount of money. The third was badly beaten and carried off as far as the town of Shuikow, before he was finally ransomed much later.

This was Dunglin's hairbreadth escape from the communists. For two days and two nights he hid himself in the subterranean entrance with Kaituan and Eldest *Go*. They crouched in the darkness and suffered from the cold, ill from hunger and almost suffocated. At last, when the guard of the communists was relatively relaxed, they fled the store one by one disguised as beggars and made their way up into the mountains behind the village of Hwang.

The occupation of the towns and villages of the region by the communists lasted only a week. Once they had squeezed enough ready money from the local bourgeoisie, they gathered up their troops and whirled away.

Dunglin had been greatly frightened by this communist terror. An old man, the fright and hardship he suffered made him quite ill after returning from the mountains. Yet when he got up from his illness he resumed his business once more. Tired and exhausted as he was the old man still went on to struggle as before for the worldly things he won only to lose so quickly. He was not rich now, yet he had more than enough to feed, shelter and clothe himself. But he was not thinking of himself. He thought as always of his sons, his grandsons and his future posterity who, he imagined, would depend upon him for support and protection and would carry on the line that he had begun.

Indeed when Dunglin returned again to the accustomed round he reflected again upon the fate of the House of the Golden Wing. In this little world of farms and villages and trading towns, political upheavals affected the lives of the people all too drastically. But they could deflect them only a moment; they could not stop them short of death itself. It made little difference, as long as the old roads of life advancement were still there. There was no distinction now between the rich and the poor, between the farmers and the bourgeois traders, between the noble gentry and the meanest beggars, for a lifetime's toil could create success for each, or a lifetime's misfortune be suddenly changed. The class struggle of the newcomers was merely one more disturbance in the local scene and one more catalysis of local character and local human ties. All such disturbances, he reflected, this like the others, whether communist or imperialist or militarist, whether political, social, or economic, were equally destructive of the life of the people, but equally unable to alter it in the end.

CHAPTER XIX

RIVER TRANSPORT

In time the disturbances created by the communist uprising, like every political and military upheaval before it, were followed by a temporary restoration of relative peace and order. In a few weeks communication and transport between the capital city and the inland towns along the Min River returned to their normal state. There were then eight steamboats plying between Hookow and Foochow. The steamboats competed with one another, striving to get cargo and passenger traffic. There were no regulations governing the rates or the fares nor any agreed-upon schedules of sailing.

About this time the Bureau of Reconstruction in the provincial government of Fukien instituted a control over communication and transport in the province. It drew up regulations and sought the co-operation of merchants and entrepreneurs, not only to advance public order but also to benefit business interests. In the matter of steamboats every inland port was asked to form a company to manage the steamboats registered in it, so that the former confusion might be remedied and competition cut down. Consequently the shareholders of the eight steamboats of Hookow gathered together and organized a company in conformity with the new regulations.

The new company was administered by a board of trustees and a committee of supervisors. A managing or executive department was set up and its personnel appointed by the board. The committee served to supervise the management of the boats and to keep a check upon the actions of the trustees, who were five in number and were elected at the periodic meetings of the shareholders. There were three members on the committee. Ma Nanshao, the richest man of the district and the most powerful shareholder, served as chairman of the board of trustees. His son-in-law, Wang Chihtan, the eldest son of Wang Yiyang, was appointed manager.

Chihtan was a college graduate who had little experience in business. It happened that one day one of the steamboats struck a rock. The wreck caused the death of two passengers. The families of the dead charged the company with mismanagement and brought an action in the provincial court. Nanshao and

Chihtan were both summoned, but they were so afraid of the outcome that they went into hiding. Naturally the company fell into an even worse state of confusion, as there were now no responsible officials. Because of this episode many shareholders became dissatisfied with the management. Chihtan was an honest man, but his secretary and subordinates were accused of " squeeze " and corruption. Soon each steamboat began to act independently as before and no longer followed the regulations and the schedules set up by the company.

As transport on the river resumed its former state of confusion and competition, many of the shareholders began to demand a reorganization. Fifth *Go*, who was now the fish dealer of the Hwang store and captain of its steamboat, called the *River Gull*, took a very active part in the demand for reorganization. He had been originally a friend and gambling companion of Chihtan, but a quarrel had broken off their friendship. Fifth *Go* intended to oust Chihtan as the manager and to take his place.

After the wreck of one steamboat there remained seven boats. Each steamboat still had its own organization with its own shareholders, dating back to the days before the new holding company was set up. The *River Gull* thus was owned in one hundred and twenty shares, distributed among various shareholders. The greatest shareholder of all was Third *Go*, who had thirty shares. The second greatest, with twenty-five shares, was Third *Go*'s newly married wife, the new Third *Sao*. Shuchen, his first wife, had died some time before, and Third *Go* had married a college graduate with money of her own. She had invested most of her capital in the steamboat. Dunglin's store owned twenty shares. Eldest *Go* had fifteen. The remaining thirty shares were divided among many small shareholders, most of them related to the larger owners. In fact, the steamboat belonged to the Hwangs as far as control went, for the family owned three-fourths of all the shares. Third *Go*, as the largest owner, acted as representative of the family in the matter. Fifth *Go*, though he owned no shares himself, was the nominal captain. He owed his position, of course, to his brother and the family.

The organization of the other six steamboats was very similar to that of the *River Gull*. There was in each case one such influential man as Third *Go* in the background, as well as a captain who, like Fifth *Go*, might or might not have any shares. Ma Nanshao, the fugitive chairman of the board, had had practical control of two steamboats and his son-in-law Chihtan, who acted as representative of the Wang family, was most influential in another. The other three boats were in a slightly different situation. There was, nevertheless, a single important figure at the back of each of the boat partnerships. These three men, Old Liang, Small Lew, and Long Deng, were all natives of the Eastern Road of the Kutien district. They acted as agents for the stores of their native places and lived in Foochow.

Thus when the steamboat company was plunged into a state of confusion the shareholders soon split into two groups. One group consisted of the shareholders who were subordinates of Nanshao. They continued to support him and his son-in-law Chihtan. The other group was headed by Old Liang, and intended to overthrow the regime of Nanshao. Nanshao held control of three steamboats, two of his own and the one of his son-in-law Chihtan. Old Liang and his friends, Small Lew and Long Deng, controlled another three. This left the two parties evenly matched. But it meant that the steamboat *River Gull*, whose owners inclined to neither of the conflicting groups, had the determining vote and exercised a balance of power.

These circumstances made it possible for Fifth *Go* to play an important rôle in the reorganization of the company. When he had become a fish dealer in Foochow he had combined the job of captain of the *River Gull* with that position, though he himself was not always on the boat. He knew Old Liang quite well. In fact as soon as the conflict arose in the company Old Liang came to see Fifth *Go*, who, as he knew, felt unfriendly towards Chihtan, the manager. Thus they joined forces in planning to overthrow Nanshao and Chihtan.

However, Third *Go* was the really powerful figure in the family's control of the steamboat *River Gull* and everybody knew that Fifth *Go* was really only his representative in what concerned river shipping. So the next move was for Fifth *Go* to introduce Old Liang to Third *Go*, who still taught and lived at Yinghwa College. He did so and the discussion between Third *Go* and Old Liang which followed led to concrete results. All too well aware of the threat to his invested capital, Third *Go* wanted to come to some arrangement among the conflicting parties that would solve the company's difficulties.

Old Liang wished to overthrow the present organization outright, as all his party hated Nanshao and Chihtan. He urged Third *Go* to come forward and said his party would support him if he took the chairmanship of the board of trustees. Fifth *Go* helped his friend urge his brother to that course of action. But Third *Go* thought differently. He was not satisfied to be a puppet of Old Liang's party. At the same time, unlike his brother Fifth *Go*, he was still on good terms with Nanshao and Chihtan. Chihtan, as the son of Wang Yiyang, Dunglin's old friend, had been a younger schoolmate of Third *Go* and had been a friend of his since their schooldays. Third *Go* also rather liked Nanshao, who was a comparatively liberal merchant and a comparatively well-educated man. He thought that people like Nanshao and Chihtan would be more reliable than those like Old Liang and Small Lew who had very little education and who had risen from being village toughs only through chicanery and sharp dealing.

So when Third *Go* went to visit Nanshao to talk things over, he did not intend to follow Old Liang's and his brother's plans. Nanshao and Chihtan both welcomed him. They too advised him earnestly to reorganize the company and hoped for a reconciliation of the two parties. They too suggested that Third *Go*, as a highly educated man and an influential shareholder in the company, was certainly the right man to compose the rival claims of the conflicting parties.

Acting as mediator, then, Third *Go* arranged matters privately with the heads of both groups. The most important steps to be taken were the rearrangement of the personnel of the board and the committee and the choice of a new manager. In a few days both parties arrived at an agreement and set a date for a meeting of all the shareholders in the seven steamboats.

At the meeting Third *Go* was elected to preside. Usually the chairman of the board of trustees presided, but in this case the meeting was aware that any appearance of partiality on the part of the presiding officer had to be avoided. An election was held, the result of which coincided exactly with what had been arranged between the two parties through Third *Go*'s mediation. On the board of trustees, aside from Third *Go* who was elected to be chairman, four men were elected to serve, two being elected from each of the opposing groups. On the committee there were to be three members, two from the party of Old Liang and one from the party of Ma Nanshao. Outwardly it looked as if the party of Old Liang had won more seats on the board and on the committee. He won four seats and Nanshao had only three, if one did not count Third *Go* who stood between the two. But in fact, as the board of trustees was legally responsible for the administration of the company, both parties were equally represented and henceforward the attitude of the chairman would be decisive if the two parties advocated conflicting policies.

Being unable to decide upon the right man for manager, the trustees appointed Third *Go*, the chairman, to take up the managership for the time being. To do so, Third *Go* set up an office in the Kutien Guild Building. As he was busy teaching most of the time, he could come to the office only occasionally, so that he relied heavily on his secretary, Wei Chenchin, a student of his who had also been a friend of Sixth *Go*'s in the primary school. In addition Third *Go* employed two clerks and a legal adviser.

The new company was thus reorganized with the whole body of the shareholders delegating their authority to a board of trustees, which in turn employed a manager and his staff. This form of corporate structure held the manager and his staff responsible to the board and the board to the shareholders; it provided a further check on the administration of the company in the supervisory committee, whose duty was to counterbalance the authority of the board and the manager and to hold them to their responsibilities. In theory the manager and his staff had the power to arrange the cargoes and schedules of each of the steamboats, to hire the captains and crews and to oversee their navigation of the boats.

This formal plan of organization of the company was in accord with the regulations promulgated by the Bureau of Reconstruction with which the company had to register. The Bureau wished the company to have a rigid organization so that the management could be unified and operation proceed smoothly. In practice, however, the real operations of the company had nothing to do with the formal structure. The company was only a nominal entity and never did quite overcome the traditional autonomy of the separate houses and the separate captains.

We remember that such steamboat purchase and traffic was originally organized by its shareholders, among whom there usually was one prominent figure who made himself responsible. Each boat was thus a world by itself. Its captain, accountant, pilot, cook, and crew of five or six sailors were in fact employed by this chief shareholder. These employees naturally were loyal to the shareholder who had got them the jobs and who could discharge them. With the organization of the company some improvement was made; each boat conformed now, as it had not before, to a common sailing schedule, in order to avoid unnecessary competition. In addition, it was in its operations subject to the Bureau, which could not give a sailing permit without proper administrative consent by the company.

But the administrative office of the company could not touch the staff of any of the steamboats, even though in theory these men were supposed to be hired and dismissed by the office. It did succeed in taking over the collection of passenger fares, without which it would have had no revenue at all. But by far the greater income of the steamboat came from freight charges, and their collection remained in the hands of the captain and the accountant of each boat, though now they rendered a monthly account to the company office. The freight charges were usually on credit and paid up annually, so in many cases they became a mere bookkeeping transaction because most of the cargoes belonged to the steamboat's own shareholders anyway, as they had originally organized to buy the boat for the sake of transporting their own goods.

Once organized in this manner the company carried on its business quite effectively, in spite of the discrepancy between its paper organization and its real mechanism. The administrative office functioned well enough and Chenchin, the secretary, took direct charge of arranging the schedules of sailings. Each boat was to sail upstream and downstream once a week, so that there would be one sailing every day, except when there were too many passengers and commodities for one boat. Then the office could call up the next boat on the schedule to sail a day ahead of the schedule.

When a steamboat, the *River Gull* for instance, was scheduled to sail upstream, its captain or his representative arranged beforehand with the dealers in the warehouses of the city to load their goods on board. Since Fifth *Go* as a rule served only nominally as captain of the Hwang boat, his representative on the boat, Weikuo, had to handle all routine matters. Once the goods were loaded on board, Weikuo recorded them in his account books, listing the amounts and kinds of the merchandise, their shippers and receivers, and the amounts of the carrying charges. As a last step Weikuo reported his boat's condition to the administrative office in the Kutien Guild Building direct to the secretary Chenchin. Chenchin sent down a clerk and two policemen who collected the passenger fares. The policemen were detailed by the government for that purpose ; otherwise the passengers would sometimes refuse to pay their fares.

Usually after the passenger fares had been collected it was flood tide, and Weikuo gave the order to weigh anchor. Upstream on the way to Hookow the boat had to pass three inland customs inspections. Weikuo had to go to each office to report his cargo and passengers and to pay customs dues. The cargo was subject to examination, by no means always perfunctory.

While the upstream trip took about a day and a night, the downstream journey needed less than twelve hours. Shipments from Hookow also were arranged for between Weikuo and the store-masters. He had once more to go over all the routine.

All the steamboats operated in this combination of conformity with the company's schedules and financial autonomy. Operations were quite successful under the reorganized administration and in less than six months the company issued a statement which showed a considerable profit.

This reorganization put the Hwang family and Dunglin's store in a very favourable position. The great staples of the Hwang store's trade were still the three lines rice, fish and salt. Steamboat transport of the rice and fish grew ever more convenient and efficient. Once again fate carried Dunglin and his family to a stability in which they found again their well-balanced life of the old days.

Even in intimate matters the power of a family head over even his grown sons still clung to Dunglin. A second remarriage for Fifth *Go* followed the old pattern. Fifth *Go* we remember was nominally captain of the Hwang boat, though his friend Weikuo did the work. Weikuo, however, got two-thirds of the salary and Fifth *Go* took only a third of it as his commission. About this time Fifth *Go*'s second wife died, leaving only a young daughter. Still hoping for sons, Fifth *Go* intended to make another marriage. One day he met a young lady on the boat who had known his sister Chumei. As Fifth *Go* grew to know her better they fell in love and the young lady consented to marry him if their families permitted. But Dunglin had other plans. He wished Fifth *Go* to marry a divorced woman who had a considerable fortune in her own name. Reluctantly Fifth *Go* followed the order of his father once again and sacrificed his love for a second time. The divorced woman was taken into the family without any kind of ceremony because she was not a virgin first wife.

But Fifth *Go*'s third wife had been brought up in the city. She had acquired habits which differed from those of the women who lived in the villages. She soon found it very difficult to get on with her mother-in-law Mrs. Hwang and her sister-in-law Fourth *Sao*. She did not like the housework or cooking, washing and sweeping, and liked titbits of nuts and cakes in addition to the regular meals, a practice scarcely known in the village world.

So perhaps Dunglin's judgment was at fault here. Fifth *Go* did not live as happily with this wife as with his first two wives. He often quarrelled with her. Once she even dared to throw a silver dollar at him and hit him with it right on the nose. He left home angrily and from then on stayed most of his time in Foochow.

One day Fifth *Go* was taken by one of his gambling cronies to a brothel where they spent their time gambling and drinking. By and by he acquired the habit of sleeping there, and took a fancy to a pretty prostitute. After a while he contracted syphilis, but he dared not tell his parents or his brothers. At last when his illness grew worse he returned home. Suddenly falling from the dinner-table one day he lay in a faint with saliva running from his mouth. Consciousness gradually came back, but after that he often fainted.

Meanwhile Fifth *Go*'s new wife gave birth to a dead boy baby. This made her parents-in-law angry about her. Fifth *Go* also hated her. The whole family expected Fifth *Go* to have a son, in order to continue his line. His daughter could not be counted as an heir. The parents had married him off three times primarily for the sake of an heir. The stillbirth brought them great disappointment.

When Fifth *Go* had outwardly recovered, Dunglin ordered him back to Foochow to resume his job as fish dealer. He went first to Hookow to stay in the store for two days waiting for a steamboat. There he wrote several letters to his brothers Third *Go* and Sixth *Go* and to his friends. After three hours of writing he suddenly fell from the chair at the counter, again spitting saliva and losing consciousness. As soon as he was put to bed a doctor was called in, but nothing could be done as the doctor did not know what kind of illness it was. This time he did not return to consciousness. After another three hours of gasping he died, without having uttered a single word.

The news of Fifth *Go*'s death gave the whole family a great shock. All the people of the House of the Golden Wing had seen him a lively man just recently. They could hardly believe that death might come so suddenly. The following day Third *Go* and Chumei came home and joined in the sorrow of the family. The old father and mother, the brothers Fourth *Go* and Third *Go* and the sister Chumei gathered to weep together, sitting about in the dead man's room. They were heartbroken, and questioned Heaven's cruelty in taking away their dear one in the prime of his life.

As old Dunglin mourned the loss of his third son, he looked for fault in himself. How could this misfortune have fallen upon his family if not in punishment of himself? This was the local code. If he had been virtuous, as believed, there could not have been in his lifetime the succession of bankruptcy and other misfortunes, and now the terrible death of his son Fifth *Go*. It was a stern code of belief, and it left him no shred of happiness. He felt himself an object of criticism from then on because his now proven lack of virtue had brought ultimate ruin upon his son.

The loss of Fifth *Go* struck Mrs. Hwang too in her dearest associations. During recent years Fifth *Go* had become the son on whom she depended most, as he came home oftenest to see his mother. His poor luck since childhood and his three marriages without an heir made him a special figure of pity in his old mother's imagination. For months after his death, when Mrs. Hwang came upon some old garment of Fifth *Go*'s, her old body could not support her sorrow and she fainted.

Fourth *Go* and Third *Go* mourned the loss of their brother too, though rather differently. They faced the loss of a strong partner in their struggles. Fifth *Go* had contributed much to the building up of the store and of the family. His interest in social welfare, in public administration and in village affairs, and his wide connections with the people of the region were indispensable to the Hwang family and to their business. His efforts in bringing about the reorganization of the steamboat company were a vivid reflection of his important place in the working mechanism of the family, the store, and the river trade.

Much as the death of Fifth *Go* upset them all, the Hwangs had to continue their daily lives. Though the days and the nights passed gloomily, daily routine and the demands of the management of their concerns gradually carried them back to a less morbid way of feeling. The coming back of Sixth *Go* from Peiping soon afterwards led the family to recall the death of Fifth *Go*. Everyone thought how much more joyful and complete the reunion would have been if Fifth *Go* were living.

Grown up now, young and promising, Sixth *Go* was not as " little " as he used to be. But everyone still called him Little Brother. He brought cheerful talk and encouraging news. With all the callow enthusiasm of youth, he advised his elders to let bygones be bygones and to look forward to a hopeful future. As Little Brother was charmingly reasonable and eloquent ; practically all his elders came to listen to him. Merriment appeared again at last in the Hwang family and another restoration to normal life came about.

Then after a round of visits in the city, the town and the village, Sixth *Go* set out again upon his studies. As the steamboat plied the river his thoughts carried him like the current. He remembered how once he had stood here with his dead brother Fifth *Go*, happily shouting together as they sailed towards home. He could not help but give way to depression, though a moment ago he had chattered cheerfully enough to his elders, intent on ridding them of their gloomy thoughts. Only now, looking at the familiar surroundings of the town, the shore, the river and the old steamboat, all the same except for the presence of the brother whose place could never be filled, did Little Brother too finally shed his own warm tears.

CHAPTER XX

THE DEADLOCK

Eventually the death of Fifth *Go* had a much greater effect upon the Hwangs than at first appeared. Not until Fifth *Go*'s influence in the family's business, in the fish trade in Foochow, and particularly in the river trade and the steamboat company was finally removed, did the latent conflict between the two factions of that reorganized enterprise flare up again into a bitter struggle. In many ways the conflict reflected the overthrow of the old ways by the new. None of the Hwangs could escape that larger conflict; certainly not those like Third *Go* and the other sons who were so rapidly forging a life for themselves in the city and along the river rather than at home among the farms of the village and the shops of the town where Dunglin was now almost ready to retire. Fifth *Go* had been a strong link among them all, just as he had been the one force that seemed to hold the steamboat company together with his friendship and sympathy for the older river merchants. And now once he was gone the remaining brothers would have to meet alone whatever came.

Thus even Sixth *Go*, home temporarily from his studies, could not escape being swept up in the train of the family's fortunes. He happened to be on hand when the company split wide open. When Sixth *Go* came back to Foochow he took up quarters with Third *Go*, who lived in an apartment house on Nantai Island, a southern suburb connected with the city by the Long Life Bridge. The two brothers, Third *Go* and Sixth *Go*, lived together happily. Quite different from the usual either hostile or merely cordial brothers, they were frank and friendly with each other and discussed all sorts of problems of human life. The elder brother, an educator and administrator, was able to contribute his practical experience from which the younger one took much profit. Sixth *Go* had a more theoretical grasp of science and history, and when he in turn expressed his ideas Third *Go* found much interest in them.

One day the elder brother came home from the administrative office of the steamboat company and told the younger brother that a certain captain had that day tried to force the secretary Chenchin to change a scheduled sailing. In the face of the secretary's refusal the captain came almost to the point of using force. This was only a sample of the company's troubles, for the company was so constructed that smooth management of its affairs seemed to be impossible. Sixth *Go* advised him to pay more attention to teaching and less to the running of the company. But Third *Go* felt there was a hope of great profit if only the company could be better organized. He was, however, fully occupied in teaching and tried to get a man to act as manager and to take the necessary steps to turn the company into a really well-operated enterprise.

At this turn of events it happened that Sixth *Go* ran into Chihtan, the ousted former manager, and invited him home for dinner. Third *Go* joined them and the three old friends had a happy time. On the strength of that reunion, Third *Go* asked Chihtan if he would like to take up the managership of the steamboat company once again and make a really promising concern of it. Chihtan seemed to be the proper man.

So Third *Go* invited the members of the board of trustees to his home to dinner and called a meeting there. But Old Liang and one of his friends, both members, refused to come. They had heard by devious channels that the meeting was called to reinstate Chihtan as manager and were strongly opposed to the plan. The meeting was held without them. Third *Go* and the two subordinates of Nanshao constituted a quorum of the board. Nevertheless, Chihtan recognized the fact that the party of Old Liang still opposed him. He begged Third *Go* to appoint his cousin Wang Chihkun instead. Chihkun was the son of Liyang and the younger brother of Huilan, the remarried widow of Mowde, and seemed equally well fitted to take his place as manager.

When therefore the meeting voted unanimously to appoint Chihkun manager, the party of Old Liang was very much dissatisfied over the decision. They charged that the vote was illegal, for they were not yet accustomed to majority rule, in which the difference of only one vote determined so important an outcome. They disliked Chihkun because he was the cousin of Chihtan and they feared he would do exactly what Chihtan had done. They feared, too, that Chihtan was in the background and that Chihkun was taking up only a nominal managership.

It was true that Chihtan was active in the background. Even before the change of managers took place Chihtan drafted a letter discharging Fat Pao from his position as legal adviser of the company. Fat Pao was an intimate friend of Old Liang who had introduced him into the office. Chihtan did this in order to test the attitude of the party of Old Liang. However, as chairman of the board and manager of the company Third *Go* had to sign the discharge, so that Fat Pao came to hate him even more than Chihtan, the enemy of his friend Old Liang. A discharge was serious, because he lost face.

Consequently when Chihkun took over the office, the party of Old Liang sent men, their captains and sailors, to wreck the administrative office. These men had begun, most of them, as street toughs. They advanced on the office menacingly and scolded and threatened the officers in the most vulgar, waterfront accents. But it happened that Chihkun was a man of strong mind. Although he had not graduated from the college where he had studied with his cousin Chihtan, he had much the greater determination and courage. He soon drove them out.

Ignoring threats and complaints, Chihkun rapidly became the manager in earnest and took up his duties seriously. First of all he went to the Bureau of Reconstruction and explained his position clearly to the officers there. He told them of his intention of running the company as a real business in line with the regulations promulgated by the Bureau long before. He thus got full support from the Bureau.

Next, the administrative office, now under the direction of Chihkun, tried to take over the collection of freight charges. This move greatly alarmed the party of Old Liang. The main reason that Old Liang had opposed the creation of legally provided organization was that he feared concentration of financial power in the hand of the administrative officers. If the plans for financial centralization should come off, the company would at last emerge with a thoroughly organized hierarchy of control, so that orders might flow from the board to the manager, from the manager to the officers, and from the officers to the crews of the steamboats. The particular control of each separate steamboat, in which the important shareholders retained the direction of their own employees, would be eliminated. Thereafter each shareholder would still have his shares in the company at large, but he would in effect have lost his steamboat. The boats would belong to the company, not to the individual merchants who had originally bought them.

Thus the conflict of the interests of the two parties came quickly to a head. Ma Nanshao had no office in the company any longer, but he remained the head of his own party and determined its action from behind the scenes. His son-in-law

Chihtan helped Chihkun actively in his reform policy. Even Third *Go* came to work in full co-operation with Ma Nanshao. In fact, their faction comprised all the men who had a better education and had learned modern methods of trade and business organization. They believed that centralized economic power in the administrative office would enable them to control more strictly the movement of each steamboat and to employ competent captains and crews. They strove to eliminate what they thought of as the corruption of the individual shareholders and captains who clung to their boats as to their own private property and cared nothing for common interests of the river trade.

The party of Old Liang regarded the issue very differently. They had originally been owners of single steamboats, who, like Dunglin, had wished merely to facilitate the transport of their own goods. Dunglin would have shared their point of view, but as Dunglin had now retired from active business his sons had the decisive influence in the company, and they had long ago come to take up the river transport system as an independent enterprise. Old Liang and his party members still looked upon the steamboats as mere auxiliaries to their regular business of rice, fish and salt. Men like Old Liang, Small Lew and Long Deng, though still influential, did not control many shares in the steamboats. They had agreed in the creation of the company in name only for the sake of the necessary registration in the Bureau of Reconstruction, without which no permit for steamboat transport could be obtained. But they wanted still to be able to ask the captains to load their goods on credit and to pay the bills only after a year or so. If the office were to collect the freight charges in actual money, they stood to lose the interest on their capital.

So when Chihkun issued his orders to collect freight charges on board the boats and in cash, Old Liang and his party members got extremely excited. They stirred up their employees, the captains and sailors, to make as much trouble as possible for the administrative office. Their employees supported them wholeheartedly, for they were told their jobs would be lost if the office succeeded in carrying out its policy.

Meanwhile Long Deng was sent to talk with Third *Go* to try to effect a compromise. He stupidly centred his complaint before Third *Go* around the appointment of Chihkun and the discharge of Fat Pao, ignoring the real and larger issues. Third *Go* answered that he did not understand why Old Liang had avoided the meeting. It seemed very unfair of them to show their dissatisfaction afterwards when the appointment had been made by a majority of the board. As for Fat Pao, he had taken a big salary without doing any work and another legal adviser had been employed at a much cheaper salary. Finally, Long Deng came out with the real wishes of his party. They wanted Third *Go* to restore the office to its former state. But Third *Go* flatly refused to consider this.

There was a deadlock. No compromise could be effected. Old Liang and his friends reflected sadly that if Fifth *Go* were still living he would have found it possible to meet their wishes somehow. Fifth *Go* had been very friendly to the party of Old Liang. He would have been the very person to advise his brother Third *Go*. Fifth *Go* had been the initiator of the first connection between Old Liang and Third *Go* and thus had made possible the reorganization which had brought the company into being. Fifth *Go* had stood at the side of the stubborn Old Liang as Third *Go* had stood at the side of the rich Ma Nanshao, and together the brothers had been able to keep the balance of power between them. They had known the inner problems of both sides. But now, unhappily, being nearer to the party of Ma Nanshao, Third *Go* was no longer able to hold the confidence of the party of Old Liang, who did not trust him. For Third *Go* too the loss of Fifth *Go* meant a great deal at this moment. So, in a way, the death of one person really destroyed the steamboat company. For after this final rebuff the party of Old Liang would not associate further with Third *Go*. They began to hate him as much as they hated Nanshao. They taunted him, demanding to know how he could hold the chairmanship of the board without their support. They accused him of intriguing with their opponents against them and decided upon forcing him out or ruining him.

Relatively free of his managership and managerial duties now that the energetic Chihkun had taken over, Third *Go* put more time and energy into his teaching. He was now professor of chemistry at Hwanan College. In that capacity he was sent as the college representative to attend a conference dealing with national defence at Nanking, the seat of the Central Government. The government was calling up all experts in the nation to help in devising a policy of national resistance and brought these men to the capital for a discussion. The Japanese invasion of China proper was only a question of time. The order from Nanking to attend the meeting was secret and Third *Go* planned to leave Foochow without stating his reasons for going.

Calling Chihkun, Third *Go* asked him to wind up the current business of the company quietly as soon as possible and to send over all papers for his signature immediately, as he was going to leave at once for Shanghai. But the news of Third *Go*'s leaving leaked out and soon spread through the city.

On the day of his departure Third *Go* went to the wharf beside the Long Life Bridge accompanied by his wife and Sixth *Go*. They went on board the steamship for Shanghai. Five minutes before sailing time, as a sailor beat a gong to warn all visitors to leave the ship, and at the moment when Third *Go* was shaking hands in farewell with his wife, two of the local police rushed into the cabin and arrested him. Sixth *Go* was already walking ashore, but he came running back. Seeing Third *Go* in the hands of the police, Little Brother begged them to take him instead. He explained that his brother had a very important mission in Shanghai. But the police replied that this was a criminal case and no one could take his place. With only a minute left before the steamship set sail, and the police holding tightly to Third *Go*, Sixth *Go* and his brother and the new Third *Sao* had no choice but to go ashore.

While the new Third *Sao* took the baggage back home, Sixth *Go* accompanied his brother to the district court. On their way the brothers saw Small Lew sitting in a ricksha beside the quay and knew immediately that he was the one who had brought the police and showed them to Third *Go*'s cabin.

They were quite right. The party of Old Liang had gathered many times again to discuss methods of dealing with their opponents. Fat Pao, the lawyer discharged from the office with lost face, plotted viciously to oust Third *Go* as chairman of the board. Fat Pao introduced the faction supporting Old Liang to Lawyer Yeh, who was famous in the city as a winner of cases through the " back door ". Hearing by grapevine that Third *Go* was going to Shanghai Lawyer Yeh snatched at once at the possibility of disgracing him. An accusation was drafted in the name of Small Lew and Long Deng, both of whom were members of the supervisory committee of the company. It was submitted to the local district court. Third *Go* was charged with having intended to escape to Shanghai with more than ten thousand dollars from the company's funds. It was on the strength of this charge that the district court had immediately sent out two police to arrest Third *Go*. Small Lew had taken the police to Third *Go*'s apartment house first, but he lied to them and said that Third *Go* was not at home. He bribed them to wait till early next morning at the time he knew Third *Go* was going to board the steamship. To capture Third *Go* on the ship would be all the greater indication that he intended to run off with the money of the company.

So now Third *Go* was taken to the district court, where he waited in the waiting-room. In a little while Chihtan, Chihkun, Chenchin and Lawyer Chao, the new legal counsel of the company, all arrived in the court to help Third *Go*. Small Lew and Long Deng and some others of their party came to press their charges. The public prosecutor called up the accusers, Small Lew and Long Deng, and the accused, Third *Go*. The hearing was held in the prosecutor's private offices. Many members of both factions eagerly waited outside for the results.

In his chambers the public prosecutor turned to the accusers first to hear their charge. Small Lew and Long Deng repeated their charge that Third *Go* had stolen ten thousand dollars and was trying to escape. When at last the prosecutor turned to Third *Go*, the accused merely presented in silence the document giving him his commission from the central government to travel to Shanghai in the interest of national defence. Third *Go* asked the prosecutor not to make public the matter of the commission because it was the government's command that it be kept secret. Having read the document, the prosecutor turned at once upon the accusers and reprimanded them for their trouble-making. Stupidly Long Deng and Small Lew still tried to press their charges and spoke of the defendant as a robber. The prosecutor ordered them to keep quiet. He said he knew now what sort of a person Third *Go* was. He warned them that they should not interfere with a man of professorial rank who intended to leave on a mission for the good of the whole nation. Turning again to the defendant, the prosecutor accorded him permission to leave for Shanghai, and said he would hold the case until his return.

After the dismissal of the hearing the two accusers, Small Lew and Long Deng, became very much alarmed. They had known nothing about Third *Go*'s possessing so important a secret document as to make the prosecutor immediately and visibly favourable to him. Lawyer Yeh advised them to examine the books of the administrative office and to find errors there, no matter how small, so that the lawsuit could be prosecuted further.

When Third *Go* returned from Nanking, the case was taken

up again. It was now assigned to another public prosecutor called Li, a man notorious for taking bribes. But Third *Go* thought his case was very straightforward. After three hearings Prosecutor Li rendered a decision to the effect that the accusers might bring their charge against the defendant in the local court of justice.

Third *Go* was angry about the decision of the prosecutor's office and that the case would have to be fought further. He regretted very much that he had not bribed Prosecutor Li. By not doing so he had lost a chance of stopping the case, because if he had won in the prosecutor's hearings, the charge would go no further. As a matter of fact his secretary, Chenchin, had attempted secret bribery with the permission of the manager Chihkun, but he had not told Third *Go* about it, for he was afraid the defendant would become nervous under questioning. Later Chenchin learned that the other party had offered a bigger sum, so that the decision turned out to be different from the one he had expected.

When Third *Go* was taken by the police from the steamship the news spread immediately to the town of Hookow and to the village of Hwang where the people talked of little else. The great son of Dunglin was in a " yamen trap " ! Dunglin was greatly worried. He had suffered the bitterness of lawsuits and the hell of prison life. Mrs. Hwang, who used to worry about even the tiniest disturbance, was especially excited by the unexpected news. The old father and mother immediately left their beloved native place for the capital city, to be on hand during the development of the lawsuit. Fourth *Go* could not bear to stay at home in the shop either. He left it to the management of Kaituan and went to Foochow. In the apartment of Third *Go* there now lived the old parents, the three brothers, and the new Third *Sao* and her children. The lawsuit was the main topic of family discussion.

Old and tired as he was, Dunglin still made a round of visits to his former friends and associates. He knew a number of people in the party of Old Liang and through them tried to persuade them to drop their charges against Third *Go*. Old Liang and his party entertained the old man cordially and praised his good intention highly. But they saw that the old man had lost his influence with his son and they did not try to make use of him.

As a matter of fact, Dunglin was becoming garrulous. He often spoke now as carelessly as a child. In the end, fearing that their old father might carelessly expose their plans to the party of Old Liang, the three brothers, Third *Go*, Fourth *Go* and Little Brother, often talked together privately without the knowledge of Dunglin. They tried to calm their parents and assure them there was no danger of losing the case.

As he grew into extreme old age, it is true, Dunglin became less influential both inside and outside the family, though he was more respected than ever as a symbol. With his bald head and his long white hair, Dunglin looked like a retired politician rather than a merchant. And nowadays he was gay again, almost childishly so ; he liked best to chat with his young grandsons and to take them with him to visit the old city and to the theatres.

Like every man of declining age, Dunglin had little further ambition except to see his offspring prosper. Yet he was more than ever the symbol of his family's solidarity and success. The belief of his people in him gave him happiness too, for all the merits and successes of his sons he now believed to be only reflections of his own virtues.

While Dunglin enjoyed his life in the city, his sons and their associates had still to deal with the running of the steamboat company and the lawsuit. In order to have further support from the shareholders, Third *Go* called a meeting of the whole body of shareholders in the Kutien Guild Building. He was confident his supporters together with those of Nanshao would command a majority and that the policies advanced by the board to date could be ratified and a vote of confidence be given him. The party of Old Liang, however, were on hand to upset the meeting and would not allow any move to come to a vote. Old Liang brought in his captains, sailors, and some street toughs to serve as proxies for the shareholders of his party. Their real job was to behave as agitators. Whenever a motion was made, these men made an uproar. Soon they were shouting, overturning chairs, throwing pencils and papers about and disrupting the meeting. Gradually the shareholders fled. So did Chihtan, a man easily frightened. Only a few remained. These were the three Hwang brothers, Chihkun and the secretary Chenchin. They were surrounded by the toughs, but they stood their ground till the meeting dissolved without result.

A second time the meeting was more carefully planned. It was held in a famous restaurant in the city. City police, equipped with pistols, were invited to sit at the back of the hall to see that no street toughs were allowed to get in, and so no one tried to make any disturbance of the meeting. When the party members of Old Liang arrived they immediately recognized the seriousness of the meeting. In the presence of the city police they knew it was impossible for them again to disrupt the meeting. They changed their tactics. They employed a few outspoken men to argue their case. But these speakers were crude and advanced unreasonable arguments. These tactics also met with failure, especially since all their arguments were refuted by several law students, friends of Sixth *Go* who had come to the meeting to help him and his brother Third *Go*. These young law students were so eloquent that they easily beat down the other party.

Seeing nothing could be done, Old Liang withdrew his whole party from the meeting. But the majority of the shareholders stayed on so that the meeting thereafter proceeded smoothly. One of the motions, duly voted and passed, was to draft a petition to the local court to state that the shareholders' meeting endorsed Third *Go*, their chairman of the board of the trustees and manager, and that they were confident he had done his job well.

But the endorsement of the shareholders had no effect. In addition to their "back door" policy, the party of Old Liang resorted to forged documents and perjured witnesses. An example of their tactics was this. A street beggar was employed as a witness to swear he had bought a shareholder's free-passage ticket for a few dollars. The office issued passes to large shareholders, good for travel without fare on all the steamboats. The accusers now charged that the office under the management of Third *Go* had sold the witness such a ticket, an indication of malfeasance. When Lawyer Chao of the steamboat company asked leave of the judge to cross-examine the beggar witness about the sights of the town of Hookow to prove whether he had ever actually been in the town or not, the beggar was at a total loss. His stupidity called up laughter among the spectators.

Nevertheless the perjured testimony and the bribery did their work, and Third *Go* was condemned to six months in prison by the local court. The decision made him and his party exceedingly indignant. They immediately carried the case to a higher court, the superior provincial court for Fukien, and prepared for a still stronger fight with the party of Old Liang.

As the conflict between the two parties grew bigger and bigger, the whole district of Kutien was drawn into it. The gentry of the district, like Lei Wuyun, Wang Chihsiang, Chen Tachuan, Chen Shankai and others, came together to Foochow to urge both parties to compromise and avoid wasting the resources of the district in further meaningless lawsuits. Geographically speaking, the party of Ma Nanshao and Third *Go* represented the dwellers along the Western Road and the party of Old Liang the dwellers along the Eastern Road, though all the contenders belonged to the same district of Kutien. Never in the history of Kutien had there been such a big conflict involving so many of the outstanding people.

The two parties were finally induced seriously to consider a reconciliation. A banquet was prepared and all the important members of both parties invited to attend. The principal contenders, the middlemen and the lawyers were present. They signed an agreement of reconciliation. Nevertheless, the main condition which the party of Third *Go* and Nanshao demanded— withdrawing the case before the courts—was never realized. The parties had pushed their misunderstanding so deeply, especially after the several trials, that they could no longer believe each other in anything. Despite the efforts of the gentry the agreement remained a scrap of paper.

So Third *Go* was still under condemnation to three months' imprisonment on the strength of some very minute mistaken entries in the books of his officers, magnified by the perjury of his opponents. He did not win his release until the case came up in the highest court. The provincial court finally had to send all the evidence of the case to the national capital, and there in the highest court, which could not be reached by bribery, the charges against Third *Go* were finally dismissed. He was free again of the threat of imprisonment, and the steamboat company had a very good chance of future development under his management. The outlook was rosy once more. The party of Old Liang was finally routed.

In fact prospects were bright for the Hwang family, the townspeople, and the whole district of Kutien. But only all too briefly. Fate had an even greater calamity in store which involved the whole of China. Suddenly, on the seventh of July, 1937, Japanese soldiers opened fire upon the Chinese at the Marco Polo Bridge outside Peiping, and the Japanese invasion of both North and South China began. In the midst of national resistance to this new and greatest threat, the Chinese government moved its capital to Chungking, prepared for a long war of resistance. Japanese planes swooped down and dropped cruel bombs, killing civilians in many cities. Foochow was no exception.

Death stalked on every hand, soon property lay in ruins everywhere, and the whole social order tottered on the brink of disruption. Bombing and blockade forced the people to migrate inland. The Hwang family retreated to the old village of Hwang, where Dunglin took up residence again in the House of the Golden Wing he had built so long ago. He left the shop to Fourth *Go*, but the business dwindled down to the very small scale on which it had originally begun. Transport between Foochow and the interior often stopped altogether. The river steamboats were destroyed and the shareholders in the company lost all their capital. Third *Go* followed the great migration of the nation's colleges, moving to the north-western corner of mountainous Fukien. There, like the others of his profession, he lived from hand to mouth. By retreating inland, back to the soil from which they had sprung, the Hwangs tried once again to survive a severe crisis in their fortunes.

In the years of resistance against the Japanese invasion, Foochow was finally occupied completely by the enemy in the spring of 1941. Following the invasion there came the enemy's savage actions : bombing and killing of helpless civilians, setting on fire of houses and properties, plundering, enslaving, raping and massacre. People were devoid of the fundamental means of subsistence. Everywhere death prevailed and disorder reigned. Communication between the inland villages and the outside world was completely cut off. The stores in Hookow, including that of Dunglin, were all unable to be the medium of the trade which kept salt fish and rice flowing up and down stream.

The House of the Golden Wing, still headed by Dunglin, had undergone a most difficult trial. This time the trial was nationwide in character. The experience and hardship that the House had suffered, the dispersion of the Hwang family as well as the impact of the new China upon its surviving members, would deserve a voluminous description. Suffice it to say here that the Hwangs, who have been swept into war and disorder, do participate in unison with the peace-loving peoples in trying to build up a better world.

Foochow was once taken back but was reoccupied by the enemy in the autumn of 1944. After that the Japanese forces thrust inland beyond the Hungsan Bridge and tried to go up to the upper Min River. This alarmed the inland villages all the more. The remaining members of the House of the Golden Wing began once more to move away from the village of Hwang.

Mrs. Hwang, Dunglin's wife, though old and tired, was forced to move several times, first out of the original house to her daughter Chumei's place and finally to mountainous North Fukien, joining Third *Go*, her eldest son. Fourth *Go*, who was wounded by the bombing at Hookow, had been ill in bed for some time. Sixth *Go*, Dunglin's youngest son, who had followed the great mass migration of the intellectuals to the far interior land and had been doing frontier work for national defence and reconstruction among the south-western provinces, was cut off completely from communication with his family. No mail could pass from the coastal provinces to the interior.

The House of the Golden Wing had contributed young men to the army. Two of Dunglin's grandchildren, one grandson and one grand-nephew, were in the ranks and fought the enemy at the front in the defence of their homeland. They were probably among the soldiers who took back Foochow in the middle of May, 1945.

Dunglin, who was now over seventy years of age, had refused the pleadings of his sons to leave the original house. He still took up the hoe and worked once again as he had done in his youth. Around him were some of the grandsons who relied upon him now for lessons in the agriculture that was their first and most enduring subsistence. An enemy aeroplane flew over their heads, making the grandchildren look up into the hostile sky, but the old man spoke to them quietly : " Sons, you are forgetting to put your seeds into the earth."

CHAPTER XXI

PUTTING SEEDS INTO EARTH

We have now learned the complete story of the development of the two related families, the house of Hwang and the house of Chang. We have seen how Dunglin and Fenchow, the heads of the two houses, had been associated and how the two families had risen and fallen. From the activities in which they had been engaged we are able to trace the changes that took place.

The changes that had taken place fall into three main stages. First, in their youth Dunglin and Fenchow had both suffered from uncertainty and poverty. A chance for success came to them only when they met and talked over the opening of a shop in the town of Hookow. Their success at business in the town was reflected in their family and village, so that they built their houses, sent their children to schools, married their sons, celebrated festivals, worshipped their ancestors and developed their farms. Their trade, which kept the rice and salt fish travelling upstream and down, became the main source of money-making on which other activities and associations depended.

In their second stage both the house of Hwang and the house of Chang began to have troubles and misfortunes. The career of Fenchow deteriorated and his maladjustment to his family and later to the store made him unhappy and finally carried his life away. His son Mowhun seemed to have a good opportunity of opening a new store and rebuilding their house, but let the chance slip away because of his mismanagement and incapacity. The house of Hwang on the other hand had internal troubles and external impacts, but Dunglin had learned from his experience how to fit himself to the tide of fate and to keep abreast of his friends so that he remained successful. The result was then an increasing difference between the further ascent of the Hwang family and the swift decline of the house of Chang.

In the third stage the house of Chang was out of the picture and the house of Hwang was struggling on. Aiming at a greater success, the Hwang family took up bigger business and became associated with local politics. Social and political change was so rapid that the Hwang members could not possibly follow. At last the national crisis caused the family to sink back to its original form.

What do we learn from the description of the history of the two families? How can we interpret the family history in order to understand the principles that operate in human relationships? From the narrative of Dunglin's relation with his family, we can see there exists a system of relationships. By a system we mean any combination of relations which can be isolated from other systems. This idea of a system is clearly given in the description of Dunglin's early life, in which the illustration of the bamboo sticks and rubber bands which are connected to form a framework is used. The whole framework can be disturbed at any time by any elastic band or by any bamboo stick. The balance of human behaviour is thus established in a similar network of relations. Each point represents a single individual and each individual will affect or be affected in the system.

The system of human relations, like the framework of the bamboo sticks and rubber bands, is in a constant state of balance which we may call equilibrium. The idea of equilibrium can further be illustrated from physiological studies. We know very well there exists in the human body a state of equilibrium. The body remains in this state, so that if a small force is impressed upon it a reaction will take place which tends to restore the system to its previous state once the impressed force is removed. In the body, when an infection disturbs the system, a series of compensatory changes take place, such as a rise of temperature or an increase in the number of white corpuscles, until the infection has run its course. Then the corpuscle count returns approximately to its old value, the temperature returns to normal, and the state of the body returns to equilibrium.

In the field of human relations a similar state of equilibrium exists. Dunglin's happy association with his grandfather is a case in point. With the death of the old man he became restless, lonesome and sorrowful. His state of equilibrium was thus disturbed. Only after a long while did daily work and routine gradually bring him back to normal.

But the disturbing force impressed on the system is sometimes too great or too prolonged, so that when it is removed the individual or group does not return to its previous state, but remains in a state of disequilibrium until after a period of time a new equilibrium is established. This new state of equilibrium differs appreciably from the old, though it may consist of a new distribution of the old elements. In the life of Dunglin the selling of peanuts was important, as it served as a stepping stone that carried him from his family to the outside world. We recall how he met Fenchow, who took him to the town where they operated a store and became partners. The business of the store opened up a new world in which the partners acquired their new ways of life, selling and buying, measuring and accounting as well as making friends with the townspeople. Under this newly established system, the store was the centre of Dunglin's activities and his family life slipped into the background.

Thus a state of equilibrium cannot be kept for ever. Change is a successive process. Human life swings between balance and disturbance, between equilibrium and disequilibrium.

As for a store such as Dunglin's, it was a tightly knit little system of its own, where its members worked smoothly and fell into an easy co-ordination. The activities of the store kept the system moving in a lively way from day to day. These activities were made up by the interaction among groups of people, that is, the relations between the individuals in the store or between the store people and the customers.

When the interactions between the individuals in a system are kept constant, equilibrium can be maintained. In the store there was frequent intercourse between the sellers and their customers. If no customers had come, the store would have become bankrupt. It is obvious then that the change in frequency of interactions affects equilibrium.

In addition to our understanding of how individuals are associated to each other by constant adjusting interactions for maintaining equilibrium, we should know that human adjustments are controlled to a large degree by the techniques, activities, symbols and habits which can be summed up under the name culture. These techniques make specific requirements on the individual's time and control his interaction with others, determining the individuals with whom he must associate and providing the basic routines upon which his institutions or systems are organized. In the little store, aside from the people who operated it, there was the environment which made up the whole atmosphere. The material things, such as tables, chairs, pots of wine, cases of medicine, scales, the counter, balance, money and account books, together with the techniques like measuring, weighing, accounting and writing, the language they used for talking and recording as well as the habits they formed in selling and buying, all made up the environmental factors which controlled human interactions. Some daily actions were repeated, but every event differed from every other over and over again, because the environmental factors above mentioned were different from time to time, though the members of the store might be the same. Therefore, in our study of human relations, we must deal not only with individuals whose relations are maintained in a state of equilibrium, but also with the cultural environment which modifies and influences their interactions.

We have mentioned above certain principles on which human relations are based. Human life changes, but not without following principles. We have taken pains in telling the whole story of the Hwang and the Chang families with detailed descriptions of daily occurrences and careful portrayal of personal associations, for the purpose of being able to trace successfully the changes that took place in the fortunes of the two families in order to find out a true picture of human life.

What do we mean by change? It is the disturbance of a system, then its restoration, or the establishment of a new system. What are the forces able to induce change or able to disturb the existing equilibrium of a system? There are, generally speaking, four forces tending to upset equilibrium.

First of all, a change in the physical environment compels a change in the techniques used in adapting to it. This consequently brings about a change in the relations of individuals in the system. The physical environment of the village of Hwang seldom changed, so that the existing agricultural routines, which were handed down from the early Hwang ancestors, worked very well without any modification. Therefore the agricultural system in which the Hwang farmers were closely associated with their neighbours had been steadily carried on from year to year.

Secondly, a change in a technique for technological reasons brings about changes in the habitual relations of the individuals. When Fenchow and Dunglin dropped their selling of wine and added the lines of rice and fish, their techniques changed completely. That was the reason why Dunglin went for the first time to the city where he made connections with the fish stores, rice shops, banks and junk owners as well as the transporting coolies. This brought Dunglin and his store to a new stage. He was cut off almost completely from his family and village, and became more and more absorbed in his life as a fish dealer in the city where he had established a new life or a new equilibrium. In this newly established system he became an important person who helped to keep commerce alive by an endless flow of fish and rice up and down the river.

As a matter of fact, the store underwent changes from time to time whenever new techniques were introduced. The change of transport to steamboats from junks greatly facilitated commerce and made possible the rapid movement of the commodities. Those stores which had not the facilities of steamships became bankrupt and were finally forced out of business.

Every time when a new line of business was taken up, new tactics were introduced and hence a new stage of human relations was reached. The salt monopoly and the wood trade are two examples. With its monopoly of salt, the store extended its power to the organization of the salt warehouse and to the control of the market. The wood trade had its stages, beginning from the wood-cutting in the forest, then the floating of logs, the collecting and making of rafts, to the display in the city market. The store was the centre which directed and kept constant contact with the different groups of people who carried out different but co-ordinated processes of the wood trade.

Thirdly, a change in personnel produces changes in the relations of individuals. Each person has different ways of interacting and different capacities for adjustment. The substitution of a new person in a group or the addition or subtraction of such a person temporarily upsets the equilibrium until the individuals in the group readjust to one another. With years of experience in the business world and wide contacts, Dunglin had become a good merchant and a trained manager. We recall that Fenchow after his retirement for a short period came back and found himself out of place. The organization of the store had completely changed since his first retirement. Dunglin had now built up a system of his own and the store functioned perfectly well without the presence of Fenchow, the senior partner. This instance well proves that the change of personnel is a factor tending to disturb the equilibrium of an existing system and causing the building up of a new system of equilibrium.

Fourthly, a change in an outside system produces a change in the relations of its members to the members of the system being considered. Dunglin was a member of both his family and the store group, so that any change in the store affected the family or *vice versa*. We have seen that the more the store expanded, the more it accumulated wealth and the higher became the status of the family. Reversely, when Dunglin was involved in a lawsuit on account of the building of his house, it disturbed not only his family and lineage but also his store and business.

The mutual effect and dependence of the systems like the store and the family is an obvious fact. The rise of the Hwang family was the reflection of the store's success. The better education of the Hwang children and their wider associations helped to expand the store. It was possible to gain the salt monopoly and connect it with the store, because of the efforts of Third *Go*, Dunglin's eldest son, and also because of the returned student from abroad. The store was again helped by the steamship company in which the Hwang sons, Third *Go* and Fifth *Go*, were important members. The death of Fifth *Go* let loose the link between the two parties in the company so that that venture resulted in conflict, in litigation and in disorganization. The failure of the steamship company, in addition to the national crisis of the Japanese invasion, greatly disturbed the systems of the store and the Hwang family, which later dwindled to a meagre existence.

From our study of human relations we have thus learned how the systems which are composed of human individuals are related, and change according to principles. The change of equilibrium and disequilibrium of the systems is not without causes. The fact that each individual is a member of many systems and that he is associated with many other individuals will cause a change in one system to change other systems. There exists an inter-relationship of systems, no matter whether they exist side by side with members in common like the store and the family, or whether they are differently related, like the family, lineage and clan.

If we review briefly the fall of the house of Chang, we shall see that the same principles were operating as in the rise of the Hwang family. When Mowhun opened a new store with Eldest *Go* and Fangyang, his ambition was to rebuild his house, and he really had a good chance. His elopement with the Chang woman and his long absence diverted him from the store business. He came back and found a serious conflict between his two partners. It was a most critical moment, but he chose carelessly, and put confidence in Fangyang. The further withdrawal of the money from the old store disturbed not only his old Uncle Dunglin, who was then the sole manager, but also Mowkwei's widow whose son had a potential ownership in the family property. See how great was the effect upon the chain of relations! A single motion of Mowhun decided the fate of the new store, which influenced the equilibrium of his own family system as well as his tie to his mother's kin.

Before that had happened some might have said that Mowhun, who had been intimately associated with Eldest *Go* since their childhood, could operate or withdraw the business in collaboration with him instead of with Fangyang. But the situation was now different. Mowhun was won over by Fangyang, who became very submissive and took a vow that he would be his faithful follower. They exchanged vows. They could talk, drink and sleep together. Why couldn't they co-operate in the store business? But since no compromise could be made between Eldest *Go* and Fangyang, Mowhun chose his new intimate. Some people had keener observation and better judgment than did he. Remember what Dunglin advised him and what Mowkwei's widow did to prevent his action. Outsiders early predicted his failure.

Science is no more than an organized knowledge of common sense. Since the aim of one branch of science is to control human life, the study of human relations should be done carefully so that predictions of future happenings can be made and measures of control can be anticipated.

We know very well that any sort of prediction is difficult, since human relations are so closely intertwined. See how our little family of Hwang gradually expanded from the corner of a small village to participation in city and national life. The Hwang members became so widely associated with institutions in their area that every movement in the local district or in the city, no matter whether it was political, military, economic or even religious, directly or indirectly influenced the house of Hwang. We remember that in his last business venture, Third *Go* laid his full confidence on the lucrative future of the steamship company. He was a highly educated and intelligent man who never thought that the possible conflict could develop into a lawsuit. Even if he might have foreseen the litigation, he could never have dreamed of the ruin the national crisis would bring to his business and his family.

Here now is laid before you a careful description of the history of two related families. It is a study made from an operational point of view. The writer hopes this piece of work presents principles for further faithful studies of human relations which may be of use to others interested in bettering humankind.

INDEX

Note: Merely incidental references to persons are not recorded in this index.

Abacus, 85, 86
Anban, 171–3, 189–93
Ancestor, First, 60
Ancestors, cult of, 61–3, 73, 126
Ancestral plot, 60
Anchi, 146
Astrology, 38
Athletics class, school, 54–5

Bandits, Long Hair, 22 ; Yunseng captured by, 30 ; Third *Go* captured by, 118–19 ; Sixth *Go* captured by, 142 ff. ; raid house of Golden Wing, 153–4 ; under Fangyang, 177–8
Banks, 8, 91
"Barbaric village", 1, 60
Bargaining for rice, 83–4
Bath, baby's first, 20 ; pre-bridal, 41
Bathing houses, 10
Bed, bridal, 40
Betrothal, 16 ; Mowde's, 38–9
Birth ceremonies, 20
Birthday celebration, Dunglin's, 182–5
Birthdays, calculation of, 68
Black Money Associations, 50
Bottom-root-tenants, 14
"Breaking Out of Hell", 110
Bribery, 29, 218–19
Buffaloes, 80 ; plague among, 154–5
Bureau of Reconstruction, 204, 213
Burial rites, of Mrs. Chang, 103–11 ; of Grandmother Pan, 131
Burial site, choosing, 23, 140

Cakes, bridal, 39
Candy, 16–17
Card, go-between's, 37
Cards, Big, Exchange of, 38–9
Chair, bridal, 41, 42

Chang, Mrs., 46, 93, 94, 102 ; death and burial, 103–8
Chang Fenchow, *see* Fenchow
Chang Mowde, *see* Mowde
Chang Mowheng, *see* Mowheng
Chang Mowkwei, *see* Mowkwei
Chang Yuehying, *see* Yuehying
Chao, Lawyer, 216, 219
Chao Meng, 172, 189–90
Chaotien, 10
Chen Chihu, *see* Chihu
Chen Shankai, *see* Shankai
Chen Shuchen, *see* Shuchen
Chen Tachuan, 172
Chenchin, 53–5, 144, 151, 204, 205, 218
Chenchung, 139
Cheng Anchi, *see* Anchi
Cheng family, 10
Cheng Lugo, 6–7, 10, 24
Cheng Seng, 144, 146–8
Chi Yakwei, Colonel, 172, 189–90
Chihkun, 211–18
Chihtan, 200–3, 211–12, 218
Chihu, 117, 159
Chimei, 161–3
Chingchia, 108
Chinma, 162–3
Christianity, 50, 65, 67, 88, 120–1, 131
Chu Fangyang, *see* Fangyang
Chuhsien, 143, 145–6
Chumei, 33, 156
Chutung, 113
Civil War, 187 ff.
Clan head, 73
Clothing, making, 79
Coffin, 105
Communists, 195–9
Condolence, meeting for, 109–10
Cooking, 78, 119
Coolies, transport, 9, 95

230

INDEX

Crown, bridal, 42, 45
Curtain, mourning, 107
Customs examination, 137
Cypresses, 194–5

Debts, collecting, 97
Deed, for family division, 125–6
Deng, Long, 202, 215–16
Dinner, wedding, 46
Division of property, 14–15, 122–6, 128
Dollars, stamping of, 85
Dowry payments, 39
Dragon Boat Festival, 56–8
Dragon King, 90
Dragon Mountain, 25, 140
" Dragon Vomiting Pearls, A ", 25, 36, 139–40, 181
Dress, mourning, 106
" Duck crossing a River ", 110
Dumplings, 57, 58, 64
Dung, as manure, 71, 75
Dungchien, 26, 28, 29, 155–6
Dungchin, 136
Dungfei, 27, 168–9
Dungheng, 49, 51, 74, 76, 129
Dunglin, childhood, 2 ; sells peanuts, 3 ; enters partnership with Fenchow, 4 ; visits Foochow, 6–9 ; opens bank account, 8 ; betrothal, 10 ; marriage, 11 ; and farm life, 13 ; family division of property from Dungmin, 15 ; reunites family, 15–16 ; death of daughters, 17, 21 ; buries grandparents, 23 ; his fortune told, 24 ; dispute with Ou clan, 26–32 ; occupies new house, 33–35 ; sends Sixth *Go* to school, 49 ff. ; at tomb sacrifice, 61–3 ; and farm work, 74 ; buys rice, 83–5 ; position in store, 87, 91–2 ; at Mrs. Chang's funeral, 108–9 ; division of family, 122 ff. ; reconstructs business, 140–1; 148–9, 151 ; and family quarrels, 153 ff. ; 168 ; and Merchants' Association, 170–1 ; sixtieth birthday celebrated, 182–5 ; in Civil War, 192 ff. ; and communists, 195–9 ; in old age, 218

Dungmin, 2, 3, 6, 11, 15
Dungtzu, 61, 89, 91, 94–6, 99, 141, 166–7
Dwarf Pirates, 66

Eggs, at birth ceremony, 20 ; as school reward, 54
" Eight characters ", 24
Evening, domestic occupations, 80, 88
Evil Eyes, Sifting the, 40

Family Division, 14–15, 122–6
Fangyang, 134, 138–9, 140, 177–80, 181–2, 187–8
Farm work, 71 ff.
Farming tenancies, 14–15
Fenchow, 3–7, 9, 15, 18, 25, 30, 36, 37 ff., 50–1, 87, 93, 101–2, 103 ff., 133
Fengwan, 145
Filial Piety Festival, 72–3
Finger, middle, pointing with, 96
" Fire-crackers, Burning the ", 65–6
Fish, dealing in, 6, 7 ; transport of, 8, 95
Five Happinesses, Bag of, 43
Five Sons, 43, 67
Flower Bridge, 26, 178
Foochow, attacked by Anban, 188–9 ; captured by Japanese, 220–1
Food, for farm workers, 71 ; preparation of, 78
Fortune-telling, 24
Fukien University, 119
" Fullness of the Month ", 20, 117

Gambling, 69, 115
Geomancy, 23, 25
Gifts, marriage, 39 ; mourning, 109
Go, Eldest, 19 ; married, 22 ; 29, 33, 65 ; farm work, 71–7, 80 ; 82–3, 86, 108 ; demands division of family, 122–8 ; starts new store with Mowhun, 134 ; 138–9, 160–2 ; withdraws from store, 165–6 ; 192, 195
Go, Second, 33, 69, 76, 114, 122, 127–8, 160–1, 185

INDEX

Go, Third, 20, 22, 30, 33 ; becomes Christian, 50 ; 65 ; betrothal, 113 ; marriage, 114–15 ; 115–21 ; captured by bandits, 117–18 ; at High School, 119–21 ; elected Conference delegate, 121 ; 146 ; returns from America, 158 ; 159, 165, 167, 175, 191, 201–4, 210–11, 213–20, 221

Go, Fourth, 33, 50–1, 53, 57, 65, 93, 115–16, 119, 122, 163 ; enters business, 166–7 ; 175, 176, 191, 195, 198, 217, 222

Go, Fifth, 33, 57, 61, 69, 76, 116, 122, 144, 149 ; and Redflower, 155–7 ; 159, 171, 175–7, 179–81, 192, 195, 201, 202, 206–7, 214

Go, Sixth, born, 19 ; first birthday, 21 ; 33, 43 ; at school, 49 ff. ; punished for truancy, 51–3 ; 61, 69, 75, 76, 86, 88, 115–16, 121 ; captured by bandits, 142 ff. ; 157–8, 159, 171, 175, 180, 208–9, 210–11

Go-between, matrimonial, 37, 41

Golden Wing, house of, 58, 153, 191, 194

Good luck cloth, 47

Grandmother, ritual respects to, 67–8

"Gruel, Filial Piety", 72–3

Guild Buildings, 182–3

Gun-firing, at New Year, 67 ; at Spring Full Moon Festival, 70

Hankan, 96–7
Harvesting, 76–7, 80
Hemp, 79
Hired labourer, 18
House, new, choosing site and building, 25 ; occupation of, 33 ; described, 33–5
Hsiwen, 143–4, 172
Huilan, marriage of, 37 ff. ; 93, 101, 103, 133
Hung Heng, 168
Hwang, Mrs. (Dunglin's wife), 16, 17, 33, 51–2, 57, 75, 116, 159–60, 208, 222
Hwang Dunglin, see Dunglin
Hwang Yuhun, see Yuhun

"Incense, kneeling", 54
Incense-bags, 57
Irrigation, 71–2, 75–6

Japanese invasion, 220–1
Junks, 8, 89–91, 95

Kaituan, 50, 87, 88–9, 97, 99, 141, 161, 165–8, 195, 198
Kettles, symbols of family separation, 126
Kwanmin, 145–50

Land ownership, 13–14
Lawsuit, Dunglin's, with Asui, 28 ff. ; over steamship company, 215 ff.
Lei Wuyun, see Wuyun
Lew, Small, 202–3, 215–16
Li, Prosecutor, 217
Li Kwan, 150–1, 153
Liang, Old, 202–3, 211–14, 218–9
Lin, Aunt (Dungmin's wife), 15, 17, 33, 127, 129, 159
Lin Chuhsien, see Chuhsien
Lin Chutung, see Chutung
Lin Tienlan, see Tienlan
Lincheng, 147
Little Brother, see Go, Sixth
Liyang, 37, 109
Long Life Bridge, 7
Long-life Feast, 182–5
Lumbering, 169, 194
Lunar time reckoning, 137

Ma Nanshao, see Nanshao
Marriage, of Dunglin, 11 ; arranging, 37–9 ; of Mowde, 38 ff. ; rites, 39 ff. ; free, 113, 180 ; of Third Go, 113
Masks, 66
Mawoo, 89–91, 94–5
Meals, 78
Merchants' Association, 100–1, 170–1, 174
Methodist Church, 120, 173
Mill, 82
Min River, 7
Mourning, 103, 106, 131
Mouse-Facing-a-Barn, 23, 63
Mowchiao, 43, 103, 133–4, 179

INDEX

Mowde, 22 ; marriage of, 37 ff. ; 93, 133
Mowheng, 37–9, 55, 56, 179–80
Mowhun, 46, 48, 76, 103–8, 111–12 ; becomes head of family, 133 ; opens new store, 134 ; marries, 135 ; and the Chang woman, 136–8 ; death, 185–6
Mowkwei, 5, 11, 46, 87 ; his widow, 139
Mowsui, 179–81
Mowyueh, 43, 103, 109, 133–4, 177–9
Music, at New Year, 68 ; at funeral ceremony, 111

Nanmin, 18, 33, 67, 71, 72, 74, 83–5, 122–3
Nanshao, 172, 200–2, 212–13, 214, 220
Nantai Island, 7
"Needlework, Begging for Skill in", 79
New Year Festival, 64–9, 98–9
Nine, unlucky number, 73
Noodles, and birth ceremony, 20

Omens, unlucky, 38
Ou Asui, 27
Ou clan, 26

Pan, Grandmother, 16–17, 33, 67–8, 129–31
Pao, Fat, 211–15
Peimin, 48, 74, 76, 108, 185–6
Pheasant Mountain, 1
Pipe, 72
Plague, buffalo, 154–5
Plays, 184
Ploughing, 80
Primogeniture, rights of, 123, 124
Procession, bridal, 43
Profit-sharing, 99
Property, marriage and, 47 ; see Division of property
Punishment, school, 54, 56
Pure Brightness Festival, 73

Rafts, 194
Realgar wine, 57–8
Red shares, 99, 141

Redflower, 155–7
Rent collector, quarrel with, 176–7
Reporting of Death, 108
Revolution, Chinese, 22
Rewards, school, 54
Rice, 6 ; cultivation of, 73–6 ; division of crop, 76–7 ; storing, 77 ; preparation for market, 82 ; sale of, 83–5 ; weighing and measuring, 84–5 ; wetting, 90 ; transport, 90–1
Rice, New Year, 66
River Gull, 201–2
Road, building of, 175–6
Robbery, 97–8
Root-holders, 13–14
"Rounding of the Year", 21

Salt, 6
Salt trade, 167–8
Sao, Eldest, 33, 57, 71, 78, 126–7, 161–3
Sao, Second, 67, 71, 77–8, 126–7, 161
Sao, Third, *see* Shuchen
Sao, Second-Third, 201, 215
Sao, Fourth, 119
Sao, Fifth, 155, 157
School, Mission, 50 ; Sixth Go at, 49–57 ; punishments and rewards, 54
Schoolgirls, and Chao Ming, 189
Sea-bags, 89–90
Self-tenant farmers, 14
Selling of rice, 83–5
Shankai, 58–9, 113, 118–19, 151, 166, 171–3
Shares, holding of, 99–100, 141 ; in *River Gull*, 201
Shipwreck, 91
Shoemaking, 79
Shoupei, 114
Shoutai, 33, 68, 159, 160–3
Shouyang, 117
Shuchen, 113, 119–20, 131, 158–9
Shuikow, 6
Sixth seventh-day rice, 110
Sleeping arrangements, 88–9
Soul cash, 104, 107
Soul table, 103–4, 107
Southern Road, 6

Spinning, 79
Spring Full Moon Festival, 69, 100
Steamboats, 135–6, 170; company, organization of, 200 ff.
Store, Dunglin's, described, 4–5; allocation of work, 5; enlarged, 18; working of, 83 ff.; profit-sharing in, 99; looted, 193
Store, Mowhun's, 134 ff.
Suihwa, 144
Sungnan, 49–50

Tally sticks, 90
Tan, Lieut., 190
Taoist rites, 104, 108, 111
Taro, as fertility symbol, 40
Taxes, 14
Teasing the Bride, 47
Threshing, 76
Tienchi Bank, 8
Tienlan, 123–5, 128, 162
Tomb Sacrifices, 59–63
Transplanting, 74
Transport, of fish, 8; river, 200 ff.
Trousseau, Huilan's, 40
Tsunching, 145–50

Vacation, how spent, 58–9
Virginity test, 22, 47

Wang Chihkun, 47
Wang Chihtan, see Chihtan
Wang Hankan, see Hankan
Wang Liyang, see Liyang
Wang village, 37

Wang Yiyang, see Yiyang
Washing clothes, 78, 119–20
Weaving, 79
Wedding, see Marriage
Weeding, 75
Wei Chenchin, see Chenchin
Weikuo, 170, 205–6
Western Road, 14, 16, 25, 220
" Wind and Water ", 18, 23, 42, 58
Wine, 88; measuring, 5
Winter, on farm, 80
Winter Festival, 63–4
Women, share in agriculture, 74; in family economy, 77–80
Wood trade, 168–70, 194
Wu, Commander, see Anban
Wu Anban, see Anban
Wu Sungnan, see Sungnan
Wuyun, 29, 143–4, 172, 179

" Yamen trap ", 217
Yang Ling, 86, 91, 165–6, 195
Yao Kaituan, see Kaituan
Yao Yunseng, see Yunseng
Yeh, Lawyer, 215–16
Yenping, 117
Yingmei, 156
Yiyang, 7, 8, 37
Yuchung, 162
Yuehying, 55–6, 179–80
Yuhun, 10, 28, 29, 32, 63, 73, 125, 128–9
Yumen, 26, 28, 29
Yunseng, 5, 18, 30, 32, 44, 86, 87, 99, 101, 109, 141, 166, 185, 195